— To —

My Dear Friends and Co-workers

Mr. and Mrs. Harold Bostrom

With Warmest Good Wishes

John A. O'Brien

Notre Dame
Sept. 18, 1968

ETERNAL ANSWERS
FOR AN
ANXIOUS AGE

Books Written or Edited by the Author

Happy Marriage

Bringing Souls to Christ

The Road to Damascus

Where I Found Christ

The Way to Emmaus

Roads to Rome

Truths Men Live By

The Faith of Millions

God and Evolution

The Priesthood in a
Changing World

Pathways to Happiness

What's the Truth About
Catholics?

Thunder from the Left

Discovering Mexico

Winning Converts

Sharing the Faith

Paths to Christ

Coming Home

The Catholic Way of Life

The White Harvest

The Vanishing Irish

You Too Can Win Souls

The First Martyrs of North
America

Sex-Character Education

ETERNAL ANSWERS
FOR AN
ANXIOUS AGE

John A. O'Brien

"The Lord ruleth me: and I shall want nothing.
He hath set me in a place of pasture."
—*Psalm 22*

Englewood Cliffs, N.J.
Prentice-Hall, Inc.

Nihil Obstat: James J. O'Connor
                   Censor Librorum

Imprimatur: ✠ Leo A. Pursley
                   Bishop of Fort Wayne-South Bend

Library of Congress
Catalog Card Number: 62–18835

Printed in the United States of America

28997–T

ACKNOWLEDGMENTS

The author wishes to express his gratitude to the publishers and individuals for permission to quote the following:

"The Healing Nun of Formosa" by W. J. Lederer, *The Reader's Digest*, August 1960. Copyright 1960 by The Reader's Digest Association, Inc., Pleasantville, New York.

"This Cop Leads a Double Life," by Eugenie Gluckert, *The Reader's Digest*, December 1956. Copyright 1956 by The Reader's Digest Association, Inc.

"The Turning Point of My Career" by A. J. Cronin, *The Reader's Digest*, May 1941. Copyright 1941 by A. J. Cronin.

"What Women Don't Know About Being Female" by Dr. Marion Hilliard, *The Reader's Digest*, May 1956. Copyright 1956 by The Reader's Digest Association, Inc.

"Whose Business Was It?" by Fulton Oursler, *The Reader's Digest*, May 1949. Copyright 1949 by The Reader's Digest Association, Inc.

"The Lady and the Gangsters" by Lester Velie, *The Reader's Digest*, January 1957. Copyright 1957 by The Reader's Digest Association, Inc.

"What We Owe to Jane Addams of Hull House" by Karl Detzer, *The Reader's Digest*, September 1959. Copyright 1959 by The Reader's Digest Association, Inc.

"It Happened on the River Kwai" by Ernest Gordon as told to Clarence W. Hall, *The Reader's Digest*, June 1960. Copyright 1960 by The Reader's Digest Association, Inc.

Man Does Not Stand Alone by A. Cressy Morrison. Copyright by Fleming H. Revell Co. By permission of Fleming H. Revell Co., Westwood, N.J.

"Blessed Crackpots" by Catherine Doherty. Copyright 1955 by Guideposts Associates, Inc., published at Carmel, New York.

"That Magic Word" by H. W. Ruopp. Copyright 1953 by Guideposts Associates, Inc.

"Spiritual Commandos" by Lee H. Bristol, Jr. Copyright 1954 by Guideposts Associates, Inc.

"I'll Get the Gangs That Killed My Father" by John M. Patterson as told to Furman Bisher, *The Saturday Evening Post*, November 27, 1954. Reprinted by special permission of *The Saturday Evening Post* and Furman Bisher. Copyright 1954 by The Curtis Publishing Company.

"Four Chaplains Join the Immortals" by Jeanne Dixon, *Catholic Digest*, August 1948. Copyright 1948 by Catholic Digest.

"We're Battling the Mobsters in Our Union" by William Wilkens as told to Bernard Bookbinder, Cornet, October 1956. Copyright 1956 by Coronet.

"Love" from *Songs from the Slums* by Toyohiko Kagawa. Copyright 1935 by Whitmore and Smith. By permission of Abingdon Press.

Christopher Notes, The Christophers, 16 East 48th St. N.Y. 17, N.Y.

CONTENTS

The Author Dedicates This Book

To
The Memory of
The Four Heroic Chaplains
George L. Fox, Clark V. Poling,
John P. Washington and Alexander D. Goode
Who Gave Their Life Preservers
To Passengers
On the Sinking *Dorchester.*
They Gave an Inspiring Demonstration
Of the Truth Spoken by Jesus, "Greater
Love Than This No One Has,
That One Lay Down His Life for His Friends."

I.

HELP FOR AN ANXIOUS AGE

"Though I should walk in the midst of the shadow
of death, I will fear no evils for thou art with me."
—Psalm 22, Verse 4

We are a "shook-up" generation living in an anxious age.
We have the unenviable distinction of living in a day when, for
the first time in history, it is possible to destroy civilization and
annihilate the human race within a few weeks. Faced with the
threat of multi-megaton hydrogen bombs, intercontinental mis-
siles and radioactive fallout, we are tense, jittery and scared stiff.

Just a few years ago we were boasting of the unprecedented
achievements of science and technology: the former was building
a new world and the latter was filling our homes with new gadgets
designed to take work and worry out of living. Suddenly we find
the tables turned on us. The marvels and miracles of science and
technology may now be used to wipe us out almost overnight!

The newspapers report the rumblings of angry threats by a
hostile power that has grown to colossal stature in less than two
decades. But a few years ago we were pouring out our resources
in manpower and matériel to save Soviet Russia from annihila-
tion by the mechanized might of the Nazi juggernaut. Now it has
wrapped its iron curtain around one-third of the human race,
while its leader shakes his fist at us and shouts "We will bury
you!"

The anxiety and tension which grip so many millions of people in the free nations today are heightened by feelings of
frustration at their inability to take any positive action to relieve

1

their fears. "What can we do?" they ask hopelessly. "The decision is not in our hands. It rests with a few men in the Kremlin."

Hence the relief which a person ordinarily secures from tension by direct action, by coming to grips with his problem and working out a solution, is denied him. The blocking of such relief increases the tension and renders more acute his brooding anxiety.

Living Under
Constant Threats

We are like the members of a fire station whose alarm bell is not actually ringing but is rumbling. It alerts the firemen with the constant threat of an alarm but robs them of the relief which comes from answering one. These rumblings of the cold war, which threatens to erupt at any moment into a flaming nuclear conflict, put the physiological and psychological anti-threat apparatus of the individual on a standby alert for immediate action.

His brain sends out signals to the pituitary and adrenal glands; these shoot their powerful secretions into the bloodstream, touching off a number of emergency measures. Millions of additional blood cells are manufactured, while the blood pressure shoots up from 130 to 200 or more. To accelerate the clotting of blood in case of a wound, fibrin is manufactured at a hastened pace.

The psychological self, the psyche, the ego—call it what you will—likewise mobilizes at the threat of attack. Feelings of anxiety and tension permeate the individual and, because they are long-drawn-out, leave him weak and exhausted. The expression "scared stiff" reflects the knotted-up feeling in the stomach, the pounding heart, the dry mouth, the flushed face, the tightened muscles and the whole state of tension.

The obsessive fears and brooding anxieties of millions of people are further aggravated by the fact that the religious faith of our forefathers and the stouthearted courage and confidence which stemmed from that faith have been greatly weakened by the corrosive acids of modern doubt and unbelief. Our fore-fathers faced the frontier of the wilderness with its lurking Red-men and hidden dangers, confident that God was not only in His heavens but also at their sides, and that nothing could really harm them. Things would somehow work out all right.

That was the priceless legacy bequeathed to us by the sturdy settlers of this country. Hither came many of them to secure a freedom of conscience and of religious worship denied them in the Old World. But the prosperity, wealth, and riches with which an industrial civilization has flooded us have weakened the fiber of our once sturdy faith and left us with few inner re-sources to face the lethal Frankensteins their industrial technol-ogy has spawned. We are frightened, anxious and appalled. Our fitful and feverish sleep is filled with nightmares. We awake not refreshed, but exhausted.

An
Ominous Lag

Frantically and desperately we reach out for the eternal truths, more certain now that while science and technology can destroy us, they lack the power to save us. The fault lies not in their products but with their users. While our scientific and tech-nological progress in the past 60 years has surpassed that achieved in the preceding 500, man's moral advance has lagged far behind. In that lag lies the ominous threat not only to our civilization but also to our very existence. Well has Edwin H. Markham said:

> We are all blind until we see
> That in the human plan,
> Nothing is worth the making
> If it does not make the man.
> Why build these cities glorious
> If man unbuilded goes?

In vain we build the world unless
The builder also grows.

Disillusioned, shaken and jittery, an anxious age is reaching out
feverish and eager hands, searching for the eternal verities which
alone make men free. They are lifting their eyes above the clouds
filled with fallout to the high heavens, seeking the omnipotent
and omniscient Being, the heavenly Father, who holds the vast
universe in the palm of His almighty hand.

The Hunger
for God

They want to see His face more clearly and to catch again the
voice that spoke to the Israelites in the desert: they yearn for the
cloud by day and the pillar of fire by night that led the wanderers
into the Promised Land. They want to see His fingerprints on
earth, sea and sky, and make contact with the infinite Source of
goodness, truth, power, beauty, life and love. More clearly than
ever before they realize that man lives not by bread alone but by
every word that comes from the mouth of God.

An anxious age wants to rediscover the bonds which bind the
creature to the Creator and the ladder upon which to climb from
earth to heaven. In short, our generation wants God and craves
to share in His life and light and love. Only in that union does
the earthly sojourner find the easement of the God-ache that has
existed in every human being since man first lifted his face to
the stars.

Sick and disillusioned with the strife and agony of war and the
threats of new and more appalling conflicts, a "shook-up" generation wants to find the paths to enduring peace, the avenues
which lead to justice, righteousness, holiness, compassion, love
and inner serenity. These are the groping questions which this
book seeks to answer. Because they concern the yearnings of the
human spirit, it endeavors to provide answers that are both timeless and eternal.

Today's
Urgent Need

A few years ago in New York I was visiting with my friend, Dr. Arthur C. Compton. He was awarded the Nobel prize for his contribution to nuclear physics and he played a leading role in the development of the atomic bomb. A deeply religious man, he had written the preface for my book, *Truth Men Live By.*

"I keep that book near my bed," he said, "and before going to sleep frequently read a few pages. They bring strength, comfort and inspiration to an anxious age such as this, for they provide the abiding answers to some of the urgent questions of our day. Bring out another book like this, which will come to grips with more of these questions, and which will be within the ken of all readers—the man in the street as well as the scientist, the philosopher and the theologian. They all need it, and it will do a world of good."

This gracious request by a man as sensitive to spiritual values as he was to the truths of science has echoed ever since in my mind. All the developments of the intervening years have made his request increasingly timely and urgent.

Embodying the results of more than forty years of study, teaching and research at the Universities of Illinois, Oxford and Notre Dame, this book endeavors to provide the eternal answers for an anxious age. I hope that it will bring to millions of worried and jittery people the perennial truths which will free them from their anxieties and give them the spiritual serenity they so desperately need today.

POINTS TO REMEMBER

1. Our age is tense, jittery and anxious because of the threat of nuclear war destroying civilization and the human race.

2. Our anxiety and tension are heightened because of our inability to take any action to relieve our fears.

3. The constant threat of a global conflict affects both the mind and the body of man and fills him with fear and anxiety.

4. Man's moral advance lags far behind his progress in science and technology; in that lag lies the threat to our civilization and our existence.

5. Our age hungers for a deeper knowledge of God and craves to share in His life and light and love.

6. This book seeks to bring strength, comfort and inspiration to an anxious age by providing eternal answers to its most urgent questions.

2.

GOD'S FINGERPRINTS

"It seemed as though my instruments, aloft in the
heavens, tracking down the cosmic rays, were fin-
gerprinting God."—*Robert Andrews Millikan*

The Empire State Building towers 102 stories above the
New York skyline. The tallest building in the world, it is one
of the great engineering and construction feats of all time. Thousands of man-hours of planning went into it long before the first
ground was broken. When the man in charge of its construction was asked what element of the work received the most attention, he replied unhesitatingly:

"The foundation. Unless the foundation was right, the building itself could never have been put up. And if it had gone up
on a faulty foundation, it would never have survived."

If your religious faith is to survive and be of use to you in the
storms and tempests of life, it too must stand on a solid foundation—and that foundation is nothing less than God Himself.
Without God, religion would rest upon shifting sands and would
crumble in the face of trouble or attack. The most important
spiritual truth to establish for yourself, then, is the existence of
God.

In this chapter I shall present evidence for God's existence
taken from the findings of modern science. While science, of
course, does not deal directly with this question, it gives us the
raw material to study, analyze and interpret.

First, we shall look at the evidence drawn from the *organization* and *operation* of matter, principally the planet Earth and
other heavenly bodies. We shall apply the simple rule of caus-

7

ality: *Things don't just happen. They have a cause. Where there is evidence of plan, order and purpose, there is proof of a causal agency at work—a directing intelligence.* It is this rule which makes up the spinal column of all philosophic and scientific reasoning. Without it, we could reach no conclusions about the cause of anything or any action.

When you see the 24 volumes of the *Encyclopaedia Brittanica* in their proper numerical sequence, you conclude that they were arranged by an intelligent being. You know the correct order didn't just happen by chance. Take Webster's *New International Dictionary*, with its thousands of pages and millions of words and marks of pronunciation and punctuation. Doesn't the order in which they are arranged offer evidence of thinking agents: editors, typists, and printers who planned and produced the whole mighty work?

Suppose someone disagreed, saying: "No. You're mistaken. That arrangement can be explained by chance. If a printer were to throw the type of those letters, words and marks up in the air often enough, ultimately they would fall into the particular order found in that dictionary."

"I can't believe it," you would reply. "Such a complex arrangement could never happen by chance."

You would be right. Your conclusion is confirmed by eminent mathematicians through a line of reasoning called the calculus of probabilities, that is, the combination of rules to express the laws of chance mathematically.

The Testimony of Mathematicians

By applying the calculus of probabilities to the conditions and elements involved in the rule of life, my friend, Lecomte du Noüy, a great French scientist and mathematician, has demonstrated, in his book *Human Destiny*, the *impossibility* of explaining this phenomenon by mere chance. It is highly technical, however, and requires considerable training in both science and mathematics to understand.

Another book which expresses substantially the same idea very simply is *Man Does Not Stand Alone*. In it, A. Cressy Morrison, former president of the New York Academy of Sciences, presents seven lines of scientific evidence which demonstrate the existence of God. Since the first one involves the calculus of probabilities and dovetails with my point, I shall sketch it briefly.

Suppose you were to put ten pennies, marked from one to ten, in your pocket and then shuffle them. Now try to take them out in sequence from one to ten, putting each coin back in your pocket after every draw. Mathematically, your chance of first drawing number one is one in ten; your chance of drawing one and two in succession is one in 100; of drawing one, two and three in succession, one in 1000, and so on. Your chance of drawing all of them, from one to ten in succession would reach the incredible figure of one chance in 10,000,000,000! This illustrates how enormously and quickly the odds multiply against chance.

By the same line of reasoning, so many precise conditions are necessary for life on earth that it is mathematically impossible for *all* of them to exist in proper relationship at any one time by chance.

First, the earth rotates on its axis at about 1000 miles per hour: a variation of *one second in a century* would upset astronomical calculations. If it rotated at 100 miles per hour, the days and nights would be ten times as long. The sun would burn up our vegetation each long day, while any surviving sprout would freeze in the long night.

Second, the sun, the source of all life on this planet, has a surface temperature of 12,000 degrees Fahrenheit. Our earth is far enough away so that the sun warms us *just enough and not too much!* If this "eternal fire" gave off only half its present radiation, we would freeze; if it gave half as much more, we would roast to death.

Third, the tilt of the earth at an angle of 23 degrees gives us our seasons. If it were not tilted, vapors from the ocean would move north and south, piling up continents of ice. Incredibly heavy masses of ice would depress the poles; the lowering of the ocean would diminish the rainfall with fearful results.

Fourth, if the moon were 50,000 miles away, instead of its present distance of 238,000 miles, the tides would be so gigantic that all continents would be submerged twice each day. The tides would create daily hurricanes and the turmoil would crack the earth.

Fifth, the earth's crust compared with its diameter is but one-half the thickness of a leaf in a thousand-page book. Upon that tissue-thin surface is written the history of all life upon this planet. If that crust were only ten feet thicker, there would be no oxygen, without which animal life cannot exist.

Sixth, if the ocean were appreciably deeper, carbon dioxide and oxygen would have been absorbed with the result that no vegetable life could exist.

Seventh, if the atmosphere were appreciably thinner, many of the millions of meteors, now burned daily in space, would be striking all parts of the earth, starting fires everywhere.

"So many essential conditions," concludes Dr. Morrison, "are necessary for life to exist on our earth that it is mathematically impossible that all of them could exist in proper relationship by chance on any earth at one time. Therefore there must be in nature some form of intelligent direction." This is but another way of saying that the evidence amassed by science demonstrates the existence of a directive Intelligence, a Supreme Being, whom we call God.

The Earth:
Our Airplane

One of the most honored names among men of science is that of Sir Isaac Newton. A profound mathematician and astrophysicist, his formulation of the law of gravitation helped to lay the solid foundation for the science of physics. His studies led him to see in the arrangement of the heavenly bodies the handiwork of God.

"This most beautiful system of sun, stars and comets," he remarked, "could nowise come into existence without the design and ownership of a Being at once intelligent and powerful . . . This Being governs all things, not as if He were the soul of the world, but as the Lord of everything; and on account of His dominion He is styled the lord God."

The truth of Newton's words was brought powerfully home to me recently. I had landed at New York after a jet flight from Rome.

"Just think," I remarked to the friend who met me, "I was in Rome only eight hours ago. Our jet must have averaged 550 miles an hour, and it was a marvelously smooth trip."

My friend, an astronomer, smiled. "Yes, it's fast," he observed, "but it's got a long way to go before it catches up with the earth. While rotating on its axis, the earth flies through space 124 times faster than your jet; yet it moves with such smoothness that you and the other passengers aren't even aware of it!"

It was a wise observation and I've never forgotten it. The earth, with its atmosphere, its great cities with millions of inhabitants, its lofty skyscrapers, mountains, rivers, and valleys, shoots through space at the startling velocity of 68,400 miles an hour. Yet so smoothly does it move that it disturbs not a babe in its cradle, nor brings a tremor to the wings of a bee nestling on the frail petals of an autumn rose.

The Clock of the Stars

And beyond our earth, the stars move in their orbits with a regularity and a precision that shames the most accurate clock made by human hands. The most perfect clock will falter by some seconds each week in the accurate measurement of time, and will have to be corrected by the "clock of the stars," as determined by the U.S. Naval Observatory at Annapolis. Here then is order, plan, purpose and design that cries out for an intelligent and adequate cause.

The simple conclusion is inescapable: As the watch implies a watchmaker, so the universe implies a God. As the watch demands an adequate cause in the form of an intelligent maker, so the universe, vastly greater in size, complexity of organization and adjustment of parts, demands an adequate cause in the form of a Being of vastly greater power and intelligence. This is the Being whom we call God.

The renowned astronomer, Kircher, had a friend who was doubtful about the existence of God. Knowing that a simple illustration would be more effective than long arguments, Kircher made a globe and placed it on his desk. His friend, calling to see him, noticed the new globe.

"This is quite good," he said. "Who made it?"

"Why," replied Kircher seriously, "it made itself."

The friend smiled.

"You smile at that as absurd," remarked Kircher, "and rightly so. But isn't it easier to believe that this little globe made itself, than the large one on which we live made itself?"

The Immensity
of the Cosmos

The findings of astronomers enable us to see more clearly the immensity of the universe, and serve to deepen our reverence before the might and power of God, who hurled the millions of worlds out into the midst of space. They serve to put richer content into the words *omnipotent* and *omniscient*, which were becoming anaemic in the nineteenth century.

In the past we have thought of our solar system as involving great distances and great masses. Thus, the sun is 94 million miles from the earth. The planet Jupiter has a diameter of 88,640 miles, and could accommodate within itself 1,400 bodies the size of the earth. But now we learn that Jupiter, and even our sun, are but specks in comparison with other celestial bodies. The nearest star is Proxima Centauri, 25 billion miles away. In fact, the distances are so great that they cannot really be understood in terms of miles.

Accordingly, the astronomers invented a new measure called a light year, to make the distance intelligible. Light travels at the rate of 186,000 miles per second. A light year, then, is the distance traveled by light during that period—6 billion miles.

Light from the moon, for instance, reaches the earth in one and a half seconds and from the sun in eight minutes. But light from the star Betelgeux takes over 100 years to reach the earth. Betelgeux, however, is small in comparison with some of the giant stars in Nubecula Minor which have diameters of over a billion miles. There are many stars such as the Cephids which are more than 60,000 times as luminous as our sun.

Moreover, the number of stars and solar systems floating about in the far reaches of space seems to be almost unlimited. The millions and billions of stars in the Milky Way are but a tiny fragment of the many worlds coursing through space. The most powerful photographic cameras are continually catching glimpses of new galaxies of stars beyond the outermost rim of the previously charted stellar universe.

Professor Harlow Shapley of the Harvard Observatory has recently reported "island universes" of stars, far outside the main sidereal system. These globular clusters are over a *million light years* distant. In other words they are so far distant that light traveling at the rate of 186,000 miles per second would take more than a million years to reach our earth.

For all that astronomers have been able to discover, this may be only the nearest fringe, the vestibule, of a universe that stretches out with its planets, suns and stars into immeasurable space. On August 21, 1961, for instance, a new and startling discovery was made. Dr. Fritz Zwicky, of Palomar Observatory in California, established the existence of the most distant supernova, or star explosion, of which we have knowledge. When do you think this took place? A thousand years ago? A million years? You aren't even close. It happened 800 million years ago! And the news of this gigantic disaster in distance space is just now reaching our earth. It took that long for the brilliant light from the explosion to arrive here, traveling at 186,000 miles a second!

So violent was the explosion, Dr. Zwicky reported, that any nearby planets and any living things on them must have been cremated within seconds. The light intensity of the explosion was anywhere from 100 to 1000 *million* times that of our sun, eclipsing the light from the entire small galaxy—or star-family— in which the disaster occurred!

The Work of His Hands

All these findings of modern science concerning the immensity and grandeur of the universe serve to emphasize the truth uttered centuries ago: "The heavens show forth the glory of God, and the firmament declareth the work of His hands." This is the same truth sounded by St. Paul when he declared: "The invisible things of Him from the creation of the world are clearly seen, being understood by the things that are made."

This mighty thought finds a more recent echo in the words of Sir Isaac Newton: "The origin of the material world must be ascribed to the intelligence and wisdom of a most potent Being, always existing and present everywhere, who controls according to His good pleasure, all parts of the universe. . . ."

Such too is the conviction of the modern astrophysicist Sir James H. Jeans: "We discover that the universe shows evidence of a designing or controlling Power that has something in common with our own individual minds . . . the tendency to think in the way which for want of a better word, we describe as mathematical." Thus does this mathematical astronomer think of God as the Divine Mathematician whose thoughts are manifested in the series of mathematical and algebraic formulae found both in a grain of sand and in the dust of the stars.

The Marvel
of the Human Body

Let us now consider the human body to see there convincing evidence of plan and purpose. The most delicate and complex machine ever devised appears as a child's toy in comparison with the human body, self-repairing and self-reproducing.

"Man," observes the noted scientist, J. Arthur Thompson, "is fearfully and wonderfully made. We never fail to be impressed with an intricate mechanical device, such as a linotype machine, a loom, a calculating machine; and we praise the maker. Why are we not more generous in our admiration of a living creature, which is more than any machine? Why are we not more inclined to do homage to the Prime Mover, who made things make themselves?"

In the human body there are 25 trillion red blood corpuscles and four billion white blood corpuscles. Each of these is a living unit of great complexity, consisting of billions of molecules and trillions of atoms. Connecting the ends of the arteries with the beginnings of the veins are the microscopic capillaries. They are so numerous that if all those in one body were placed end to end they would stretch across the Atlantic!

Especially striking is the awesome organization of the cerebral cortex, the seat of the higher intellectual processes. Though its nerve cells weigh only about half an ounce, they number approximately 9,200,000,000—more than three times the number of people living on the earth. Yet each cell is like a busy telephonic switchboard, receiving calls and bringing one part of the body into communication with another.

Visit the telephone plant of a great metropolis like New York and gaze at its marvelous network of mechanical and electrical equipment, making it possible for millions of people to communicate with one another. What would you think of the individual who would say that such complex and intricate machinery happened by chance? You would probably say, "That man has taken leave of his senses."

That must be the verdict passed on the individual who could say that the brain of man evidences no plan, coordination or purpose and is the result of blind chance. Common sense dictates that it is the work of a Supreme Intelligence and the law of causality confirms that conclusion.

The
Human Mind

Our last illustration of the evidence of an Infinite Creator is the mind of man. This is the pinnacle of all creation, the apex in the pyramid of values and the basis of the dignity of man as a moral personality. No scale can measure the human intellect because it transcends the properties of matter and reaches into the world of spirit.

How wonderful indeed is the mind of man which measures the girth of Betelgeux and weighs stars a million light years from our planet. "I have sat," said Loren C. Eisley, a noted anthropologist, "under the slit dome of a mountain observatory and marveled, as the great wheel of the galaxy turned in all its midnight splendor, that the mind in the course of three centuries has been capable of drawing into its strange, nonspatial interior that world of infinite distance and multitudinous dimensions."

When confronted with the workings of the human intellect, the materialist and the atheist become strangely silent: they have no formula to explain its achievements. Those feats trumpet the existence of an order of reality that transcends matter and has a kinship with the divine. This fact was acknowledged by Julian Huxley, when he said: "Our knowledge of physics and chemistry neurology does not account for the basic fact of subjective [mental] experience, though they help us to understand its workings.

The stark fact of mind sticks in the throat of pure rationalism and reductionist materialism."

Here then is the climactic evidence of plan and purpose and the crowning argument of God's existence. No wonder that Shakespeare felt compelled to cry out : "What a piece of work is man! How noble in reason! how infinite in faculty! in form and moving how express and admirable! in action how like an angel! in apprehension how like a god! the beauty of the world! the paragon of animals!"

Such insight into the awesome organization of the universe and the operation of its laws, as we have sought to afford in the instances cited, reveals nature as a vast mirror, reflecting the power and intelligence of a Supreme Mind. Glimpses of the workings of that Mind and of the divine plan may be had by the person who carefully reads the marvelous story written in the vast book of nature. Therein he discerns the record of plan, order, coordination and design. Purposiveness, spelled out on each page of nature's story, is the universal language by which mind discerns the work of mind and in consequence man loses his sense of loneliness in the realization of God's presence and activity throughout the universe.

"The deeper one penetrates into the secrets of nature," points out Dr. Arthur H. Compton, "the clearer becomes his awareness of law, order and purposiveness evident in all that happens. The constancy of the laws of nature gives a unity to all truth and makes our world a cosmos rather than a chaos. By learning these laws one can learn more about the Supreme Mind, God Himself, in whom we live and move and have our being."

The whole universe rests upon the all-encompassing network of the laws of God. If we could look deeply enough into the mysterious and unfathomed network of law in any single object in all creation, we would see God and understand man, nature, and God. Tennyson gave admirable expression to this mighty truth when, in passing through a woods, he beheld a flower bursting out in the crevice of a wall, which he thus apostrophized:

Flower in the crannied wall,
I pluck you out of the crannies,
I hold you here, root and all, in my hand,
Little flower—but if I could understand
What you are, root and all, and all in all,
I should know what God and man is.

*The evidence of God's existence is as inescapable as it is over-
whelming. Everywhere on earth, in the sea, or in the sky, there
are the clear and unmistakable fingerprints of the divine Architect
of the universe, the almighty and eternal Being who is our Father
and our God.*

POINTS TO REMEMBER

1. Just as a building needs a strong foundation, so does
religion and the spiritual life. God is the rockbound
foundation of all things spiritual.

2. The existence of God is not an uncertain thing—it
can be demonstrated from the findings of modern
science.

3. The world's great *mathematicians* have stated that
the universe could not have come into existence by
chance—there must have been, and must be, a Supreme
Being who created it all.

4. The world's great physicists, looking at the staggering complexity of the universe, have stated that there
must have been, and must be, a supreme Intelligence
who put it all together and makes it work.

5. Wise men through the ages have agreed that the
universe proves there is a God:

St. Paul, 2000 years ago: ". . . the firmament declareth the work of His hands."

Sir James Jeans, today: "We discover that the universe shows evidence of a designing or controlling
power."

6. The organization of the human body and especially of the brain shows plan and purpose.

7. The achievements of the human mind demonstrate the existence of a Supreme Being, the Author of the laws of nature, whom we call God.

8. By learning these laws one can learn more about God Himself, in whom we live and move and have our being.

9. The evidence of God's existence is everywhere—and it is overwhelming.

3.

WHAT GOD MEANS TO US

"I, Lord, went wandering like a strayed sheep seeking Thee with anxious reasoning without, whilst Thou wast within me . . . I went around the squares and streets of the city of this world, and I found Thee not, because in vain I sought without for Thee who wast within myself."
—*St. Augustine*

Endowed with intellect and will, man is fashioned in the image and likeness of God. He towers above all the brutes of the field because he possesses a spiritual nature, an immortal soul, destined for an eternal life with God in heaven.

The more profoundly one studies the moral and spiritual endowments of man, the more clearly does he perceive not only the existence of a moral Lawmaker but also the claims of that divine Legislator upon man's allegiance, obedience and love. This leads us into the realm of religion, which concerns itself with the relations between the creature and the Creator. When we enter this realm, we come into possession of new sources of knowledge concerning God.

The picture provided by the findings of science is indeed a majestic and awesome one: divine omnipotence written in capital letters upon the star-studded sky and divine omniscience shining in all its brilliance in the feat of a fecundated human ovum and in the mysterious operations of the mind and conscience of man. But the picture is still meager and sketchy. It needs the clarity and wealth of detail which can be provided only by divine revelation.

Where the findings of research in the natural sciences end,

divine revelation begins. Consequently it is necessary to supplement our knowledge of God with the penetrating insights and
the richness of the revelation of God supplied by the Bible.
"God," says the Apostle Paul, "who at sundry times and in
divers manners spoke in times past by the prophets, last of all in
these days hath spoken to us by his son." These divine communi-
cations were transmitted to us through the inspired writers of the
Old and the New Testament—the holy Bible. What a song at
twilight is to a weary worker, what the sight of home is to a lonely
wanderer, what a compass is to a pilot on a stormy night, the
Bible is to us—"a lamp unto our feet and a light upon our path."

Biblical
Science

The scholarly study of the Scriptures has led to the development of various branches or specialties within the general field
of Biblical science: hermeneutics, which formulates the general
principles for the determination of the meaning of the Scriptures;
exegesis, the application of these principles to specific texts to
interpret them correctly; textual criticism, which seeks to determine the precise wording of the passage. Biblical science includes also lexicography, which is concerned with the correct
translation of the words; historical criticism, which establishes
the authorship and the historical setting of the passage; lin-
guistics, which embraces Hebrew, Greek and Latin—the languages particularly involved in the study of the Bible and the
early commentaries on it; form criticism, which attempts to recover the units of oral tradition which were in circulation before
the Scriptural texts, especially the Gospels, were written.

From this brief description of the various branches of Biblical
science, it is evident that the same painstaking efforts made by
scholars in the secular sciences to discover objective truth are
matched by their counterparts in the sacred sciences. Dovetail-
ing into the work of the Scriptural scholar is that of the trained

theologian whose field embraces the whole content of divine revelation. Theology may be defined as the *science of religion:* it
studies in the light of reason and divine revelation the relations
between God, man, and the universe. Its two chief branches are
dogmatic theology and moral theology.

As we come now to treat of the *nature* of God and our *relations* with Him, it is necessary for us to avail ourselves of the
great fund of scientific knowledge resulting from the research of
Scriptural scholars and trained theologians. Utilizing the blazing
light of divine revelation, these scholars throw upon our subject
an illumination much greater than any which the workers in the
natural sciences can provide. This they do, not by exhortation or
preaching, but by simple exposition: a dispassionate objective
presentation of the facts.

The light furnished by the natural sciences discloses simply the
power and *intelligence* of the Creator. It reveals nothing of His
solicitude and *love* for man. These are qualities and values—
realities outside the scope of the physical sciences which are
concerned with material things and their quantitative aspects.
Faith, hope, love, devotion, beauty, goodness, honor and sacrifice
never grace the vocabulary of the physical scientist because, elud-
ing all the senses, they can neither be weighed nor measured.
They are as far beyond the reach both of the microscope and the
telescope as God is. They are, however, the realities which constitute the core of human life and give it purpose, meaning and
value. They stem from the source of all moral and spiritual
values—the infinite Creator of the universe.

God Revealed
in Christ

One day a brilliant young instructor in the physical sciences
came into my office in the Newman Foundation at the University
of Illinois, where I was teaching courses in the philosophy of
religion to upperclassmen of various faiths.

"Dr. O'Brien," he said, "as a scientist I know that the network
of law, which governs all the phenomena of the physical uni-

verse, indicates the existence of a Supreme Intelligence and
Power. But how do I get to a *personal* deity, whom I can adore
and *love*, with whom I can *communicate*, and from whom I can
receive grace and help in time of need? These are the vital questions which physical science doesn't answer for me."

"My friend," I replied, "I could refer you to many learned
works treating the nature of God and His relations with man.
But that would necessitate reading for many months and unfortunately most of these scholarly works are in the technical
language of philosophy and theology. You want an answer here
and now. I can give it to you, for fortunately there is a short cut.

"The best picture of God that we can ever acquire is that
afforded us by the person of Jesus Christ, the untarnished mirror
of the Most High. Uniting in Himself the nature of man and
the nature of God, Christ is God incarnate. God stands revealed
to us in the character of Him who cleanses the lepers, heals the
sick, restores sight to the blind, forgives the woman taken in
adultery, washes the feet of His disciples, sheds His blood for
the redemption of mankind and, dying on the cross, pardons
His executioners.

"See the gentle Christ," I continued, "as He walks over the
dusty roadsides of Judea and Galilee and says to His disciples,
'Learn of me, for I am meek and humble of heart.' It is His
ministry of mercy and love that prompts the Beloved Disciple
St. John to give the noblest and most penetrating definition of
God ever uttered, when he says simply, 'God is love.' That lays
bare the very heart of God and His essential nature. Jesus confirms that answer when He says, 'If anyone love me, he will keep
my word, and my Father will love him, and we will come to him
and make our abode with him.' "

Love
Opens Eyes

The young instructor was silent for a few moments, evidently
reflecting upon what I had said. Then he remarked: "That makes
sense to me. It opens my eyes to an important fact, namely, that

I must use not only my intellect but also my heart. One can read a lot about love, analyze and dissect it, but still be ignorant of its essential nature and distinctive ethos. One must *experience* love to understand it."

"You're right," I remarked. "Jesus implies this in His answer to the doctor of the law as to which is the great commandment: 'Thou shalt love the Lord thy God with thy whole *heart*, and with thy whole soul, and with thy whole mind.' Hence it is only in *loving* God with all our faculties—heart, mind and soul—that we really *know* Him."

About a month later the young physicist returned. Gone was the look of puzzlement and inner disturbance. In its place was a smile of serenity, peace and inward joy.

"Dr. O'Brien," he said, "God is no longer a wraithlike vague abstraction to me. I see Him through the mirror of Christ as the very personification of Beauty, Truth, Goodness and Love. He is the answer to the cry for help in all my trials, the invisible Companion always at my side and the source of all my inner peace and joy.

"Life," he continued, "is no longer a desolate treadmill taking me nowhere. It now has direction, meaning and purpose. Every day I read a chapter of the Gospels and follow Christ in His journeying, and listen to Him teaching along the roadside. I find myself echoing the words of the disciples who walked with Him to Emmaus after the Resurrection: 'Was not our heart burning within us while he was speaking on the road and explaining to us the Scriptures?' "

Such, I think, is the experience of all who not only study the life and teachings of Jesus but also cultivate a personal devotion to Him and keep Him in their hearts as well as in their minds. His presence brings them the joy of a good conscience and warms their hearts with the radiance of a love that embraces all mankind, even one's enemies.

As the young scientist bore witness to the vivid and enthralling insight into the nature of God given to him by Christ, I thought of the words which Shakespeare has King Henry VI

address to the Duke of Gloucester after relieving him of his office
of royal protector:

> God shall be my hope,
> My stay, my guide, and lantern to my feet.

Yes, a good conscience is a wall of brass and God is the sure defense of every virtuous soul.

Seeing
God

In *Pathways to the Reality of God*, Rufus Jones tells of a
little boy who was being put to bed by his mother. Kissing him,
she said, "Good night, Johnny. Sleep tight." Then she turned
out the light and started for the door. A sudden fear came over
the child as the darkness closed in on him.

"Am I to be left all alone, Mommy," he asked, "and in the
dark too?"

"Yes, my dear," replied the mother. "But you know you have
God with you all the time."

"Yes, I know God is here," said the boy, "but I want someone who has a face."

Such too is the anxious, wistful cry of men and women everywhere. "We know in the abstract," observes Rufus Jones, "that
God is Mind and Spirit and that He is near us. But we want to
have a more vivid sense of His reality and His presence in our
world, and above all, we want to see Him and to discover Him
as a real Person with an actual Life and Character." This is precisely what Jesus does for us. It is in Him that we see not only
the face of God but also His personal character.

"The glory of Jesus," says Dr. Joseph R. Sizoo, "was that He
lived with gentleness. He introduced a new virtue into the world,
for the most beautiful and arresting thing about Him was that

He was gracious. He was never impatient, never unkind; He never spoke an unlovely word nor did an unlovely deed. He met rudeness with respect, pertness with politeness and coldness with courtesy. The inbred calm, the compassionate understanding and the serene magnanimity of Jesus will live to hallow and haunt all those who would live the good life."

The Clean
of Heart

To know God mere intellectual groping is not enough. More helpful in seeing God than intellectual subtlety are a pure heart and a clean conscience. Christ did not promise the beatific vision to the keen of intellect but He did say: "Blessed are the clean of heart, for they shall see God."

These words must have burned their way into the mind of Ignatius, Bishop of Antioch. Condemned to death by the Emperor Trajan for his refusal to worship the nation's idols, he was being led through the streets of Rome to the Flavian amphitheater to be torn limb from limb by the savage beasts in the arena. A Roman soldier mocked and scoffed him.

"Who," he sneered, "is this Christian God of yours?"

The venerable bishop gazed for a moment into the soldier's sensual dissipated face.

"You shall know Him," he replied, "when you are worthy of Him."

The person who suffers persecution for justice's sake, who sacrifices for truth, who hungers for righteousness, who lives a godly life, penetrates to the deepest understanding of God. Virtue is more important than knowledge in enriching one's vision of God. Live a holy life and God will dwell in you and make Himself known to you.

"God's thoughts," observes George Macdonald, "His will, His love, His judgments are all man's home. To think His thoughts, to choose His will, to love His loves, to judge His judgments, and thus to know that He is in us, to be at home."

When God dwells in the soul of a person, a radiance shines in his face, a spiritual resonance in his voice, and peace fills his heart. Nothing in the universe can supply the radiance lost when God is banished from a human life. The experience of humanity the world over verifies the finding of St. Theresa: "Where God is, there is Heaven. Where God is not, there is Hell." Plato too caught a glimmering of this mighty truth when he declared: "To escape from evil we must be made, as far as possible, like God; and this resemblance consists in becoming just, holy, and wise."

The Answer
to Our Cry

God, then, is the answer to the cry of the human soul for happiness. In the partial possession of God in this life, we catch glimmerings of that supreme ecstasy which the soul will experience when it shall be in intimate union with infinite Beauty, Truth, and Love. Then the unveiled majesty of the eternal King will ravish the soul with beauty and still its restless yearning with a love that knows no ending.

"Eye has not seen," says St. Paul, the great Apostle of the Gentiles, "nor ear heard, nor has it entered into the heart of man, what things God has prepared for those who love him." A foretaste of that ineffable bliss is experienced by all who walk in the paths of peace and righteousness, who keep always the joy of a good conscience, and who feel the love of God warming their hearts with its divine radiance.

This is illustrated in the life of St. Paul. Word reaches the Apostle in his prison cell in Rome that he is soon to be executed. Is he upset and terrified at the grim news? On the contrary, he was never more serene. "I have fought the good fight," he says, "I have finished the course, I have kept the faith." Turning with confidence to the Lord whose name he has carried afar unto the Gentiles, he continues: "For the rest there is laid up for me a crown of justice, which the Lord, the just Judge, will give to me in that day."

Albert Schweitzer, a noted Biblical scholar, philosopher and musician, gave up his professorship at the University of Strassburg and undertook the study of medicine that he might minister to the Lambarenes in the French Congo, who were without the services of any physician. For many years he has labored among them, working far into the night at the little hospital he has built in the African jungle. Does he feel lonely, discouraged, downcast?

Far from it. The consciousness that he is fulfilling Christ's law of love has buoyed him up and filled his heart with a quiet joy which neither fame nor worldly honors could provide. Stressing the supremacy of the commandment of love and its ability to effect the most intimate union with God, Schweitzer says: "The essential element, in Christianity, as it was preached by Jesus . . . is this, that *it is only through love* that we can attain to communion with God."

The Nature of God

We supplement the knowledge of God provided by the person, character, and life of Christ with that afforded by Scriptural scholars and theologians studying the contents of divine revelation. As we have previously indicated, the findings of their painstaking research are as worthy of the term "scientific" as are those of the physical scientists.

Human language is unable to express adequately the attributes of the deity and it is impossible for finite minds to comprehend the infinite. The language even of the inspired writers of holy Scripture groans, staggers and falters under the awesome burden of divine revelation. Perceiving this, the writer of *Ecclesiasticus,* speaking of God and His infinite power, says significantly, "We shall say much, and yet shall want words." But struggling bravely under his burden, he adds, "The sum of our words is: He is all."

God is revealed to us as a spirit, all-wise, all-powerful, eternal and omnipresent—existing everywhere. "God is a Spirit," says Christ, "and they that adore Him, must adore Him in spirit and in truth." God is present everywhere in three ways: by His essence, by His knowledge and by His superintending power.

Just as the soul pervades the body and is necessary for every movement I make, so God's concurring power is necessary for every deed I do, for every word I utter, and for every thought I think. Just as God brought us into existence out of the yawning abyss of nothingness by His creative power, so He sustains us in existence by His conserving power. Were God to withdraw His sustaining hand from us for one instant, we would fall back into the nothingness from which we came. God is as necessary for our life as the air we breathe.

In the tabernacle of every faithful and devout soul God dwells in a particular manner. Attentive indeed are His ears to the prayers of him who communes with Him within this living temple. It is of this divine Presence that St. Paul writes to the Corinthians: "Know ye not that you are the temple of God, and that the Spirit of God dwelleth in you? But if any man violate the temple of God, him shall God destroy. For the temple of God is holy, which you are." With Tennyson can the devout soul say:

> Speak to Him, thou, for He hears, and Spirit
>   with Spirit can meet—
> Closer is He than breathing, and nearer
>   than hands and feet.

God
Intimately Present

God is present in an especially intimate manner in the soul that is filled with the love of God. It was in this manner that God took up His abode with the prophets, Apostles, martyrs, saints and all the holy souls who clung to Him in deeds of righteousness, in prayer and in acts of love. God and one constitute a majority. When God is with one, he need fear no power in heaven, on earth or under the earth.

This is illustrated by an incident in the life of St. Francis of Assisi. In 1219 he set out to preach the Gospel to the Saracens who were then at war with the Crusaders. Though Francis was aware of the fearful punishment and death inflicted by the Moslems upon Christians who fell into their hands, he walked fearlessly into the camp of the enemy.

"Take me," he said to the astonished Moslems, "to your leader, the sultan, for I bear tidings of great moment."

Led to the sultan, who was curious to learn what news this Christian emissary could have, Francis said:

"I bring you the good tidings of man's redemption. Christ the Savior died for all men and opened for them the gates of heaven. His love embraces all and His religion is one of universal love. His commandment is twofold: "Love God with your whole hearts and your neighbor as yourself. God is love and He wants His children to love all men, even their enemies."

In this vein Francis continued for some time. The sultan listened in amazement not only at the preaching but also at the absolute fearlessness of the preacher, armed only with innocence and love. He could not find it in his heart either to kill or imprison such a man and sent him back unharmed to the Christians' camp.

The realization of the intimate presence of God in the souls of those who love and serve Him is a powerful bulwark against temptation and an incentive to strive constantly to make one's soul a more fitting habitation for the Most High. For this reason there are few exercises of the spiritual life more profitable than that of the practice of the presence of God, the constant recollection, even if only subconscious, of the indwelling of our Maker, our best Friend, and our ultimate Judge. When we forget about God, and turn our backs upon Him, danger stares us in the face.

Experience
of the Race

Other people can at times take on such a garb of attractiveness that, almost before we realize it, we find our hands stretching out to possess them. The experience of the race, sad and tragic as it is, shows us, however, that these experiences are like Dead Sea apples that crumble at the touch. They do not yield the promised joy but only boredom, nausea and remorse.

We shall be spared from learning by the costly method of painful experience, if we remember the all-important fact of God's presence. Thus sin becomes an offense not to a distant Being in the far-off firmament, but an insult to One present within us. Is it likely that an individual will deliberately insult a friend in his very presence?

In his great work, *The Varieties of Religious Experience*, William James treats at length of the serenity and peace which result from the practice of the presence of God. He tells how it leads to "the disappearance of all fear from one's life, the quite indescribable and inexplicable feeling of inner security, which one can only experience, but which, once it has been experienced, one can never forget."

Probably few men practiced the presence of God more frequently than the intrepid Apostle of the Gentiles. Though he was often imprisoned, scourged, stoned, shipwrecked, and suffered from hunger, cold and nakedness, he experienced an inner glow from the consciousness of the divine presence within him. Indeed he had come to feel the divine life throbbing within him to such a degree that he was able to say: "It is now no longer *I* that live, but *Christ* lives in me."

Indeed one cannot flee from God's presence, even if he would. He may separate from His friendship but not from His presence. Even though guilty, he must still face his Maker and his Judge. What experience in life is more embarrassing and painful than that of facing a friend with whom you have not kept faith? What gnaws more deeply into the marrow of your being than the agony which comes from the realization that you have shattered the high ideals that he has held of you?

The shame you experience is hotter than a red-hot iron, more piercing than a serpent's tooth. How can one escape that bitter humiliation, that cup of gall, if one fails to keep faith with his Lord and Master who has deigned to make His abode within the individual's heart and soul?

Our Best Friend

The realization of God's abiding presence is helpful not only in resisting temptation but also in bearing with patience and even with joy the hardships and the pains which life in this valley of the shadow of death inevitably brings. Is it not easier to bear sickness and pain when we know that we are in the presence of friends, doctors and nurses who will not fail to do all in their power to help us? So likewise the consciousness of the presence of our best Friend will not fail to give us strength to carry our burden and to bear our suffering with patience and resignation.

God will not fail to make each moment of pain bear its rich fruition in the ineffable joys of life everlasting. Such tribulation as He permits to fall upon us is but the "shade of His hand outstretched caressingly." In all the vicissitudes of life, in times of joy, temptation, or suffering, the consciousness of the presence of God will not fail to give us the humility, the protection, and the strength which we need.

When my students at Notre Dame came to me to say goodbye before they were sent to the far-flung battlefronts of World War II, I could think of no truth more comforting to propose to them than that of the constant presence of God.

"Remember," I was accustomed to say, "whether you are sent to the Solomon Islands in the South Pacific, or to the Aleutians in the far North, to Tunisia or to any of the countries of Europe;

whether you are assigned to a submarine to prowl in the depths of the sea, or to an airplane to wing your way through the trackless skies, or to be encased in a mighty iron tank to penetrate to areas where no other vehicle could travel, remember that God is with you wherever you go."

It has not always been easy for youth to leave home and friends and native lands to go out to face death in all its hideous forms in the far corners of the world. But what, perhaps more than anything else, nerved them for the difficult task which their country asked of them, was the realization that God went with them all the way. It is a truth, as helpful as it is comforting, for old and young. To clasp the outstretched hand of God in all our gropings and wanderings is to find a sure and a safe road.

God Infinitely Perfect

No catalogue can list all the perfections of God, for He is infinitely perfect. No words can adequately describe His beauty, holiness and love, for they transcend the mind of man. In seeking to depict the wisdom and the knowledge of God, we find ourselves exclaiming with St. Paul: "O the depth of the riches of the wisdom and of the knowledge of God! How incomprehensible are His judgments, and how unsearchable His ways! For who hath known the mind of the Lord? Or who hath been His counselor? . . . For of Him, and by Him, and in Him are all things: to Him be glory forever. Amen."

Not infrequently the tribulations, which God in His infinite wisdom permits to fall upon us, turn out to be blessings in disguise. This is illustrated in the life of Sir Walter Scott. He was about to retire to his beautiful estate Abbotsford to spend the remainder of his days, living the comfortable life of a country gentleman. But through the indiscretion of his business partners he was suddenly faced with bankruptcy and a debt of 100,000 pounds.

To meet his obligations Scott arose at four o'clock every morning, and wrote the famous Waverly novels, which have so greatly enriched our literature and brought joy to countless readers. No wonder it was that the author acknowledged in his diary that the apparent misfortune proved to be "a tonic and a bracer"—a blessing in disguise.

While we can neither scale the heights of God's knowledge nor plumb the depth of His wisdom, we can secure some feeble concept of the perfections of the Almighty when we realize that the admirable and lovable qualities found in the noblest of human beings are all found in their plenitude in Him. These qualities can exist in only a limited way in human beings because their containers are limited.

Years ago I sat one evening at sunset looking out over the waters of the sea of Galilee along whose shores the divine Master had so often walked with His Apostles. Suddenly my reverie was broken by the arrival of a group of native women.

They had come, as their forbears from time immemorial had come, to fill their vessels from the waters of the ancient sea. Then, placing their vessels on their heads, they returned to their homes. They come to a goodly lake, but they go away with such a tiny bit. Not because there is no more water to take, but because that is all their receptacles will contain.

How like a picture of humanity! We come from the illimitable ocean of the being and perfections of the infinite Creator. But we carry away only a few tiny drops of that vast ocean because that is all our finite human nature will bear. What the mighty expanse of the waters of the Pacific is to the thimbleful scooped out by a little child, the immeasurable being of the infinitely perfect God is to the finite being of man. We are a drop of water: He is the mighty sea. We are a grain of sand: He is the vast seashore. We are a splinter of time: He is the ageless sequoia. We are a farthing candle: He is the blinding sun.

In short, God is the answer to the cry of every lonely soul for friendship and love. He is the fulfillment of our ceaseless quest for life and happiness. He is the end of the rainbow, the Alpha and the Omega, the beginning and the end of all things. He is the light of the world, and they who follow Him do not walk in darkness, but shall have the light of life. He is love unutterable, and the only love that can still our restless hearts.

"Our hearts," says St. Augustine, "have been made for Thee, O God, and they shall never rest, until they rest in Thee." The practice of the presence of God fills our heart with a quiet peace and makes our face to shine with a radiance which neither clouds can obscure nor grief banish. To know God is to love Him, and to serve Him is to reign.

POINTS TO REMEMBER

1. The findings of the natural scientists are sufficient to establish the existence of a Supreme Being. To learn about the nature of God and His relations with man, however, it is necessary to have recourse to divine revelation recorded in the Bible and to the findings of Biblical scientists and theologians.

2. The best picture of God that we can ever acquire is that afforded us by Jesus Christ, the untarnished mirror of the Most High. Jesus is God incarnate, and He reveals the love and mercy of God for man.

3. A good conscience and a pure heart are of greater help to one in seeing God than intellectual acumen devoid of humility.

4. Live a holy life and God will dwell in you and make His presence known.

5. God is a spirit, all-wise, all-powerful, eternal, infinite and present everywhere.

6. A good conscience is a source of strength, security, peace and joy.

7. The practice of the presence of God within us banishes fear and enables us to withstand adversities.

8. Because God is infinitely perfect the human mind cannot grasp all His perfections.

9. God is the answer to the cry of every lonely soul for friendship and love.

4.

WORSHIP:
THE HEART OF RELIGION

"Where there are two or three gathered together
in my name, there am I in the midst of them."
—Our Savior, Jesus Christ

One day a middle-aged businessman came into my office with a problem I've encountered many times. He was well groomed and apparently prosperous.

"My wife is a good Christian woman," he said, "and our son and two daughters go to church with her and then attend Sunday school. They seem to get a lot out of religion. They're cheerful and happy when they return. I'm beginning to feel as though I'm the 'black sheep' of the family. But I've been so engrossed in business for many years that I've forgotten how to worship.

"Worse even than that," he continued, "I've come to look upon religion as a mere matter of listening to a sermon and singing hymns, and I don't feel the need for either. Am I right in thinking that religion is good for those who feel the need for it but isn't necessary for folks like me? I don't want to go just out of social pressure, for I'd feel like a hypocrite."

"I think the solution of your problem," I replied, "lies in getting a better understanding of what religion really means. It isn't merely a matter of attending church and singing hymns. It's much more than that. It's essentially the recognition of God, your Creator and heavenly Father, and the fulfillment of your duties to Him.

"Let me illustrate. You have a son whom you have clothed, fed and sheltered. You are providing him with a good education and are showering him with something more precious still—your love and care. You expect him to recognize you as his father, and to show some gratitude for all you've done for him and to reciprocate your love.

"Suppose that you come home after a hard day's work at the office and find your son sitting in a chair reading the newspaper. He doesn't look up at you. He doesn't greet you. In fact, he ignores you in every possible way. Wouldn't you feel hurt? Indeed you would be inclined to say, 'What kind of an abnormal son do I have? Doesn't he have even a spark of gratitude and love for the father who helped to bring him into being and has provided for his many wants?' "

I paused to let the words sink home. The smile on his face showed that they had.

"Golly," he said, "I had never realized the way I've ignored my obligation to my Creator. It's about time I quit being an ingrate and began to pay the homage of my gratitude to the God who created me and to the Christ who redeemed me."

Meaning
of Religion

The incident brings out vividly, I think, the fact that most people want to pay their just debts, but that many of them fail to realize *they owe a debt to God.* Religion is not a matter of mood, caprice or sentiment. It is essentially the paying of a debt —the greatest and most important debt in our lives.

In its broadest sense, religion is the sum of the relations between the creature and the Creator. On the part of the creature, it means the acknowledgment of his complete and abiding dependence upon the Creator and the latter's absolute and sovereign dominion over him.

This sense of dependence upon God, this keenly felt need of divine assistance, coupled with man's conviction that he can place himself in friendly and helpful communion with the deity, and his efforts to do so, are the essence of religion. At the very heart of religion, then, lie two ideas: the consciousness of man's need of God, and the conviction that the humble and reverent expression of the need for divine aid can and will be answered.

God, we cannot emphasize too often or too forcefully, is not an impersonal force. He is neither nature, nor the cosmos, even when these words are written with capitals. He is a Person. Man admires the crimson and gold which gild the leaves of a mighty forest with autumnal splendor. He stands in awe before the majesty of mountains whose snow-crowned peaks tower into the heavens. He marvels at the delicate fragrance of an Easter lily whispering of life soon to replace the snows of winter. He is thrilled by the prodigality of gorgeous colors with which nature splashes the skies at sunset. All these he can admire, but he can *love* only a *person* and *worship* only a *God.*

Religion is thus seen to be essentially a *personal* relation. Man raises aloft his hand to clasp the hand stretched down from on High. He opens his lips to a listening ear. He pours out the love of his heart to a heart which reciprocates with an overwhelming love. Reciprocation is of the very essence of religion. God both listens and replies. James Russell Lowell wrote:

> God is not dumb, that he should speak no more;
> If thou hast wanderings in the wilderness
> And find'st not Sinai, 'tis thy soul is poor.

Don't Cut Down
the Tree

Here it seems appropriate to come to grips with a difficulty sometimes urged against the practice of religion. The difficulty was voiced by a university student who remained after one of my class lectures.

"I'm taking a course in comparative religion," he said, "and it shows that many primitive peoples employed a good deal of magic and superstition in their religious practices. Doesn't this tend to discredit all religion?"

"No," I replied. "The conclusion is much too wide for the premises. If that line of reasoning were to prevail there would not be today a single valid science. In their early stages all branches of science were infested with error. Medicine is a capital example. Many false potions, treatments and remedies were mixed up with the early practice of the healing art. Does it follow that the whole modern science of medicine is therefore without any solid basis?

"Until recent decades physicists believed that all matter consisted of hard *inert* pellets called atoms. Does that erroneous notion discredit the modern science of physics? Thousands of years ago Cicero punctured the fallacy of those who tried to discredit religion by pointing to the superstitions encumbering it, when he said: 'Religion is not removed by removing superstition.'"

"Yes," agreed the student, "I see that the conclusion is far too wide for the premises. You don't cut down an apple tree because you discover a few bad apples."

God's Solicitude
for Man

There are two kinds of religion: *natural* and *supernatural*. Natural religion is the sum of man's duties to God in so far as they can be ascertained by the light of reason alone. The principal duties of man according to the law of nature are expressed in the Ten Commandments, except that the day designated to be kept holy would not necessarily be the Sabbath.

Supernatural religion is the sum of man's duties to God as made known by divine revelation. There are certain truths, such as the Trinity and the Incarnation, which are beyond man's capacity to discover. There are other truths, such as that God is one, eternal and infinite, which man could arrive at by his reason. Many of the truths of natural religion are also divinely revealed. They are supernatural only in the manner in which they have been made known to us.

Divine revelation is a beautiful and striking expression of God's solicitude and love for man. If left entirely to himself, man would fall into many errors and abominations, as the history of pagan antiquity abundantly shows. By revealing religious truths, God removes all uncertainty about them. This is of great importance. Without that divine assurance, man would be paralyzed by doubt.

The great Scottish writer Thomas Carlyle once said of the poet, Robert Burns: "His religion at best is an anxious wish—like that of Rabelais, a great Perhaps." Man won't, however, resist a driving passion or face the martyr's fire on the strength of a mere Perhaps. He needs the certainty that comes most impressively from God's assurance that a thing is true.

God's Right
to Our Worship

The duty of worshiping God is a truth made known by our reason and revealed by the Almighty in both the Old and the New Testament. It is a truth therefore of both natural and supernatural religion. Let's look at it first in the light of reason alone.

A man who paints a picture, owns it. He has put onto the canvas all the colors that give it value. It's his because he has made it. His title to such a painting is universally recognized. Similarly the sculptor, who takes a rough block of marble and carves out of it a great statue, owns that sculpture because he has made it.

In each instance, however, the artist used material already in existence. The painter created neither the canvas nor the colors; the sculptor created neither the marble nor the chisel. Hence the title of neither to the work of his hands is as absolute as

God's title to the ownership of His creatures. He has not only shaped and fashioned them but also created them out of nothing by an act of His all-powerful will. As this point is of crucial importance, I shall illustrate it with an example.

One day Michelangelo was walking along a street in Florence, when he spied a large block of Carrara marble. It had been hacked, cut and spoiled by an unskillful craftsman and then discarded as worthless. The keen eye of the gifted sculptor perceived in it the possibilities of a great statue, and he had it hauled to his studio.

There, day after day and week after week he carved and chiseled, seeking to fashion the marble into the likeness of the youthful David. After months of painstaking labor the unsightly block had disappeared: in its place there stood the figure of the gallant young conqueror of Goliath, so lifelike that it seemed almost to be breathing.

Transported by its perfection, the great sculptor seized a mallet and struck the base of the statue. "Speak! Speak!" he cried, seeking to have it burst into life.

While it has not spoken in words, the mute eloquence of its beauty, symmetry of form and perfection of detail has for four centuries provoked the admiration and the praise of visitors from all lands. Indeed it is acclaimed by not a few connoisseurs as one of the greatest masterpieces of the sculptor's art.

On the day when I first saw it in the Pitti Palace in Florence, several American physicians were grouped around it. They were loud in their praise of the fidelity with which Michelangelo had reproduced the muscles and sinews of the human body.

As I listened to the words of praise that came so spontaneously to their lips, I could not help but reflect: "Their eulogies are indeed well merited. But how strange it is that people, who pour forth their meed of admiration and praise for the sculptor who reproduces the inert likeness of the human figure, seldom pause to ponder upon the far greater feat of the Creator who not only fashioned the human figure but also brought it into existence and endowed it with life. If the sculptor of the likeness of the human figure is worthy of praise, how much more so is the infinite Creator of the living human being!"

A Demand
of Truth and Justice

It is therefore a stern dictate of both reason and common sense that we should acknowledge the Creator's absolute *dominion* and *sovereignty* over us and our utter *dependence* upon Him. This is a demand of both truth and justice. The rendering of such acknowledgment constitutes the worship of God, which is the heart of religion. The person who refuses such worship is living a flagrant lie and perpetrating a monstrous injustice. He is subverting the whole moral order and all nature cries out at him, "Liar! Ingrate! Robber! Thief!"

This dictate of reason is confirmed by the voice of divine revelation. The pages of the Old and New Testament are vocal with this message. "Let all the earth adore Thee," cries the Psalmist, "and sing to Thee: let it sing a psalm to Thy name." And again he exclaims: "Come, let us adore and fall down: and weep before the Lord that made us. For He is the Lord our God: and we are the people of His pasture and the sheep of His hand." We should worship God not only because He is our Creator, but also, as the Psalmist points out, because He is holy: "Exalt ye the Lord our God, and adore at His holy mountain: for the Lord our God is holy."

Shortly after the birth of Jesus, the Magi came and, relates Matthew, "falling down they adored Him; and opening their treasures, they offered Him gifts: gold, frankincense and myrrh." After Satan had sought to tempt our Lord, Jesus says: "Begone, Satan: for it is written, The Lord thy God shalt thou adore, and Him *only* shalt thou serve."

To the Samaritan woman at Jacob's Well, Jesus says: "But the hour cometh, and now is, when the true adorers shall adore

the Father in spirit and in truth. For the Father also seeketh such
to adore Him. God is a spirit; and they that adore Him, must
adore Him in spirit and in truth."

The obligation to worship God *binds all human beings,* for
they are all indebted to the Creator for their existence as well as
for the endowments of their bodies and minds. It is a duty from
which not even God can dispense His children since it is rooted
in the *moral law:* this binds a father to require the respect, honor
and love of his children and obliges the children to render the
same.

Social Worship
Is Required

How many kinds of worship are there? There are two chief
kinds: internal and external. Internal homage consists of the
thoughts of praise and adoration and of the sentiments of reverence, devotion and love. External worship is the expression of
such thoughts and sentiments in prayer, hymns and ceremonies.
Since God is the Author of body and soul, we must render to
Him the homage of both. Otherwise we would be defrauding
Him by paying only *half* the debt.

"The tongue blessing God without the heart," points out the
British theologian Ralph Venning, "is but a tinkling cymbal; the
heart blessing God without the tongue is sweet but still music.
Both in concert make their harmony, which fills and delights
heaven and earth."

External worship is of two kinds, *private* and *public,* and both
are required. An individual alone in his room may render external homage to God. But more than this is required: he must
join with others and render public or social homage to the
Creator. Why? Because God has endowed man with a *social*
nature, and man must use that endowment to worship God.
Otherwise he is not fully acknowledging His indebtedness to the
Almighty. This is a truth of great practical importance, which I
shall illustrate.

Solving Problem
of Nonattendance at Church

A minister in one of my classes said: "I'm always greatly worried about the weather on Sunday morning. I work diligently on my sermon for several days, polish it carefully, and then commit it to memory. This is no small chore. But if it's raining hard on Sunday, the attendance falls to a handful. I go through with the sermon as best I can, but it's tough going, and I feel disappointed because it reaches so few. How can I solve this problem?"

"Reverend," I replied, "I think the solution lies in stressing the serious *obligation* to render public *social* homage to almighty God, rain or shine. People must be made to realize that this is not a matter of mood or whim, or dependent upon the weather. Where there's a will, there's a way.

"This is shown by the fact that people, who have theater tickets, or a dinner engagement or other appointments, find ways of getting there. They must be made to realize that on Sunday they have the *most important date* of the entire week—a date with the Almighty.

"The Catholic Church drives this truth home to her children from the time they attain the use of reason. The Church teaches that this obligation binds under pain of grievous sin, from which one is excused only for some serious reason.

"The emphasis here," I continued, "is, however, chiefly on the *worship* of God through participation in the Holy Sacrifice of the Mass and not upon listening to a sermon, helpful though it may be. But certainly the primary consideration must always be the *worshiping* of God. This gives proper direction to the duty and shows *to* whom it is due: to God and not to any clergyman. Hence when people set out through the pouring rain, they realize they are keeping an *appointment with their God* and not with any man."

"I see," remarked my ministerial friend, "that there is a world of difference. Your explanation enables me to understand why your churches are so crowded on Sunday morning, frequently from early morning till nearly noon. It reminds me of the sensation created in New York when one of the city's prominent ministers proposed a moratorium on preaching. I know what he was driving at: more worship and less oratory. Put the spotlight upon God instead of upon the preacher."

"Yes," I said, "I can recall the comment of Rev. Dr. Harry Emerson Fosdick, pastor of New York's Riverside Church, on that proposal: *'That minister is concerned because the great multitude of our Christian people do not really worship. They must have someone forever talking to them. They do not know how to make high use of the power and joy of united reverence. His concern was justified.'*"

The Cancer of Worldliness

It is estimated that on any Sunday more than a hundred million people in the United States attend no church and hence engage in no public worship. Indeed there are millions who do not enter a church throughout the whole year. Back of nearly all this neglect of divine worship is the failure to understand that God *wants* it, has explicitly *commanded* it, and is *entitled* to it by the most compelling of all reasons, namely, that of creating us.

This truth, above all others, needs to be driven home to the people of our country, both young and old. It must be stamped upon the minds, written upon the hearts, and woven into the wills of all so that it becomes one of their most profound convictions. Otherwise worldliness and indifference to spiritual values will continue to eat like cancer into the warp and woof of their moral nature until they become pagans in everything but name.

This is the truth which Thomas Merton expressed so well in his memorable bestseller, *The Seven Storey Mountain:* "It is a law of man's nature, written into his very essence, and just as much a part of him as the desire to build houses and cultivate the land and marry and have children and read books and sing songs, that he should want to stand together with other men in order to acknowledge their common dependence on God, their Father and Creator."

Calling at my office one day, a middle-aged businessman said: "I've been away from the practice of religion for twenty years. I had gotten so engrossed in business that the accumulation of the almighty dollar became the be-all and the end-all of my existence. But I always felt that I was cheating God out of something to which He is entitled—homage and worship. This feeling became more acute on Sunday mornings when I heard church bells summoning my neighbors to worship.

"I'd try to escape from that sense of guilt by burying my head in the Sunday newspapers. But it was only a temporary escape. Remorse would bite into my peace of mind and haunt me through the week. I want to pay my debt of homage to my Creator and make up, if possible, for lost time. I'm a social creature and I want to stand with my fellowmen in worshiping the God who made us all."

His experience is typical of that of all persons who stop to think of the *debt* which they owe to God for all the blessings and gifts which He has lavished upon them. Among those gifts is the faculty of *speech* which the individual should use in union with his fellows in worshiping and thanking God. Until the debt of public worship is paid, remorse will disturb the peace of mind of every person with a sensitive conscience.

When Great Britain was at the zenith of her imperial power, exercising sway over one-fourth of the earth's surface and population, Rudyard Kipling, the poet laureate, sounded a note of warning in his famous *Recessional*, lest the nation forget the Source from whom all power and blessings flow. He wrote:

> God of our Fathers! Known of old,
> Lord of the far-flung battle line
> Beneath whose awful hand we hold
> Dominion over palm and pine.
> Lord God of hosts! Be with us yet,
> Lest we forget. Lest we forget!

That is the note that needs to be sounded in America today.
We must not forget the divine Being who has poured out His
blessings and favors upon us with so lavish a hand. Common
decency requires us to acknowledge our indebtedness to our
Creator and to return to Him the homage of our worship, gratitude and love.

Worship Deepens
Our Spiritual Life

Worship is not only the fulfillment of our most basic duty to
almighty God but it is also a means of enriching and deepening
our spiritual nature and securing for us many precious values and
blessings. "There is no other form of human endeavor," points
out Professor Henry Nelson Wieman of Chicago University, "by
which so much can be accomplished." Speaking of friendship,
love, beauty and other precious things in human life, Professor
Ernest Hocking of Harvard observes, "Worship is the whole
which includes them all."

My old friend and colleague at the University of Illinois, Professor Guy Tawney, says of worship, "It is indeed so important
that one finds oneself sometimes wondering how any of us can
afford to do anything but educate ourselves in this art." The
well-known British theologian, Gerald Vann, goes so far as to
say, "Worship, then, is not a part of the Christian life: it is the
Christian life."

Obviously the worship about which these scholars are speaking is not a mere casual sauntering into a church, gaping idly at
the service and then sauntering out. It is not the mere passive
role of an onlooker: it implies the actual participation of mind
and heart in the divine service. It means union of the soul with
God through acts of homage, adoration, gratitude and love. The
world fades away when the soul is lifted up to God in the most
intimate of all unions.

In worship one acknowledges his utter dependence upon God without whose divine assistance he is unable to advance in virtue and holiness. He realizes that he is as helpless as the babe, unable to take a single step without the supporting arm of its mother. As man reaches up his hand to clasp the outstretched hand of God, he is keenly conscious of the necessity of that indwelling which Jesus thus describes so clearly:

"Abide in me, and I in you. As the branch cannot bear fruit of itself unless it abide in the vine, so neither can you *unless you abide in me*. I am the vine; you the branches: he that abideth in me, and I in him, the same beareth much fruit: for *without me you can do nothing*."

Worship Provides Perspective and a Sense of Values

In worship one is brought face to face with his Maker and there he is reminded of the supreme values of life. He is freed from the tyranny of the visible and the transient and is enabled to perceive the invisible and the eternal. He is aided in forming a proper *hierarchy of values* and of putting first things first instead of last, as so often happens in the pressure of daily life.

He is enabled to recall more vividly the momentous words of the divine Master in pointing out to us life's supreme and primary objective: "What doth it profit a man if he gain the whole world and suffer the loss of his own soul?" In that moment of union with his Creator, the worshiper feels like the soldier, home on furlough, after years at a bleak and lonely outpost.

Worship lifts us out of ourselves and elevates us to a lofty eminence, and thus widens our horizons and gives us a sense of direction. "The greatest need of mankind today, socially and individually," says Canon B. H. Streeter of Oxford, "is a true sense of direction." The pilot of a vessel lost in a fog is unable to get his bearings and hence unable to steer the ship into the port.

A hunter and his guide lost their way in a dense woods in the Northwest and found to their dismay they had been walking in circles for three days. When finally spotted in a clearing by a helicopter pilot, they were rescued.

"If only there had been a hill," remarked the hunter, *"we could have gotten our bearings."*

Worship is the holy hill which we can climb each day and thus get our bearings in the midst of life's strangling close-ups and confusions.

In the Parable of the Prodigal Son Jesus tells us that when the son, returning to his father, "was yet a *great way off,* his father saw him, and was moved with compassion, and running to him fell upon his neck and kissed him." This seems to indicate that the father, eager to catch the first glimpse of his son, went to a hill from which he could survey the countryside. Who can doubt that each morning, as he stood on that elevation scanning the far horizon, he lifted up his heart and mind to God in acts of homage and supplication?

In worship one becomes more clearly conscious of the majesty, might, power, sovereignty and eternity of God. Unbidden to his lips, come the words of the Psalmist: "Lord, thou hast been our refuge from generation to generation. Before the mountains were made, or the earth and the world was formed, from eternity to eternity thou art God."

Centuries later the great Apostle to the Gentiles, St. Paul, sounds a similar note in proclaiming the paternity of the Almighty: "I bow my knees to the Father of our Lord Jesus Christ, of whom all paternity in heaven and earth is named, that he would grant you, according to the riches of his glory, to be strengthened by his Spirit with *might unto the inward man."* Yes, in true worship the Spirit of God flows into the human soul and gives it a *power and strength* which the things of this world cannot give. *Worship washes away man's tensions, gives him serenity, deepens his faith and strengthens him to undertake the noblest and to achieve the best.*

External Worship
No Substitute
for Virtue

Here I would like to come to grips with an objection often voiced against worship and those who engage in it. It was aptly stated by a man, long estranged from religion, who called one day at my office. Seeking to justify himself, he said: "I haven't attended church or engaged in worship for years. I know some people who are regular worshipers on Sunday but who aren't so scrupulous about trampling on some of the commandments on the other days of the week. I concluded that if that's all the good public worship does them, I might as well stay away."

"I've heard this objection," I replied, "a hundred times, but I don't think it's well founded. Its conclusion is too broad for its premises. You don't cut down a grapevine because you find on it a few bad grapes. Similarly you can't condemn a congregation because a few of its members don't live up to their moral code. They're the exceptions which prove the rule. It's a question whether such persons really engage in true worship.

"It's one thing," I continued, "merely to *attend* divine service and it's quite a different thing to *enter into its spirit and really engage in that elevation of mind and heart to God, which alone is worthy of the name of worship.* People who come for worldly motives and who simply go through the external actions are not really worshipers. They're hypocrites. They may deceive men but not God. 'Be not deceived,' warns the Apostle Paul, 'God is not mocked.' You can't throw dust in the eyes of the Almighty. He reads the thoughts of your mind and the secrets of your heart as the pages of an open book.

"By bringing one face to face with God, worship rebukes the evil in one's life. It makes him so clearly conscious of it in the presence of the infinitely holy God, that the sense of guilt scorches his conscience like a red-hot iron. The white radiance of God's presence lights up the dark places in one's conscience and

enables one to see more clearly where his conduct has been out
of step with God's law."

Ceremonies and rites of worship are, however, no substitute
for a virtuous life. Recall how emphatically the prophet Micheas
thundered this great truth to the people of Israel when he said:
"What doth the Lord require of thee, but to do justly, and to
love mercy, and to walk humbly with thy God?" This same
truth was stressed by Jesus Himself when He warned: "If therefore thou offer thy gift at the altar, and there thou remember
that thy brother hath anything against thee; leave there thy
offering before the altar, and go first to be reconciled to thy
brother: and then coming thou shalt offer thy gift."

"The Turning Point in My Life"

That the words of the Savior are hearkened to is evident from
the frequency with which news items appear telling of various
business firms and government offices receiving so-called "conscience" money. Let me cite a couple of examples.

Some time ago newspapers carried the story of a U.S. government office receiving $15,000 in payment of the tax on smuggled
goods. The smuggler explained that while attending divine services the consciousness of guilt became so clamorous that he decided then and there that he would make full restitution.

Even more striking and dramatic is the following case, related
to me by a prominent businessman in Chicago. "A sudden drop,"
he said, "in the value of several thousand shares of stock, in
which I had invested the profits of my business, washed out the
earnings of twelve years of hard work and threw me into bankruptcy. I was so upset that I went into a drugstore and bought
a deadly poison. While returning to my hotel, I passed a church
into which people were flocking.

"Before I realized it, the surge of the incoming worshipers had
drawn me along with them. I entered a rear pew. The sight of

all those worshipers kneeling in prayer, the beautiful hymns and
the soaring music of the organ combined to lift me out of myself. I suddenly found myself face to face with my Maker. New
streams of energy, power, hope, confidence and trust flooded my
soul. When the service was over, I poured the poison in the
gutter, and faced the situation with courage and common sense.

"In a few months the stocks began to pick up, and in a couple
of years my business was prospering more than ever before. *It
was that hour of worship which proved the turning point in my
life.* It has enabled me to see that no situation is really hopeless
when one turns to God in worship and unfaltering trust and
confidence."

Worshiping God
by Our Deeds

Life is a voyage made not in a canoe coursing effortlessly
along, with the occupant dipping a single paddle into the water.
It is made in a sturdy rowboat with the occupant struggling valiantly with both oars for every foot gained. One oar is *effort* and
the other is *worship*, and when only one oar is used, the voyager
finds himself traveling in circles.

True worship consists not only in words, but also in deeds.
God wants the homage of our *wills* as well as of our *intellects:
these are but the two sides of the same coin.* The notion that
worship has no connection with moral conduct is grotesque. "By
their fruits," declares Jesus, "you shall know them." Then He
continues, "Not every one that saith to me, Lord, Lord, shall
enter into the kingdom of heaven: but he that *doth* the will of
my Father who is in heaven, he shall enter into the kingdom of
heaven." This truth is central in the teachings of Christ. It is
stressed by every writer on the spiritual life. It is echoed by
Thomas à Kempis in his great masterpiece, *The Imitation of
Christ:* "Sublime words make not a man holy and just, but a
virtuous life maketh him dear to God."

To render God the praise of our words and to deny Him the homage of virtuous deeds is to hand Him a branch from which the fruit has been plucked. It is like the action of the man who places on the collection plate on Sunday an envelope, impressive enough on the outside but empty within. Worship is not an empty sham. It is a *living* tree, producing the fruit of morality, and both the tree and the fruit derive their vitality from God.

Well does the English poet, W. S. Blunt, say:

> The temple I would build should be all white,
> Each stone the record of a blameless day;
> The souls that enter there should walk in light,
> Clothed in high chastity and wisely gay.

POINTS TO REMEMBER

1. Religion is the sum of the relations between the creature and the Creator. On the part of the creature, it means the acknowledgment of his complete dependence upon the Creator and the latter's sovereign dominion over him.

2. At the heart of religion are two ideas: the consciousness of man's need of God and the conviction that the reverent expression of the need for divine aid will, in some way, be answered.

3. Natural religion is the sum of man's duties to God in so far as they can be ascertained by reason. Supernatural religion is the sum of man's duties to God as made known by divine revelation.

4. Because God created us, He has a right to our worship. This duty is dictated by reason and revealed in Holy Scripture. It is a demand of both truth and justice.

5. We must worship God with our minds and our bodies and join with others in public acts of social homage because our minds, bodies and social nature stem from God.

6. The duty of worshiping God is not satisfied by mere attendance at divine service and listening to a sermon, but requires the lifting of our minds and hearts to God in adoration, thanksgiving, propitiation and praise.

7. Worship deepens our spiritual life, unites us with God and provides perspective and a sense of values.

8. External worship is no substitute for virtue.

9. Worship renders one painfully conscious of his sins, and increases his horror and hatred of them and his purpose of amendment.

10. True worship consists not only in words but also in deeds. "By their fruits," says Jesus, "you shall know them."

5.

BRINGING RELIGION
INTO DAILY LIFE

"All things whatsoever you would that men should do to you, even so do you also to them; for this is the Law and the Prophets."—*Jesus* (Matthew 7:12)

"By their fruits you will know them."—*Jesus* (Matthew 7:16)

"Religious people have their heads in the clouds. Dreaming of happiness in heaven, they do little to bring it to earth. We'll make our own heaven on earth by fighting for social justice, a square deal for every worker and the equal distribution of property and of profits. We're no longer interested in a religion whose only promise is, 'There'll be pie in the sky when you die.' We want our pie now! We want our heaven here!"

Thus shouted a communist speaker from his soapbox in Hyde Park, London, where speakers solve with ease the vast complex problems of the world. As I stood in the motley crowd of listeners, I could not help but feel that he was echoing the cry of increasing millions in every land. They want action *now*. They want justice *now*. They want a more abundant life here—not merely in a future life. They want their pie *here and now*—not in the distant sky of another world.

Is there some grounds for this indictment of church-going people and of the religion they profess? Let us listen to the testimony of a speaker in our own country and see if it too stirs some soul-searching on the part of all religious people.

George E. Q. Johnson, Chicago's District Attorney, was battling the notorious mob of gangsters headed by Al Capone. Their bootlegging had mushroomed into a $50,000,000 racket; they had muscled into control of a number of labor unions; they were collecting millions from merchants for "protection." Scarcely a week passed without someone being murdered, often under ghastly circumstances, as a result of their network of activities.

Religion Needed
Seven Days
Each Week

Explaining to one of my university classes his difficulty in securing a conviction, Mr. Johnson said: "Persons who were shot, but did not die, were too afraid to reveal the name of the would-be murderer. Witnesses were called in, only to experience an attack of forgetfulness; other witnesses disappeared before the case came to court. When word got out that a witness was talking, he would be "taken for a ride," gangland style. Even hospitals were invaded and injured victims finished off to keep them from talking. Capone and his mob had paralyzed law and order. They had Chicago by the throat and were laughing in unholy glee."

"What was the matter with the citizens?" asked a student. "Didn't they have any spunk?"

"They seemed cowed," replied Johnson, "and wanted no part in our efforts to convict notorious and brazen killers. Even though we would promise witnesses police protection, they would either 'clam up' or suddenly forget all they knew. These citizens would go to church on Sunday, pray, sing hymns and listen to sermons. But they were afraid to put their religion into practice on weekdays, afraid to bring it into the courtroom, afraid to take the witness chair. This is the great weakness of so many church-going and religious people."

"Mr. Johnson," asked another student, "what is the cause of that?"

"It is traceable, I believe," he replied, "to the failure to realize that religion is a seven-day-week affair, that it must be brought into the market place, shop, office and courtroom. Citizenship calls for the discharge of duties, which at times may be more hazardous than those of a soldier. Religion calls for the performance of duties outside the church and synagogue as well as within them.

"This is the truth that was driven home to me when I was battling the Capone mob. Thank God, there were some citizens who realized this, and risked their lives to testify and thus help us send Capone to Alcatraz and ultimately break up the mob."

The Hyde Park talk and Mr. Johnson's story both dramatize the urgent need for all religious people to bring their religion into their daily lives, to make it serve as a leaven to transform the world, to eradicate its evils and heal its wounds.

Jesus Stresses Superiority of Works over Deeds

A religion which is donned on Sunday like a suit of clothes, and then is discarded the rest of the week is a mere caricature of the real article. Running through all religion that is worthy of the name is an insistence upon coming to grips with evil in all its forms. It declares eternal warfare against sin, vice and crime; its inner dynamism allows neither rest nor peace of mind until an individual has done his best to eradicate these cancers from the body of society.

Christ demands not mere words but deeds: these are the golden key which alone opens the door of heaven. Stressing the duty to follow His example, Jesus says: "I have given you an example, that as I have done to you, so you do also." What was that example? The Apostle Peter thus sums up the life of his Master: "He went about doing good." He healed the sick, restored sight to the blind and hearing to the deaf, cleansed the lepers, cured the paralytic, restored vigor of limb to the lame, forgave the sinner and cast out devils.

It was to these works that Jesus appealed as the evidence of His divine character. "If I do not the works of my Father," He says, "believe me not. But if I do, though you will not believe me, believe the works: that you may know and believe that the Father is in me, and I in the Father."

Thus dramatically did our Lord appeal to the superiority of deeds over mere words as an evidence of His divinity and of the truth of His teachings. As it was with the Master so it will always be with His disciples: the example of our lives will outweigh our words as an evidence of the power of the religion, which we profess, to leaven society and sanctify the individual.

This is the thought so well expressed by Peter, the chief of the Apostles: "Dearly beloved, I beseech you as strangers and pilgrims to refrain yourselves from carnal desires which war against the soul, having your conversation good among the Gentiles: that . . . they may, by the good works which they behold in you, glorify God in the day of visitation."

Example Speaks Louder
Than Words

The age and the country in which we live are particularly prone to judge institutions, creeds as well as persons by their deeds. This was the criterion which the Master proposed to His disciples to enable them to distinguish the true prophet from the false. "Beware of false prophets," He said, "who come to you in sheep's clothing, but inwardly are ravenous wolves. By their fruits you will know them."

Example is not only contagious but also infectious. It is as pervasive as the atmosphere, and its power transcends that of all spoken words. "People look at me six days in the week," remarked the English divine Richard Cecil, "to see what I mean on

the seventh." While precept merely points out the way to travel,
example draws one consciously or unconsciously along it.

Actions speak louder than words. "Of all commentaries upon
the Scriptures," observed John Donne, the English poet, "good
examples are the best and the liveliest." In his *Canterbury Tales*
Chaucer has the following significant couplet about the country
parson:

> This fine example to his flock he gave,
> That first he wrought, and afterward he taught.

How to Put Religion to Work

In short, the most urgent task facing Christians today, as in
the past, is to *put into daily practice in every area of human life
the great ethical principles and spiritual ideals which Jesus both
taught and exemplified.* This is the truth which our Lord
stressed in season and out of season: it runs like a thread of gold
through all the pages of the New Testament. The necessity of
bringing religion and its ethical teachings into daily life was
echoed and reechoed by Moses and the prophets in the Old
Testament, "What doth the Lord require of thee," said the
prophet Micheas, "but to *do justly,* and to love mercy, and to
walk humbly with thy God?"

"I'm convinced," remarked a businessman to me recently,
"that most religious people want to put their spiritual ideals into
practice, but don't always know how to do so. If you could show,
particularly by examples, how they can do this, you would render
a much needed service."

I'll try to do this. "The way is long by precept," runs the adage,
"but short by example." Accordingly I shall present some notable
examples showing how you can put your religion into practice,
help your fellow man and make the world a better place in which
to live.

Ministering
to the Poor and Hungry

In an article, "Blessed Crackpots," in *Guideposts*, Catherine Doherty, a former Russian baroness, relates that she and five friends were seated around a table one night in 1930 in Toronto. They were discussing the sad plight of the poor and unemployed. Thousands of them were unemployed and their families were hungry, living in unheated houses. The six decided to *do* something about it. They quit their jobs, sold all their property and gave the money to the poor.

They opened a two-room headquarters from which to work, and the doors were always open. During the four following years they fed and housed 40,000 unemployed, wandering men and cared for 700 children. They found jobs for impoverished fathers; they went into private homes; they nursed the sick. They didn't "talk religion"; they let their actions speak for themselves.

They established Friendship Houses where the poor and unemployed found shelter and food. The movement has spread, and now such houses are found in large cities in Canada and the United States. The workers in these houses are motivated by the love of God and His love of the poor. They seek to draw the poor to Christ not by words but by their deeds of kindness and love.

"One wintry night," relates Catherine, "a young man, lonely, sick and hungry, came to our Toronto house."

"What am I expected to do," he asked, "in return for food and shelter?"

"Nothing," replied Catherine. "Just stay until you find a job."

A few days later he said, "I think I'll go around to the communist meeting. Do you care?"

"Of course I care," answered Catherine, "but go if you wish. I warn you, though, I'll be praying for you."

He continued to attend the communist meetings, but never discussed them. On Christmas Eve, Catherine was busy, preparing a party for 600 orphans the next day. Late at night she hurried off to midnight mass. Later as she moved up the crowded aisle to the Communion rail, she felt someone nudge her. It was the young man.

"Merry Christmas!" he whispered, as he walked along at her side to the rail.

"He had come back to God on his own," commented Catherine, "without a word of preaching. It was the best Christmas present I ever received."

What a striking illustration of the power of example to draw souls to God! The young man perceived the love of God shining through Catherine's deeds. That love found a response in his own heart and brought him willingly to his knees in prayer, adoration and love.

A Word of Thanks
Warms Human Hearts

A word of thanks for a kindness, favor or gift would seem to be the least that might be expected in return. Of the ten lepers whom Christ cleansed, only one returned to thank Him. Jesus felt the sting of their ingratitude as evidenced by His words: "Were not the ten made clean? But where are the nine?"

That most of us are like the nine was shown by a study made by a postal employee of the mail addressed to Santa Claus that ended in the Dead Letter Office in Washington, D.C. There were thousands of letters asking for gifts of all kinds, but only one letter expressing thanks.

This is the theme developed by H. W. Ruopp in "That Magic Word" in Guideposts. He relates that Dr. William L. Stidger, a professor at the Boston School of Theology, was discussing with a group of friends the hardships and sufferings which people were experiencing from the depression then gripping the country.

"There sure isn't much to be thankful for," remarked one.

"Well I, for one," said Dr. Stidger, "am grateful to Mrs. Wendt. She was a teacher of mine when I was a kid, and some thirty years ago she introduced me to Tennyson and kindled a love of poetry and literature that has remained through the years."

"Did you ever thank her?" someone asked.

"Come to think of it, I haven't. But I'll do so this very night."

A few weeks later came the reply.

"MY DEAR WILLIE:

"I want you to know what your note meant to me. I am an old lady, living alone in a small room, cooking my own meals, lonely and seeming like the last leaf on the tree. . . .

"You will be interested to know, Willie, that I taught school for fifty years and in all that time yours is the first letter of appreciation I ever received. It came on a blue, cold morning and it cheered my lonely heart as nothing has cheered me in many years."

Most of us feel grateful for kindnesses and favors but, unless the sentiment is expressed, it never reaches the benefactor. The mere feeling of gratitude is not enough: it must be communicated.

God's Commandos
Answer Cries
of Distress

Lee H. Bristol, Jr., shows how a person can be a commando for Christ and thus weave the ideals of religion into his daily life. In "Spiritual Commandos" in *Guideposts* he describes the remarkable feat of Wallace Speers, vice president of a large clothing store in New York, and the chairman of the Laymen's Movement for a Christian World. It is a unique organization whose members try to apply Christian principles on a round-the-clock basis. These spiritual commandos respond to any call of need or distress: visiting a man in prison, helping a youngster who has gotten into trouble, or simply calling upon a new family that has just moved into the neighborhood.

One day one of its members, Joe Mitchell, got a telephone call from a displaced person whom he had never met.

"You don't know me," said the man, "but I've heard of your group of Christian commandos and I'm calling for help. There are 86 political prisoners who should have been released at the end of the war who are still languishing in prison. Nobody seems to be interested in getting them out. Will you try?"

"I'm just a man in the dry goods business here in New York. I know nothing about the procedure in international relations. How would I start?"

"I heard that you once met the Pope. Won't you write him?"

Joe is a Presbyterian, but he got all the details and sent an airmail letter to the Vatican. Two weeks later the D.P. called. He was almost hysterical with joy.

"I didn't know you could do it so fast. You've gotten 84 out of the 86 prisoners released!"

Sure enough, about a week later came a letter from the Vatican, thanking Joe for calling to their attention a situation of which they were unaware. Through their prompt intercession with the Italian government, all but two of the prisoners were immediately released. The cases of the other two were to be reviewed.

It's a far cry from the office of a dry goods store in New York to Rome, but the cry was made, heard and answered within two weeks. The sky is often the limit for what an ordinary person can do, if he acts unselfishly for others. We usually read of commandos blowing up bridges, exploding a bomb in the camp of the enemy or setting fire to an ammunition dump. Peace has its heroes, however, as well as war, and it has urgent need for brave and resourceful commandos to answer the cry of distress in a hundred fields.

Healing the Sick
and Afflicted

In "The Healing Nun of Formosa," in *The Reader's Digest*, the noted writer, William J. Lederer, describes the incredible achievements of a medical missionary. Here are the highlights of his moving story in condensed form.

At St. Joseph's Hospital in Kaohsiung, about 200 miles south of Taipei, Formosa, Sister Hilda, a member of the Missionary Sisters of the Immaculate Conception, has been ministering as a physician and surgeon to the natives and the U.S. military men and their wives for many years. She has become a legend in her lifetime. In a typical day that often stretches to midnight, she examines, diagnoses and treats 91 new patients, with ailments ranging from a broken leg to food poisoning, dysentery, pneumonia, earaches, burns and flesh wounds. In addition, convalescing patients and 20 expectant mothers come in for checkups. In one decade she has delivered more than 4,000 babies.

When Sister's medical duties do not confine her to the hospital in Kaohsiung, she travels through a 35-mile area, serving as physician and surgeon to some 50,000 people. Some of them are dark, pygmylike people who live in isolated mountain areas. For Sister Hilda who is about fifty and afflicted with arthritis, the climbing of these mountains is quite a strain.

She has, however, nothing but a cheery smile and a word of encouragement for the motley crowd of patients awaiting her. She often works for six hours at a stretch, without stopping for rest or food. On one of these trips she was accompanied by the writer, W. J. Lederer.

"Sister," he remarked, "I'm amazed at your inexhaustible strength and vitality. Nothing seems to tire you."

"You think I have a lot of pep," said Sister, grinning. "Actually I don't. But when I run low, I pray. God always hears me and replenishes my supply."

The next morning—the day before Christmas—Sister Hilda had an unusual treat: a visit from her sister who is a religious superior at a nearby mission. Recalling their Christmas celebrations as children in Westphalia, they laughed with joy at the remembrance of opening packages and of the grand dinner they had after church.

"It was wonderful," remarked Hilda, "but today we receive far more presents than we did as children—and far more precious ones. Come, Sister and Mr. Lederer, and I will show you today's multitude of gifts."

What Faith
and Love
Can Do

They went into a slum area a few blocks away. When people caught sight of Sister Hilda, they ran into the street, waving, laughing and shouting her name. From tumble-down shacks, men, women and ragged children came streaming, shouting, "Greetings, Sister Hilda!" They pressed little cakes and flowers upon her, while the youngsters sang a hymn for her in a high childish soprano.

"These," said Sister Hilda, beaming with joy, "are our Christmas presents. God is generous. For us the joys of Christmas come every day of the year."

When at last the greetings, singing and excitement died down, Sister went about visiting the sick. Lederer watched her, as she bent down slowly, because of the painful arthritis, to examine the bandages on an old man's arm. As the wind fluttered her white-and-blue habit, Lederer marveled at the gay smile on her face and the tenderness with which she treated the penniless and ragged patient. If he had been a king, she couldn't have shown more anxious solicitude.

For 30 years she hasn't been home, Lederer reflected, and every minute of that hard-working time she has spent ministering with tender and loving hands to the poor, the sick and the afflicted. "During 30 years of world travel," he said, "I have, perhaps, met more than my share of famous people. But the one person whose company has given me the most enduring pleasure is Sister Hilda."

High praise indeed! But it is matched by the tribute paid by an American physician practicing in Taipei.

"When I get discouraged and tired," he told Lederer, "I go to Kaohsiung and watch Sister Hilda practice medicine. Then I return home with confidence that everything is possible to the man who has faith in God and love in his soul. That's something you can't learn in medical school."

Though Sister Hilda has preached no sermon in Formosa, few, if any, of its people have been given a more impressive manifestation of Christ's love than the suffering and poor of Kaohsiung and the surrounding countryside. She has spoken through her deeds. But they speak a universal language which even the deaf can hear, for they are a symphony of love.

Redeeming
Hopeless Drunkards

One of the most unique organizations in America is Alcoholics Anonymous, generally called "A.A." Back of its establishment is a remarkable story of the faith, gratitude and spiritual insight of its anonymous founders, known only as Bill and Dr. Bob. Anonymity is of great spiritual significance to the members of A.A. and serves as a constant reminder to place principles above personalities and to help others with no thought of recognition by anyone save God.

It was conceived by Bill, an alcoholic, in New York in 1934, and was established in Akron, Ohio, the following year with Dr. Bob playing such an important role that he is generally considered a co-founder. Its one purpose is "to help the sick alcoholic recover, if he wishes." Like the Christophers, it has virtually no formal organization, no pledges or constraints, no records and no quotas.

Close to the last stages of alcoholic disintegration, Bill conceived the idea that if he attempted to aid other alcoholics he might thereby help himself. While working on others, Bill was able for the first time in years to remain sober himself. But the inebriates, whom he tried to assist, failed to respond. Discouraged and heartbroken, Bill was on the verge of a relapse when he met another alcoholic, Dr. Bob, in Akron.

It then dawned on Bill that one-sided preachment is futile: help must flow two ways. When help is offered by an alcoholic and accepted by another, each of whom is seeking to help himself by aiding the other, a new element enters the situation. As a consequence of this aid from one who was helpless himself, Bill remained sober and Dr. Bob got sober, and the nucleus of A.A. was formed.

At the end of the second year it had 15 members and in 1962 it had 350,000, divided into 8500 local groups. It is established in some 90 prisons and more than 100 clubs exist to foster the A.A. idea, though not formally affiliated with it. In metropolitan areas such as New York, Chicago and Los Angeles, A.A. groups range from 100 to about 300. Established in every state, it has spread to more than 70 countries.

While the organization avoids the use of the word "cure," insisting that an alcoholic always remains one, its success has been phenomenal. About half of all who make a sincere effort to stop drinking get sober at once and remain that way. Another one-fourth become sober after some relapses, while the remaining one-fourth show improvement.

"I had been in and out of hospitals and sanitaria for twenty years," related a lawyer, "but got no lasting relief. After a few weeks or at most a month, I'd go on another binge. It wasn't until I joined A.A. and began to put its principles into practice that I really became a free man again. Finding A.A. was the greatest discovery in my life. It will help any man who co-operates 100 per cent with it."

Basic Principles of A.A.

The basic principles of A.A. in summary form are these:

1. The alcoholic humbly acknowledges that by himself he is powerless over liquor. Without this frank admission he does not undergo the deep deflation of his ego which seems to be the first step toward recovery.

2. He comes to believe that only a Power greater than him-

self can lift him up, and he turns his will and life over to God. He undergoes a genuine "conversion" in the broad sense of that word.

3. The alcoholic undertakes a searching moral inventory of himself, acknowledges to God and to at least one human being his shortcomings, begs God to remove them, and tries to make the human amends possible.

4. He endeavors through prayer and meditation to improve his contact with God, praying only for the knowledge of God's will and the strength to carry it out.

5. After having had such a spiritual experience, he tries to bring the message to alcoholics and to apply these principles in his daily life.

"Our deep kinship," Bill said in an address to the American Psychiatric Association in 1949, "the urgency of our mission, the need to abate our neurosis for contented survival—all these, together with *love of God and man*, have contained us in surprising unity."

"A.A. brings one into intimate contact with God," related a university professor. "A member must acknowledge that in himself he's powerless, at his wit's end. Then he raises his hand toward God and cries, 'Help me, O Lord, for only you can lift me up.' When he utters that cry and means it, *things begin to happen*. Faith can move mountains. Through the channel of faith God sends the divine power which transforms the weakling and makes him a spiritual giant. I know, because I've gone through this transformation."

"Is faith in God necessary?" I asked.

"Yes," he replied, "absolutely necessary. Nothing starts to happen until an alcoholic makes that act of faith—trust in God. If he doubts, he sinks like the Apostle Peter; but if he really believes, God will give him the necessary help. The secret of the marvelous success of A.A. is that it puts two religious principles to work: faith in God and love of neighbor."

The organization is founded on the Christian principle of

love. While some moderns scoff at it, the members of A.A. do not hesitate to proclaim from the mountaintops their faith in this enduring and self-authenticating principle. They find that, like ceasing to drink, loving one's fellow man makes no impossible demands on an ordinary, all-too-human being. "In a world whose spiritual values have dropped close to the vanishing point," observes *Fortune* magazine, "the strange society of A.A. places its entire proposition upon the *reality* of spiritual experience."

Through their exciting and startling discovery that mutual love and service floods souls with a power that frees them from one of the most galling tyrannies to which man is subject, and their making that principle basic in A.A., anonymous Bill and Dr. Bob have already aided uncounted thousands and ultimately will aid millions throughout the world. They seem to have achieved the impossible: the transformation of hopeless drunkards into crusading missionaries, eager to go at any hour of the day or night to aid a tempted brother and remain with him until the temptation is past.

What a superb example of bringing the great moral teaching of Christ into a workaday world and applying it to one of the areas of human life where it is most desperately needed! Well might there hang upon the wall of every home the motto of A.A.: "God grant us the serenity to accept the things we cannot change, courage to change the things we can, and wisdom to know the difference."

The Battle
Against Labor Racketeers

In the war to protect the rights of workers against the ruthless racketeers who have seized control of many local unions, brave commandos ready to risk life and limb are urgently needed. Such a commando is William Wilkens, crane operator and a staunch union man in Long Island, New York. Bill spent 15 months in a

Nazi prisoner-of-war camp, where he was starved, beaten and spit on. In "We're Battling the Mobsters in Our Union" in *Coronet*, he tells of the work of spiritual commandos in the labor field. Here in condensed form are the highlights of his stirring story as told to Bernard Bookbinder. As a member of the Long Island Local 138 of the International Union of Operating Engineers, Bill soon discovered that the brown-shirted minions of Hitler didn't have a monopoly on ruthless brutality.

Entrenched in control of labor unions were their counterparts: unscrupulous vicious gangsters, fattening on the graft stolen from the workers whose interests they were supposed to protect. On attending a union meeting, Bill was shocked to see the czarlike manner in which it was conducted by William C. (Big Bill) De Koning, Sr., later sent to prison for extortion. No reports were read, no motions made, no questions raised, unless De Koning so directed.

The comparatively few members who attended voted by voice. De Koning would bark in a rasping voice, "All in favor?" Woe betide the individual who raised a dissenting voice. The answer always was an obedient "Aye." A fear, comparable to that of the Nazi prison camp, dominated the union and all its activities.

In 1950, *Newsday*, published in Garden City, Long Island, disclosed that the deed for the Labor Lyceum, consisting of the union hall, restaurant and bar built by union members with materials donated by contractors, was in the name of De Koning's wife, Rose. As the racketeer had always said that the Lyceum belonged to the union and would eventually become part of a home for old engineers, a few of the men asked him about the story.

"Are you gonna believe them or me?" bellowed De Koning.

No more questions were asked. When the czar signaled for the adjournment of a union meeting, his stooges filtered through the hall announcing, "Bill wants you to stop by for a drink." The drinks, however, were on the men. Later investigations disclosed that De Koning was reaping more than $70,000 a year from the operation of the bar and restaurant.

Stirring
the Nation's
Conscience

In 1953 when Bill and his wife Ruthie were expecting their third child, they needed money badly. Bill got an extra job at Roosevelt Raceway, the night harness-racing track in Westbury, Long Island. Unfortunately De Koning ran the union there too. Bill made $8 a night collecting tickets at the gate. But after a few evenings a De Koning henchman told Bill to report at the Lyceum that Friday night. There flunkies took $8 from Bill and the other union members. He was told to come back every week during the summer racing season.

"I felt sick," said Bill. "The $8 which had been extorted from me would have bought a quart of milk a day for a month. What was I doing? All I wanted was the same things that everyone wants: a good wife, a nice family, and a decent job. Did I have to pay off a union leader in order to work?"

Later that summer, as a result of prodding by Newsday, the Long Island District Attorney obtained an indictment against De Koning, his son and a dozen of his lieutenants on charges of extortion, coercion and grand larceny. With the De Konings in prison, Bill and other reform members elected a new official. They enlisted the support of newspapers, obtained legal counsel and drew up a 12-point program calling for such basic rights as secret ballot elections, extension of voting rights to all members, regular audited financial reports, equal distribution of work, and an end to one-man rule.

Bill and his chief ally, Pete Batalias, appeared on the radio in New York with labor columnist Victor Riesel. They described the racketeering, hoodlumism and corruption which had long dominated their union. A few hours later Riesel lay on a hospital bed, blinded for life by an acid-thrower. But the continuing fight of Bill, Pete, Riesel and other brave commandos has stirred the nation's conscience, brought about U.S. Senate investigations of the gangsters throttling millions of union members, and brought some reform measures.

Union Members
Must Fight
Racketeers

Much more needs to be done to free union members from their worst enemies: the racketeers who annually defraud them of millions. The movement has the powerful support of the top leaders of the American Federation of Labor, which has already expelled some of the unions dominated by gangsters. It will require the support of the nation and particularly of the union members themselves.

Bill Wilkens and his little group of brave commandos have shown, however, what even a few can accomplish when they fight unselfishly for the right at the risk of brutal beatings and even assassination. They have given the nation an inspiring demonstration of the manner in which brave individuals can bring the ethical principles and the spiritual ideals of religion into the union hall, the newspapers, the general public and into every nook and cranny of daily life.

"I know now," says Bill, "that we are going to win. But maybe that's not the most important thing. Maybe the biggest fight for us—and for everyone—is the fight against fear. And I've won that."

All Citizens Needed
in Battle on Home Front

Unlike military warfare, the war against racketeers, gangsters, thugs, hoodlums, swindlers, crooks and vice syndicates offers an opportunity to men and women of all ages to serve. During the Capone era one of the judges who earned the hatred of the mob for the stiff sentences meted out to their members was

John P. McGoorty. He was a member of our Newman Foundation Advisory Board at the University of Illinois, and I had occasion to visit him from time to time. Arriving at his home on
Chicago's south side one evening, I was surprised by a policeman
who stepped out of the darkness, with a drawn gun.

"The state's attorney," explained the judge later, "is keeping
a twenty-four-hour guard around the home. Threats are tele-
phoned to me at all hours of the night. Members of the mob
say they will wipe out my family if any more of their men are
convicted in my court. They are getting frantic with fear and
would stoop to anything."

"Judge," I said, "you're in about as dangerous a spot as a soldier in the front line trenches."

"Yes," he remarked, "there are battles on the home front as
perilous as those overseas. It's a privilege and an honor for every
citizen to serve his country. We of the older generation must not
let our boys carry the whole burden. We have the chance to
serve our country and our God. We can put our ethical and
spiritual ideals into action without carrying a gun."

Helping Convicts
Get a Fresh Start

"Amen I say to you, as long as you did it for one of these, the
least of my brethren, you did it for me." This utterance of Jesus
haunted the mind of Charles S. Wade of Reading, Pennsylvania,
and prompted him to put it into practice in his daily life. Wade
selected ex-convicts as "the least of his brethren." They stand
desperately in need of help to get a fresh start in life. The service
which he has rendered to a great multitude of these unfortunates
is an inspiring example of how one can bring his religion into
the market place. In "This Cop Leads a Double Life" in The
Reader's Digest, Eugenie Gluckert relates the fascinating story.
Here are its highlights in condensed form.

Just before dawn one cold autumn morning in 1955 a cordon
of police, armed with machine guns and tear gas, watched a house

in which a desperate young ex-convict parolee had barricaded himself. He had engaged in a series of burglaries and taken shelter in his sister's home.

"Come and get me!" he shouted, waving a shotgun. "I've got plenty of ammunition and I'm a sharpshooter."

If the police had accepted the challenge, they would doubtless have succeeded. But the cost in life, limb and property damage would have been high. Detective Wade thought of a better plan. Stepping under a street light so he could be seen, he handed his automatic to a policeman.

"I'm unarmed," he shouted, "and I'm coming up." Tense, worried and anxious, the police waited, wondering if he would emerge alive. Three hours passed, while Wade reasoned with the trigger-happy youth.

"He was just a scared kid," Wade explained later. "He seemed relieved when I took his gun. I told him I'd have to turn him in and he'd have to serve his time. But I promised to help him all I could, and assured him of a job working for me when he got out."

For years Charles S. Wade has lived a double life: a detective by night and the manager of an insulation and weatherproofing business by day. As a detective he has sent many a lawbreaker to jail and as a successful businessman he has given many of them employment and a fresh start.

Wade Puts Preaching into Practice

"Most lawbreakers," he says, "get started on the wrong foot because they can't cope with financial worries. Then when they get out, no one will hire them, and soon they're back at the old racket again. What they desperately need is someone who will trust them enough to give them a job."

Wade practices what he preaches. Of his 45 employees more than half are ex-convicts, but only Wade knows which ones they are. He treats them all alike and encourages them to develop skills that will bring them higher wages. When they arrive in the morning, Wade joins them for coffee and doughnuts. Then they have a brief session of group singing, which seems to warm their hearts as much as the coffee warms their bodies.

Though Wade's salesmen collect as much as a thousand dollars a day, neither he nor his customers have ever been defrauded. Only once has his trust backfired. A new employee pulled a gun on him and attempted to rob the box in which receipts were kept.

"If that's the way you want it," said Wade, looking the ex-con squarely in the face, "I'll open the box. But remember, Joe, you're taking something out of here that money can't buy. *That's my faith in you.*"

Thoroughly ashamed, the gunman handed over his revolver. Fearfully he related that he was in financial straits and at his wit's end. Wade's double faith in him paid off, and the man became one of his most valued employees.

To obtain a parole, a convict must secure a sponsor and a job. If these are unobtainable, the inmate can become so embittered as to make rehabilitation practically impossible. To prevent this, Wade is now organizing a nation-wide ex-con employment service.

The people of Reading call Wade "the cop with the big heart," and the army of ex-cons he has helped esteem him as "the best friend they ever had." But what especially warms his heart and inspires Charles Wade to carry on is the consciousness that he is keeping step with the music and the melody of the words spoken long ago: "As long as you did for one of these, the least of my brethren, you did it for me."

Vice Moguls Take over
Phenix City

Racketeers, gamblers and mobsters usually center their activities in large cities, where the "take" is greater, but they do not pass up smaller ones where they can easily set up shop. Phenix

City, Alabama, is a capital illustration. In that sprawling city of 24,000 on the west bank of the Chattahoochee River, across from Columbus, Georgia, there was staged one of the most dramatic duels between a public spirited citizen and the vice syndicate in the history of our country. That duel is described by John M. Patterson in an arresting article in The Saturday Evening Post, "I'll Get the Gangs That Killed My Father" by Furman Bisher. Here in condensed form are its highlights.

The main stem of the city was a hodgepodge of gaudy brawling neon-lighted hotspots, doing a land-office business. Honkytonks and taverns fronted for houses of prostitution, gambling rooms and narcotic dens. Stripteasers did their stuff to the syncopation of ribald remarks from the rowdy customers. Throaty songs of torch singers, drunken laughter and the clink clank of slot machines clashed in a weird cacophony of sin. In the back rooms the operators were fattening on the proceeds from this proliferation of vice in all its forms.

The chief contributors to an annual gross of $100,000,000 were the soldiers from Fort Benning across the river, the largest infantry camp in America. They were milked of their pay checks as systematically as cows in a dairy. Few were the law enforcement officers or public officials not linked to the rackets.

With the cash registers playing a loud staccato, the local merchants and the bulk of the citizens turned a deaf ear to the staggering total of 230 burglaries and the 27 unsolved murders in the preceding decade. Even the discovery of a black market baby ring and a school for training burglars failed to stir them to action.

"As long as I'm showing a profit," remarked a merchant, "I'll take no heed of what goes on downtown or at the courthouse."

It reflected the general apathy. It explains why no policeman lifted a finger to stop the degrading brothel business: service men stood 200 to 300 deep in line in front of Ma Beachie's two-story house. The racketeers and gangsters seemed to have a strangle hold on the city, which had become a modern Sodom and Gomorrah.

In the 1952 primary election Hugh Bentley, Hugh Britton and his 16-year-old son were watchers at one of the ballot boxes. A gang of seven racketeers pounced upon them, knocked them to the ground and started kicking them. A woman ran to a state trooper looking idly on.

"Help them, officer," she begged. "They'll kill them if you don't."

"Lady," he replied nonchalantly, "they're not going to hurt them. They're just using their fists and feet on them."

The pictures of the three beaten men, their faces streaming with blood, appeared in papers across the country and shocked the nation.

Patterson Challenges the Mobsters

One man stepped forth to challenge this Goliath. Albert L. Patterson, a state senator, had gotten a close-up in his law practice of the manifold operation of the mob and had seen the breakdown of law enforcement on the local level. If elected Attorney General, he knew he could get action. He ran on a reform platform, vowing to clean the Augean stables of Phenix City at all costs.

Alarmed, the vice lords poured great sums into the campaign to defeat him by hook or by crook. Despite all their bribery and corruption, Patterson was swept into office. The mob's only weapons now were those of violence and murder.

One night his phone rang. "You've got to change your mind," warned the caller, "or you won't be here over the weekend."

"The odds are against me," Patterson told the Methodist Men's Club. "I have only a hundred-to-one chance of ever being sworn into office. If they make up their mind to get you, they'll get you. You can't be ready all the time, and they'll pick the right time and the right place."

Within 24 hours the gangsters struck. Leaving his office at

nine o'clock on the night of June 18, 1954, Patterson walked to his car and got in. A murderer stuck a gun in his face and pulled the trigger three times. Patterson staggered to the sidewalk, and sat down on the curb to die.

"He refused to fall," related his son John. "His strong point was the bridle that led him to death. He refused to fall for the murderer, just as he had declined to abandon his fight to clean up the town."

He fought more effectively in death than in life. Declaring that "the local police officers are unable or unwilling to do their duty," Governor Gordon Person sent the Alabama National Guard to take over. Entering the city in a heavy rain 100 guardsmen seized the police station, city hall and courthouse. All city officials were relieved of law-enforcing duties. The noisy honkytonks and brawling taverns became as quiet as cemeteries.

Gambling apparatus and lottery books were piled high behind the Russell County Jail. Stripteasers, B-girls and prostitutes fled like rats from a sinking ship. Hoyt Shepherd, the big boss of the machine, pleaded guilty to leasing places for gambling and was sentenced to jail. Big signs at bridges across the Chattahoochee proclaimed Phenix City as "off limits" to the military personnel at Fort Benning. Patterson's son John was elected Attorney General to carry out the program of his father.

Albert L. Patterson was a deeply religious man. He believed that religion shouldn't be kept in moth balls but should be put in action in every aspect of daily life. He lived up to his conviction at St. Mihiel in 1918, when he led a charge against the German lines. Wounded by a machine gun bullet in his right leg, he lay in a trench for two days without water or food. Under cover of darkness he finally managed to drag himself back to his own lines. He was awarded the Croix de Guerre for heroism.

Though crippled for life, he served his community with distinction, battling for civic decency against the entrenched forces of racketeering and corruption. At the bottom of his briefcase they found a worn and frayed clipping which reflected his philosophy of life. On it were the words of Edmund Burke, the famous English statesman and author: "The only thing necessary for the triumph of evil is that good men do nothing."

POINTS TO REMEMBER

1. Religion must be put to work every day in the week.

2. What you are speaks so loudly that people cannot hear what you say.

3. A simple word of thanks warms the human heart.

4. Everything is possible to the man who has faith in God and love in his soul.

5. "God grant us the serenity to accept the things we cannot change, courage to change the things we can, and wisdom to know the difference."

6. Every citizen can do his part in the battle against crime.

7. "As long as you did it for one of these, the least of my brethren, you did it for me."

8. "The only thing necessary for the triumph of evil is that good men do nothing."

6.

PRAYER:

MAN'S LINK WITH GOD

"When we pray we link ourselves with the inexhaustible motive power that binds the universe."
—Alexis Carrel

One of the most fundamental of all the religious activities
in which man engages is prayer. It is as universal as the belief in
a Supreme Being, and it follows as a natural consequence of that
belief. It is most worthy of careful study. Accordingly we shall
consider the nature and meaning of prayer, its various kinds, the
qualities true prayer should possess, its role in human life, its
divine basis, and indicate some of its fruits. But first it is well to
remove some common misconceptions of prayer, which have
both clouded and impaired man's spiritual life.

Prayer is not a mechanistic gimmick like a vending machine in
which one inserts a penny, pulls a lever and out comes a stick
of gum. It is not a form of magic, wherein one recites *abraca-
dabra* or any other verbal formula and *presto chango!* he receives
whatever he requested. It is neither a pep talk to oneself nor an
effort to lift oneself by tugging at his bootstraps; neither is it a
form of Couéism nor an exercise in the power of positive thinking
or autosuggestion. Neither is it the asking of the Almighty simply
to rubber-stamp all one's desires and plans without a single
change.

Prayer is the lifting of our minds and hearts to God to adore,
thank, propitiate or petition Him. At the heart of the whole
concept of prayer is the notion of an actual living *contact* with

our Creator, in which there is a union of our minds with His mind and of our hearts with His. Hence it differs radically from mere daydreaming, idle reverie or the mechanical utterance of words, in which neither the mind nor the heart participates.

Early in 1918 the all-out German offensive seemed about to overwhelm the Allies. Appointed Generalissimo of the whole Western Front, Foch determined to launch a great counterattack on which hung the outcome of the war. It was set for July 18, and all preparations were completed. Telling his staff officers to leave him undisturbed for an hour if possible, Foch left his office.

A motorcyclist arrived with an urgent telegram of the greatest importance for the General. His officers found him at the village church, kneeling in prayer before the altar. After reading the telegram, Foch dictated a reply. As the officers left the church, they saw the General back on his knees, his eyes on the tabernacle.

"Always when I leave God's temple," said Foch, "I feel stronger, and above all more certain. It is there that I made the crucial decisions during the war."

No wonder it is that history records his leadership as one of the decisive factors in winning that mighty conflict. In prayer he made contact with God, the source of all wisdom and power.

Conversing with God

Prayer is essentially conversation with Almighty God, our heavenly Father. Conversation means both speaking and listening, and in prayer the latter is not less important than the former. God wants us not only to speak to Him, to pour out our hearts in homage, praise and love but also to listen to Him in return. The good resolves which well up within us come as the echoes of His voice, caught by the sensitive ear of conscience.

"My wife and I," relates Otto Whitington of Louisville, Kentucky, "were standing on a street corner waiting for a bus. We saw a youngster suddenly dart up the steps of a fine brick residence, ring the doorbell vigorously, and then run away. When a kindly-faced gentleman opened the door, he looked up and down the street, but could see no caller. Disappointed and a bit perplexed, he closed the door.

" 'I'm afraid,' I remarked to my wife, 'that's the way many of us pray.'

" 'Yes,' she agreed, 'many of us call on God for guidance but don't wait to receive it. He too must be disappointed.' "

You have had persons call you on the telephone, saying that they wanted to have a little chat with you. Then they talked continuously for five or ten minutes, scarcely allowing you to get a word in edgewise. Didn't you feel that it was really no conversation at all because you were reduced to the status of a mere listener? In conversing with God, pause occasionally to meditate and listen, and you will find God responding with words of cheer, encouragement, guidance and help. New resolutions for a better and holier life will crystallize in your mind under the influence of divine inspiration and grace.

Grounds for Divorce

One of the strong bonds holding the members of a family together and deepening their love is communication. If that be impaired or destroyed, the family is in for trouble. On the very day I write these lines, newspapers tell of a woman who came into the circuit court of Judge Phillip F. Locke in Chicago, seeking a divorce on quite unusual grounds.

"On what grounds," inquired the judge, "are you asking for a divorce?"

"Cruelty," replied the wife.

"What was the cruelty?"

"For sixteen months," she explained, "my husband hasn't spoken a word to me."

She was granted a divorce, alimony and the custody of the two little children. In addition, the husband, an advertising sales manager, was ordered to keep in force a $55,000 insurance policy for the benefit of the children.

If the failure of a husband to converse with his spouse for sixteen months be a serious violation of the vow of conjugal love and devotion, as it is, how much greater is the offense of the creature who neglects not merely for months but even for years to render the homage of prayer to the God who made him? Receiving the blessings of life, health of mind and strength of body from the Creator, the creature who fails to acknowledge them by so much as a "Thank You, Almighty God, for all these gifts!" is indeed an ingrate and a cheat. He is cheating God of the tribute to which He has a strict right.

Deepens Union
with God

As conversation helps to bind more closely the members of a family, so prayer helps to unite us more intimately with our Creator and deepens our friendship and love. What sunshine is to plants, what moisture is to parched lips and what oxygen is to lungs, prayer is to the mind, heart and soul of man. It taps a wellspring of divine power, bringing strength to the weak and energy to the exhausted. Without prayer man is like a weary traveler wandering aimlessly in a desert, void of life and meaning.

"The purpose of religion," observes Rufus Jones, "is to make a person conscious of the presence of God. There are many paths to this end—great art, nature, music, truth, great literature, poetry and the unselfish acts of men. But the final climb is the path of prayer."

Holy Writ abounds with exhortations and commands to pray. "Let us lift up our hearts with our hands," exhorts Lamentations, "to the Lord in the heavens." "Ask," says Jesus, "and you shall receive, that your joy may be full." In times of discouragement one should have speedy recourse to prayer. "And He [Jesus] told them a parable," relates Luke, "that they must *always* pray and not lose heart."

In times of spiritual danger, vigilance and prayer are of the utmost importance. "Watch and pray," admonishes the Savior, "that you may not enter into temptation." Reflecting the teaching of his divine Master, the Apostle Peter warns, "Be prudent therefore and watchful in prayers."

Such prudence implies that we pray for what is right and just. This was always uppermost in the mind of President Lincoln, especially during the grim days of the Civil War.

"Let us have faith, Mr. President," said a visitor, "that the Lord is on our side in this great struggle."

"I'm not at all concerned about that," replied Lincoln, "for I know that the Lord is always on the side of the right; but it's my constant anxiety and prayer that we are on the Lord's side."

By sharpening our perception of right and wrong, prayer helps to put us on God's side.

Greatest
Unused Power

In the early days of our country an engineer and a minister were gazing at one of our country's most awe-inspiring spectacles —Niagara Falls. As the engineer watched the mighty stream of water plunging over the precipice, he remarked, "There is the greatest unused power in the world."

The minister was silent for a few moments. Then he replied, "No, the greatest unused power in the world is the Spirit of God, and that energy is harnessed by prayer."

History confirms the truth of his reply. Think of what the
twelve Apostles, filled with the Holy Spirit, were able to accomplish. Spreading the Gospel throughout the Greek and Roman
Empires, they gave a new depth to human life and thought.

Motto
of St. Francis

In every age, men and women filled with the Spirit of God
have exerted a profound influence upon the moral and spiritual
life of society. Think of the far-reaching influence of the God-
intoxicated man, St. Francis of Assisi, upon the life of thirteenth-
century Italy. He kindled a torch of love—love of God, man and
all His creatures—that has lighted the path for all succeeding
generations. God-illumined and love-anointed, he sang a sweet
canticle of adoration, which has warmed the hearts of men and
opened their minds to the realization that the power that moves
the earth, the sun and all the stars is love, and that God Himself
is love.

Conscious that prayer is the channel through which the Spirit
of God comes into the heart of man and takes possession of him,
Francis spent long periods in prayer. He realized that it would
be the power of God working through him that would accomplish the great tasks which transcended his ability. Hence his
motto was: "More than *I* can do."

God working in and through him was the secret source of the
mighty spiritual reformation which the gentle Poor Man of
Assisi wrought. Like St. Francis, our motto too should be: "Not
able of ourselves, but *enabled* by God through prayer."

When confronted with tasks which appall us, we would do
well to remember the assurance given by Christ to the Apostles
as He sent them out on their world-transforming mission. "When
they deliver you up," He said, "do not be anxious how or what
you are to speak; for what you are to speak will be given you in

that hour. For it is not you who are speaking, but the *Spirit* of your Father who speaks *through* you."

A World-Famous
Prayer

During some of his protracted periods of fervent, soul-absorbing prayer and meditation, St. Francis experienced ecstasies and raptures, achieving such intimate union with God that he might well have cried out with St. Paul: "It is now no longer I that live, but Christ lives in me." Out of these intimate colloquies with his Lord, Francis distilled his famous Prayer for Peace, acclaimed by many as second only to the Lord's Prayer in beauty and spiritual insight. Worth memorizing and saying daily, it runs:

Lord, make me an instrument of Thy peace. Where there is hatred, let me sow love; where there is injury, pardon; where there is doubt, faith; where there is despair, hope; where there is darkness, light; where there is sadness, joy. O, Divine Master, grant that I may seek not so much to be consoled as to console; to be understood as to understand; to be loved as to love; for it is in giving that we receive, it is in pardoning that we are pardoned, and it is in dying that we are born to eternal life.

Christ
at Our Door

In Keble College, Oxford, England, there hangs a world-famous painting, "Christ—The Light of the World," by Holman Hunt. It has been widely copied and now hangs in many homes. Often during my student days at Oxford University, I would come to draw inspiration from it. It depicts Jesus standing before a thatched cottage, holding in one hand a lantern, and knocking at the door.

The artist drew his inspiration from the words of the Apoc-

alypse, also called Revelations: "*Behold, I stand at the door and
knock. If any man listens to my voice and opens the door to me,
I will come in to him and will sup with him, and he with me.*"
The painting brings out vividly the important truth that God is
not distant from us but is at our very door. He is eager to enter
with His light, strength and grace into every home and every
heart.

Prayer is the *opening* of the door of the human heart to allow
God to enter and set up His throne. There He will guide, enlighten and inspire us to live an upright, holy and noble life. In
that intimate union with our Creator we surrender our mind,
will and heart to Him. It is in this *surrender* of the human will
to the divine will that we perceive most clearly the essential
nature of prayer.

"Not My Will, but Thine"

We do not come to prayer to *impose* our wishes and our will
upon God, to insist that He but rubber-stamp our plans, but to
submit them to Him for approval, correction or rejection. Many
times the things we ask for so feverishly would be not to our advantage but to our detriment. Like little children asking for a
bottle labeled "Poison!", we often ask for things which would
prove fatal to our spiritual life. In His infinite wisdom God favors
us by withholding them.

Submissiveness to the divine will is then an essential requisite
for true and fruitful prayer. Who has better illustrated this fact
than Christ Himself? Kneeling in the Garden of Gethsemane,
the God-man perceived the Passion and death which He was
about to undergo. His human nature cried out in agony: "Father,
if it is possible, let this cup pass away from me." Then He added
the all-important words, "Yet not as I will, but as thou willest."
These made it a perfect prayer and a model for all our suppli-
cations.

Four Kinds
of Prayer

Most people think of prayer solely as petitioning God for favors, blessings and help. This is but one kind and the lowest in the ethical and spiritual scale. There are three other kinds. The first and most important is the *prayer of adoration*, in which we acknowledge God as our Creator and Sovereign and our complete and abiding dependence upon Him. The second is the *prayer of thanksgiving*, in which we lift up our voice to thank God for all the blessings and graces we have received. The third is *propitiatory prayer* in which we seek to atone for our sins, acknowledging our guilt, professing our sorrow and purpose of amendment, and imploring forgiveness.

These four kinds of prayer—adoration, thanksgiving, propitiation and supplication—abound in the pages of the Old and the New Testament and are contained in the Lord's Prayer given to us by Christ Himself. Spiritual writers are unanimous in pointing out that we should cultivate the habit of saying more prayers of adoration and thanksgiving, thus focusing our attention more upon God and less upon ourselves and our wants. The latter are already known to God, and surely He will not fail to minister to the needs of those who adore, praise, thank and love Him.

In certain parts of Germany people greet one another not with "Good morning" or "Good evening" but with "Praised be Jesus Christ!" To which the person answers, "Praised forevermore!"

In a pastoral letter Cardinal Bertram of Breslau relates the following incident. In a German hospital a working man lay on the operating table to undergo a serious operation for the removal of a growth in his tongue.

"If there is anything you would like to say," the surgeon remarked, "you had better say it now. After the operation you will no longer be able to speak."

The man was silent in thought for a few moments. Then his face lighted up.

"I want my last words to be, 'Praised be Jesus Christ!'"

"Praised forevermore!" answered the surgeon, as he signaled the anaesthetist to begin his task. In that brief prayer there were blended sentiments of adoration, thanksgiving, propitiation and love. How much nobler and more praiseworthy than the prayers in which we seek merely our own selfish interests!

Our prayers are less egotistic when they are directed to the homage and worship of God. In *losing* our lives for God, we *find* them; in singing the praises of God, our own tears are washed away. "Rejoice always," says St. Paul. "Pray without ceasing. In all things give thanks; for this is the will of God in Christ Jesus regarding you all."

The Psalms sound like a many-tongued canticle, in which heaven and earth sing the praises and glory of God. How typical are the verses: "The heavens shew forth the glory of God and the firmament declareth the work of His hands . . . O Lord our Lord, how admirable is Thy name in the whole earth! For Thy magnificence is elevated above the heavens . . . I will give praise to Thee, O Lord, with my whole heart: I will relate all Thy wonders. I will be glad and rejoice in Thee: I will sing to Thy name, O Thou most high."

It is this pervasive spirit of exultant joy, praise and thanksgiving that has made the Psalms an unsurpassed book of prayer. In singing the praises of the Almighty and rejoicing in His wondrous works, the singer finds his own heart filled with joy and gladness. As the countenance of Moses shone with glory as He descended from Mount Sinai after His communion with God, so the face of every person arising from prayer should be radiant with serenity, peace and joy.

The Perfect Prayer

Our Savior spent long hours in prayer, thus setting an example for all men. On one occasion when He had just arisen from prayer, one of His disciples said, "Lord, teach us to pray." Whereupon Jesus replied: "In this manner therefore shall you pray:

" 'Our Father who art in heaven, hallowed be Thy name. Thy kingdom come, Thy will be done on earth, as it is in heaven. Give us this day our daily bread. And forgive us our debts, as we also forgive our debtors. And lead us not into temptation, but deliver us from evil.' "

Here is the perfect prayer, the model for all others and the one most widely said. Here is the beautiful blending of adoration, thanksgiving, propitiation, supplication and joyous submission to God's holy will. In its brief compass it sounds all the essential notes in the diapason of perfect prayer.

Like a lovely melody, it grows sweeter and more endearing with every utterance: its beauty, freshness and appeal increase with the passing years. An angel trumpeting our praise to the Most High, a helmet and a shield in time of danger, a contrite and humble heart pleading for pardon, a deliverance from all harm—it is all of these and more. Its music should echo in our hearts often during the day and its refrain be with us still when night's slumber comes to release us from the tumult and the fever of the day.

Manner
of Prayer

How should we pray? First, with attention, placing ourselves in the presence of God; second, with the realization of our own helplessness and dependence upon God; third, with sincerity, earnestness and submission to God's will; fourth, with profound faith and trust in His providential care and love of us; fifth, with perseverance. These are the qualities which should characterize all our prayers. The more earnestly we strive to embody them, the more successful we shall be. We would not speak in a careless and indifferent manner to an earthly king; neither should we speak in a slipshod, slovenly manner to our God.

If the prayer is expressed in words, it is called oral; if it is silent, it is termed mental. In both, attention is of the utmost importance; if it is lacking, it can scarcely be said to be prayer at all. Since the essence of prayer is the *lifting of our minds and hearts to God*, making a living contact with His mind and heart, it is evident that neither the mere movement of our lips nor idle reverie satisfy this indispensable requirement.

"How can you ask God to listen to you," asked St. Cyprian in the third century, "when you do not listen to yourselves? You wish Him to remember you at the very moment in which you forget yourselves."

In some non-Christian lands the natives are reported to paste written prayers to their windmills, believing that as long as the wheels are revolving, the prayers are being said. But surely the Creator wants from the creatures whom He has endowed with the Godlike faculty of reason a homage more meaningful than the mere movement of lips or windmills. This is clear from the words of Our Lord: "This people honoreth me with their *lips*; but their *heart* is far from me. And *in vain* do they worship me."

With his keen insight into the workings of the human mind, Shakespeare brings out this truth in *Hamlet*, where he has Claudius say:

> My words fly up, my thoughts remain below:
> Words without thoughts never to heaven go.

In spite of our best efforts to concentrate, however, distractions will occasionally occur. These should not discourage us. We should, of course, strive to banish them and, with God's help, we will succeed. Indeed He will not fail to reward us for our efforts. He knows the weakness of our natures and does not ask the impossible.

While journeying on horseback one day, St. Benedict met a peasant walking along the road.

"You've got an easy job," said the peasant. "Why didn't I become a man of prayer? Then I too would be traveling on horseback."

"You think praying is easy," replied the saint. "If you can say one Our Father without any distraction, you can have this horse."

"It's a bargain," said the surprised peasant.

Closing his eyes and folding his hands, he began to say the Our Father aloud: "Our Father, who art in heaven, hallowed be Thy name, Thy kingdom come . . ."

Suddenly he stopped and looked up.

"Say, shall I get the saddle and bridle too?" he asked.

Squaring Deeds
with Prayers

If prayers are to be most fruitful, we must say them not only with attention but also with a willingness to conform our conduct to God's commandments. To pray without sorrow for past sins and a firm purpose of amendment is tantamount to asking God to approve immoral conduct and therefore makes a mockery of prayer. Indeed it is virtually impossible even to ask God's blessing if one is living unrepentantly in sin.

Shakespeare portrays this truth in a memorable scene in Macbeth. After murdering his guest, King Duncan, Macbeth hears two of the king's grooms utter brief prayers. He attempts to join them but cannot. He thus relates his terrifying experience to Lady Macbeth:

> One cried, "God bless us!" and "Amen" the other:
> As they had seen these hangman's hands.
> Listening their fear, I could not say "Amen,"
> . . . I had most need of blessing, and "Amen"
> Stuck in my throat.

Praying with sincerity means that we must try to square our deeds with our prayers. Otherwise our prayers aren't worthy of the name. They point accusing fingers at us and say, "You hypocrites! Do you think you can deceive Almighty God who reads the heart of man as the pages of an open book? You profess one ideal with your lips, but the opposite with your conduct."

Well does Chaucer say:

> Whoso will pray, he must fast and be clean,
> And fat his soul, and make his body lean.

I've often told my students of a curious prayer that St. Augustine frequently started to say during the years before his conversion, when he was still manacled by habits of lust. "Give me chastity, O God," he would cry, but then realizing the abandonment of the sensual pleasures this would entail, he would sadly add, "*but not yet.*" Then I would end with the comment, "Thus did his prayer die stillborn."

Invariably some students would ask, "But was that really a prayer?"

"No," I would reply. "It started as a prayer, but the second half canceled it out. Augustine was keen enough to perceive the folly and the mockery of petitioning God to bestow chastity upon him, unless he would strive to amend his life and make his actions square with the ideal to which his conscience aspired. Unless there is the willingness to co-operate with God's grace, one doesn't really pray. Prayer doesn't mean that God is to take over and do all the work: it means sincere and wholehearted collaboration with Him."

Incidentally the *yet* was a long time coming for Augustine. He was shipwrecked not only in morals but also in faith. Heresy darkened his intellect as vice padlocked his will: a double thralldom. But when he finally did escape from this galling imprisonment, he was never again to be taken captive. For eighteen years his mother, St. Monica, prayed without ceasing for his conversion and finally her prayers were answered. In *Giants of the Faith*, I tell at some length this moving story, which illustrates both the power of prayer and the necessity of co-operation with the requested grace.

Pray
Daily

In the Lord's Prayer we say, "Give us this day our daily bread." Thus did Jesus teach the necessity of praying often and even daily. Life is lived one day at a time. We are better off to concentrate our efforts upon achieving our best today instead of

dreaming about what we are going to do in some far-off tomor
row. We do not ask God to fill our larders with provisions foi
years to come, but simply for "our daily bread." This brings us
daily to the Throne of Grace and keeps us closer to our Heavenly
Father.

In an art shop in Dublin, Ireland, I spied a beautifully dec-
orated parchment on which was printed a prayer, "Just for
Today," by Sybil F. Partridge. It now adorns my study. I would
like to share with my readers the inspiration which the prayer
has given me daily through the years by quoting it here. Some of
you have probably heard it sung as a hymn, for it is both a
prayer and a hymn.

> Lord, for tomorrow and its needs I do not pray,
> Keep me, my God, from stain of sin, just for today.
> Let me both diligently work and duly pray;
> Let me be kind in word and deed, just for today.
>
> Let me in season, Lord, be grave, in season gay;
> Let me be faithful to Thy grace, just for today.
> So, for tomorrow and its needs I do not pray;
> But keep me, guide me, love me, Lord, just for today.

When Cardinal Newman was a young man of 32, he took a
Mediterranean trip, visiting Sicily, Naples and Rome. Upon returning alone from Rome, the vessel became becalmed in the
Strait of Bonifacio between Corsica and Sardinia. While walking
the deck and gazing up at the darkened sky, he was inspired to
write the famous prayer, "Lead, Kindly Light," which is sung
as a hymn in so many churches. In the spirit of the Lord's Prayer
and "Just for Today," it too asks for light to see but one step
ahead. I quote the first stanza:

> Lead, kindly light, amid the encircling gloom,
>   Lead Thou me on!
> The night is dark, and I am far from home.
>   Lead Thou me on!
> Keep Thou my feet; I do not ask to see
>   The distant scene—*one step* enough for me.

The more frequently we pray, the greater becomes our ability to pray. The famous Polish pianist Paderewski once remarked: "Normally I practice many hours every day. When I miss a day, I know the difference. When I miss two days, the critics know the difference. When I miss three days, the whole world knows the difference." So it is with prayer. The practice of daily prayer enables us to achieve perfection in this important spiritual art.

Morning Offering
Sanctifies Whole Day

A lover can't speak too often to his beloved: neither can the soul commune too frequently with God. Every contact is a source of both joy and strength. Pray often: morning, noon and night; before and after meals, in times of danger or temptation, when the road is steep or the burden heavy. Start the day by offering all your thoughts, words, deeds, silences, joys and sorrows to your Heavenly Father, thus transforming them into so many prayers.

That day there will be no indifferent, neutral or merely worldly actions: the whole day will be consecrated to God and will ascend before His Throne with the sweet odor of incense. Walking thus toward the light, the shadows will flee behind you.

I've had occasion to do a great deal of flying. While waiting for the plane to take off, I've noticed an invariable procedure. Whether it was in America, Europe or Africa, there was a careful check-up. After the ground crew had reported on their fueling and inspection, one of the flight crew would then check on the amount of gas and another check the instruments on the panel. The lives of the passengers were dependent upon that twofold check-up.

Yet how many persons start the day without recharging their spiritual batteries, without being sure they have equipped themselves with the spiritual resources necessary to carry them safely through the day? Is it any wonder that so many crash one way or another: become irritable, uncharitable, inconsiderate, selfish, fault-finding, profane in speech, backbiting, and "blowing their top" with little or no provocation?

Especially commendable is the custom of family prayer. The family that prays together, stays together. The dagger of dissension and the sword of divorce will never pierce the sturdy armor of family prayer. An excellent time is at the end of the evening meal, when all are present. Beautiful is the custom in many a home, where the father reads aloud a chapter of the Bible and then one of the children recites a prayer. In many Catholic homes the family joins in the recitation of the Rosary, which recalls to their minds the chief events in the lives of Christ and His Blessed Mother. All such homes may truly be called Houses of God and Gateways to Heaven.

"Our home is a different place," remarked a friend, "since we began the practice of evening prayer. Previously there was a good deal of squabbling among the children as to what TV program was to be turned on. But now after we kneel together in prayer for five minutes, with the children taking turns in leading the prayers, a spirit of consideration and kindness toward others is evident in all."

"Yes," his wife chimed in. "It's a powerful discipline, though of course this is merely an incidental effect. I venture to say that any family that follows this practice for a few weeks will never abandon it. It builds our home life around God."

Faith and Trust
Essential

One should pray with profound faith and unfaltering trust in God. "All things whatever," says Jesus, "you ask for in prayer, *believing*, you shall receive." Faith is the power that moves mountains: without it, nothing great can be achieved. In season and out of season, Our Lord emphasized the incalculable dynamism of a living faith. "If thou canst believe," He says, "*all* things are possible to him that *believeth*."

Reflecting the teaching of the Divine Master, the Apostle Paul says: "Let us therefore draw near with confidence to the throne of grace, that we may obtain mercy and find grace to help in time of need." Similarly the Apostle James bids us to "ask with faith, without hesitation. For he who hesitates is like a wave of the sea, driven and carried about by the wind."

Job was tested by so many terrible trials and afflictions that the mere reading of them distresses the soul. Did they destroy his trust in God? "Although he should kill me," replies Job, "I will trust in him." Here is the supreme expression of faith, the greatest the mind can conceive. When this living dynamic faith undergirds our prayers, they can move mountains.

Faith is the antiseptic which cleanses our prayers of the bacteria of paralyzing doubt and crippling egotism and enables us to throw ourselves with unfaltering trust upon the infinite power, mercy and love of God. Prayer permeated with such confidence enables us to tap new fountains of power and energy, and to become the mighty instruments of the omnipotent God.

Such faith enables us to conform our will to His so perfectly that the power of God works unobstructedly through us. "And the confidence," says the Beloved Disciple John, "that we have toward Him is this, that if we ask anything according to His will, He hears us." Thus does prayer permeated with profound faith, confidence and trust enable one so to blend his will with the divine will that he achieves an intimate union with God: the secret of all sanctity and the goal of all our striving.

St. Theresa of Avila, a Carmelite mystic, was well known for her deep piety, profound faith and marked serenity. She wrote a few lines in which these three virtues shine forth most clearly. Known as "St. Theresa's Book Mark," it is a spiritual classic. For forty years it has hung in my study, so its message will greet me daily. Worth memorizing and reciting daily, it runs:

> Let naught disturb thee,
>   Naught fright thee ever.
> All things are passing,
>   God changeth never.

> Patience e'er conquers,
>   With God for thine own,
> Thou nothing dost lack.
> He sufficeth alone.

Perseverance
Is Necessary

We should pray with perseverance. Unlike mortals who grow vexed if a supplicant becomes too persistent, God welcomes such an expression of faith and trust. The Scriptures relate how the Israelites in Bethulia prayed all night, when Holofernes besieged the city. Despite their continued prayers, the situation grew more desperate. Their faith and their prayers were undaunted, and finally God sent them a deliverer in Judith.

In her continuing prayers for her wayward son, Augustine, St. Monica prayed specifically that he be deterred from going to Italy. Despite the fact that her prayer was unanswered, she continued to pray for his conversion. It was in Milan, through the good offices of Bishop Ambrose, that the conversion was effected. In denying that specific request God was thus actually doing her a favor.

The Apostle Paul prayed repeatedly that he might be relieved of a certain affliction. Finally God answered him with the assurance: "My grace is sufficient for thee, for power is made perfect in infirmity." By bearing that affliction willingly and bravely, Paul transformed it into a ladder on which he climbed to the Throne of God. Impatience therefore should have no place in our prayer life. "We have to wait a whole year," remarks St. Francis of Sales, "before the seed we sow in the ground bears fruit. Should we be less patient in regard to the fruit of our prayers?"

The fruitfulness of persevering prayer is illustrated in the case of the Canaanite woman who besought the Savior to cure her afflicted daughter. She was evidently very importunate and persistent, for the disciples came to Jesus, saying, "Send her away, for she is crying after us." She would not be put off, however, but continued to follow Him, crying, "Lord, help me!" Then Jesus said to her, "O woman, great is thy faith! Let it be done to thee as thou wilt." That moment her daughter was healed.

After Eddie Rickenbacker's plane crashed in the South Pacific during World War II, he and some of his companions drifted in a rubber raft for weeks. Their food supply was exhausted, but they persevered in prayer. On one occasion shortly after finishing their prayer, a strange thing happened.

"A gull," reported Rickenbacker, "came out of nowhere and lighted upon my head. I reached up my hand very gently. I killed it, and then we divided it equally among us. We ate every bit, even the little bones."

The incident helped them not only physically but also spiritually: it deepened their confidence that God's providential care would abide with them till they were rescued.

"I'm rather glad," remarked one of Rickenbacker's companions, "that plane crashed because it took a lot of nonsense out of my life. There is something inside me now that won't allow me to forget that God stayed right by us out there."

Prayer:
A Form of Companionship

The very act of praying exercises a wholesome, spiritualizing influence upon a person because it brings him into the presence of God, infinitely just, holy and perfect. The longer we remain in that presence, the more sensitive becomes our conscience and the more responsive to virtue becomes our will. In the radiant presence of Infinite Holiness our imperfections not only stand out clearly but assume disturbingly large dimensions. We feel ashamed of them and determined to get rid of them. Inherent in all genuine prayer therefore is the cleansing, purifying, uplifting influence of noble and inspiring companionship.

"Tell me with whom you go," runs an old saying, "and I will tell you what you are." Everyone has experienced the salutary influence of being in the company of a genuinely good and holy person. Like warmth, goodness radiates out to others and deepens the hunger of the heart for virtue and holiness.

"Are your plans after graduation," I asked a senior in one of my classes, "pretty well worked out?"

"Yes," he replied. "I plan on being married six months after graduation. I'm engaged to a lovely girl, Marjorie, and that has prompted me to put more pep, vigor and drive into my studies and all my work."

He paused for a moment. Then he added, "She's done more than that for me. Some of her goodness and holiness must have rubbed off on me. I never feel better or more virtuous than when I'm in her presence. I know how high her standards are, and I try to match them. Even when we're separated, the very thought of her is a help and inspiration to me."

A manly boy and captain of the golf team, he wasn't ashamed to bear witness to the powerful influence for good which was exercised upon him by his association with a genuinely good girl. Can't we all testify to the wholesome and inspiring influence we have experienced from being in the company of thoroughly good people? Yes, we all feel as if some of their "goodness were rubbing off on us."

If such an influence is exerted by the presence of a virtuous person, how much greater is the influence exerted by the presence of God who is the source of all virtue and holiness? Prayer is *keeping company with God*, sharing His thoughts, His ideals, His principles, His values, His loves. Who can emerge from that company without being purified, sanctified and ennobled?

Maintain Contact
with God

Not only theologians, ministers, priests and rabbis but scientists as well testify to the power of prayer. One of the greatest scientists of the twentieth century was the Nobel Prize winner

Alexis Carrel, author of the classic, *Man the Unknown*, upon whom I was privileged to confer the Cardinal Newman Award. Here is what he said about prayer: "When we pray we link ourselves with the inexhaustible motive power that binds the universe. Pray everywhere; in the street, in the subway, in the office, the shop, the school, as well as in the solitude of one's own room or in a church. True prayer is a way of life. Today as never before prayer is a binding necessity in the lives of men and nations."

A man in prayer is like a bar of steel in touch with a magnet. The bar itself becomes magnetized and can hold suspended in the air another piece of steel as long as it maintains contact with the original magnet. The man of prayer is in touch with the magnetism of God and attracts others to him. But break that contact and his magnetic power is gone. Prayer is contact with God and as long as man keeps that contact, the infinite power of God works in him.

An incandescent bulb shines brilliantly when in contact with electricity. Break that contact and immediately its radiance disappears. Similarly the person in touch with God through prayer glows and sparkles. Break that connection and his brilliance fades.

How maintain the luster? Pray always. This can be done by living an upright and virtuous life. God wants the homage not only of our prayers but also of our deeds. A virtuous life is a continuous prayer of blended adoration, thanksgiving, propitiation and supplication. "Not everyone," Jesus reminds us, "who says to me, 'Lord, Lord,' shall enter the kingdom of heaven; but he who does the will of my Father in heaven shall enter the kingdom of heaven."

Does Prayer Undermine Initiative?

Doesn't prayer incline one to throw upon God the burden of doing tasks which one ought to do himself? Doesn't it thus rob one of initiative, vigor and determination? No. It increases them by inspiring one with the confidence that with God's help he can accomplish things which far surpass his own power. "Without me," says Jesus, "you can do nothing." The branch torn from the vine, bears no fruit: united with the vine it bears fruit abundantly.

The motto of St. Ignatius of Loyola offers practical guidance for us here. "Pray," he counsels, "as if everything depended upon God: act as if everything depended upon you." In other words, we are to do our level best; then when we reach the limit of our resources, God comes to our assistance with new power and energy. We then become the instruments of His power and the channels of His grace.

Possible Only with God's Help

Abraham Lincoln remarked, "I have been driven many times to my knees by the overwhelming conviction that I had nowhere else to go; my own wisdom and that of all around me seemed insufficient for that day." His experience is typical of that of great and inspired leaders in every age. When they had done their best, and the goal was still beyond their reach, they stretched out their hands in prayer and found there a divine hand, ready to help them reach the goal.

I once wrote an article called "Can Christians Unite?" for the *Saturday Evening Post*. In it I cited the words of Christ: "There shall be one fold and one shepherd," indicating the unity which should characterize His Church. Those words have inspired the ecumenical movement which seeks to achieve the unity of all Christians. After pointing out the grave and formidable obstacles that seem to be humanly insurmountable, I ended with the following paragraph:

"What is impossible for men, however, is simple and easy for God. The foolishness of God is wiser than our wisdom and His weakness is greater than our strength. Only God can bridge chasms so deep and so ancient. Through humble and persistent prayer, Christians believe, God will be moved to make up for our deficiencies, our awkwardness and ineptness, and thus fulfill the prayer of Christ 'that all may be one.' In penitence, humility, trust, confidence and persevering prayer we shall do our best and leave the outcome in the hands of the God who assured us that no prayer asked in the name of Christ will go unanswered."

Mail coming to me from members of all branches of the Christian faith in all parts of the United States, Canada and even foreign lands echoed and reechoed this same general conviction. It will encourage Christians everywhere, I hope, to work harder and to pray more fervently for the achievement of the great ideal which for centuries has haunted the broken Body of Christ— Christian unity.

God Hears
Our Prayers

One final question: How do we know that God hears prayers? We know this on the greatest authority in the world: God himself. There is no theme that Christ, who is God Incarnate, stressed more forcibly and frequently than this. "If you ask the Father anything in my name," Jesus assures us, "He will give it to you. Hitherto you have not asked anything in my name." And again: "If you abide in me, and if my words abide in you, ask whatever you will and it shall be done to you."

There is not a hair of our head that God has not numbered. There is not a sparrow falling to the ground that escapes His all-seeing eye. There is not a sigh or a whisper that escapes His ear. The marvels of radio enable us to hear voices and music thousands of miles away, even from the other side of the globe. If we can hear voices at such a distance, why should anyone wonder that God, who is infinite, can hear our prayers? This thought finds apt expression in the lines of Francis Kane:

If radio's slim fingers can pluck a melody
   From night and toss it over continent or sea;
If the petaled notes of a violin
   Are blown across a mountain or a city's din;
If songs like crimson roses are culled from thin blue air,
   Why should mortals wonder that God hears prayer?

POINTS TO REMEMBER

1. Prayer is the lifting of our minds and hearts to God to adore, thank, propitiate or petition Him.

2. Prayer is essentially conversation with God and conversation implies both speaking and listening, and the latter is not less important than the former.

3. In times of spiritual danger, vigilance and prayer are of the utmost importance.

4. The famous Prayer for Peace by St. Francis of Assisi is ranked by many as second only to the Lord's Prayer, and is worth memorizing and saying daily.

5. In prayer we do not seek to impose our wishes and our will upon God but to submit them to him for approval, correction or rejection.

6. We should pray with attention, with the realization of our dependence upon God, with earnestness and submission to His holy will, with profound faith and with perseverance.

7. In spite of our best efforts to concentrate, distractions will occasionally occur. These should not discourage us. With effort and God's help we will succeed in banishing them.

8. Praying with sincerity means that we must try to square our deeds with our prayers.

9. Pray often: morning, noon and night; before and after meals, and in times of danger and temptation. Start each day by making the Morning Offering which consecrates your whole day to God.

10. One should pray with profound faith and unfaltering trust in God.

11. St. Theresa's Book mark is a beautiful prayer, well worth memorizing and reciting daily.

12. The very act of praying exercises a wholesome spiritualizing influence upon a person, because it brings him into the presence of God, infinitely just, holy and perfect.

13. A virtuous life is a continuous prayer of blended adoration, thanksgiving, propitiation and supplication.

14. We know that God hears prayers on the authority of God Himself. "If you ask the Father anything in my name," Jesus assures us, "he will give it to you."

7.

STRATEGY IN
THE SPIRITUAL LIFE

"Strategy prevails where force fails."—*François Rabelais*

"Walk in the Spirit and you will not fulfill the lusts of the flesh."—*St. Paul*

A famous Greek legend tells the fascinating story of the fall of Troy, a city in Asia Minor, in 1200 B.C. For ten years the soldiers of Greece had tried to capture the city only to have the Trojans repel every assault. So evenly balanced were the contending forces, it seemed the struggle would end in a stalemate. Then it was that the wily Greeks hit upon a ruse calculated to tip the scales.

They built a gigantic wooden horse, inside which they secreted a number of warriors. Then they withdrew across the Hellespont to the island of Tenedos. Seeing the abandoned horse, the Trojans thought the struggle had ended. In the effort to get the structure into their city, they had to tear down a portion of the walls. That night they feasted and drank in celebrating their apparent victory.

While the city slumbered, the warriors emerged, climbed the walls and with torches signaled the army waiting on Tenedos. Quickly the Greeks hurried across the Hellespont and took possession of Troy. Hence the term *Trojan horse* has come to signify a type of strategy that enables one to achieve a victory through a ruse, maneuver or stratagem where force alone would fail.

Strategy
Wins Victories

Its lesson has not been forgotten by military leaders in all the subsequent centuries. Whenever opposing forces are struggling for mastery, their respective leaders strive to work out a plan of campaign that will secure victory with the least cost. When the Allies were facing the formidable task of invading Europe, which Hitler had converted into an apparently impregnable fortress, they assembled the best brains in all their forces to work out an effective strategy. Upon its success hinged not only the lives of millions but also the future of civilization, democracy and human freedom.

Throughout that long and costly conflict the military leaders who devised the most effective stratagems were those winning the battles. Rommel, the desert fox, pouncing suddenly upon the foe, and Patton, rushing his armored divisions with lightning speed through hostile territory, are but two of the many strategists whose skillful maneuvers paid off in brilliant victories.

The importance of a carefully worked out plan, making generous use of surprise, deception and craftiness, is recognized in all competitive sports. It is no accident that the teams coached by acknowledged strategists are the ones which pile up most of the victories. In football the names of Rockne, Warner, Yost, Wilkinson, Paul Brown and Lombardi come instantly to mind.

To guard against opposing teams "pulling the unexpected," coaches send out scouts who chart the plays and report the positions of weakness and of strength of forthcoming opponents. What they dread most of all is to have their players caught flat-footed by the tricks and wiles of the enemy. Against such deception the only defense is knowledge.

"I've sent assistants," related George Halas, famous coach of the Chicago Bears and one of my former students at the University of Illinois, "to scout teams hundreds of miles away. I've done this even when I thought our team was much superior. But I didn't want our players to be taken by surprise. Besides, you can only work out an effective strategy when you know the positions where your opponents are strong and where they're weak.

"The scout charts their chief formations and plays, and we train one squad in their use. Then our defensive unit scrimmages against those plays. In this way we alert them to all the opponents' tricks so that we'll be able to nip most of them in the bud. Today a winning team must have not only a lot of power and speed but also the ability to diagnose the opponents' plays and react quickly. Strategy in both defense and offense is of the utmost importance. Without it, a team won't go far."

When two boxers of equal punching power face each other, victory usually goes to the one who employs the better strategy. It enables him to outfeint and outsmart his opponent and thus to land several blows to his adversary's one. "If I were to fight Bobo Olson again," said Kid Gavilan, "I would use both hands." His poorly thought out plan of depending entirely upon left jabs cost him the victory. Effective strategy makes good use of all available power and adds the element of surprise.

The Spirit
Against the Flesh

Man's spiritual life is a warfare of the spirit against the flesh. "The flesh," says the Apostle Paul, "lusts against the spirit, and the spirit against the flesh; for these are opposed to each other, so that you do not what you would." In this domain, where victory means a crown of imperishable glory, man has to fight not merely external foes but the enemy entrenched in the citadel of his own soul. Here the struggle is the most difficult and the most persistent, for there is no possibility of escape.

With the penetration of a master psychologist, St. Paul lays bare the anarchy enthroned in our very nature as a result of original sin. "I see another law in my members," he says, "warring against the law of my mind and making me prisoner to the law of sin that is in my members." Who is not conscious of the pull of

his lower sensual nature which, like the force of gravitation, seems
to be operating upon him from adolescence to the grave?

The consequence is that man must struggle constantly against
the current. If he relaxes his vigilance and effort but momentarily, he finds himself heading downstream. His spirit seeks to
lift him up to the stars, but the flesh mires him fast in the mud.
He wills one thing but does the opposite. Mirroring the experience of all humanity are the telltale words of the Apostle to the
Gentiles: "To wish is within my power, but I do not find the
strength to accomplish what is good. For I do not do the good
that I wish, but the evil that I do not wish, that I perform."

In each of us there is a saint and a demon, a Dr. Jekyll and a
Mr. Hyde, struggling for mastery. Spiritual writers are fond of
comparing man to the rider of an unruly and stubborn horse;
the rider wants to go in one direction but often the steed gets the
bit in his teeth and takes off in the opposite one. If the rider is
to reach his destination, he must subdue the horse and bring him
under control so that he responds to the tug of the reins. So man
must discipline his unruly nature, his flesh, and bring it under
the direction of his conscience and will.

Such then is the spiritual warfare which characterizes man's
life upon this earth. If he is to gain the victory he too must work
out an effective strategy. He must not go it blindly, as so many
do: they stumble repeatedly over the same obstacles and fall
into the same traps. They are pushovers for the world, the flesh
and the devil. They make no intelligent effort to profit from their
blunders. The consequence is that their spiritual progress is nil.

"I'm a credit manager," a man told me who came to talk over
a passion for gambling which was getting the better of him. "I'm
familiar with all the confidence games and the tricks which dead-
beats try to pull. I flash the 'no sale' sign at once. But when it
comes to gambling, I'm like a country sucker. I know the odds
are piled high against me, but I fall for the racket time after
time. I'm jeopardizing my home and the security of my family."

"Why walk into those gambling dens?" I asked. "With this
craving so pronounced in you, why don't you give them a wide

margin? Put them off limits, and don't go within a mile of them. Then you'll have a chance. You can't play with pitch without being tarred."

"Yes," he said, "I can see that I'll have to use in this matter the same hardheaded tactics I use in business. I'll try and follow the strategy you suggest."

Work Out
an Effective Strategy

How does one go about the business of working out an effective strategy for his spiritual life? He does it in much the same manner as a military leader goes about his task. The latter reconnoiters the position of the enemy; he ascertains where it is strong and where it is weak. Accordingly he maps a campaign which will exploit its weaknesses and be on guard where it is powerful. This is substantially the strategy for success in both the temporal and the spiritual domains.

One of the important exercises in the spiritual life is the daily examination of conscience. Each evening it is a good idea to look back over the past day and see what blunders, large or small, were made. What were the circumstances surrounding them? What persons, things, or places were involved? Such a review quickly alerts the sensitive conscience to the dangers to which one is subject. Then a quick review of the past few months or year will pinpoint the chief fault or sin into which one has fallen.

Spiritual writers call this the predominant passion or weakness to which one is subject. They urge that it be faced frankly as the chief threat to one's spiritual welfare, progress and eternal salvation. No effective spiritual strategy can be charted until that danger or weakness has been carefully determined. Resolutions of improvement must not be blind general ones: they must have eyes and they must focus upon the particular fault or weakness that must be conquered before a person can hope to emerge from the first stage of the spiritual life. This is called the purgative way, the stage in which one has freed himself from the tyranny of mortal sin and hence from the slavery to a besetting vice.

Determine
Your Chief Weakness

What is your predominant passion? That is for each one to determine for himself. With some it is anger, the habit of flying into a rage at the slightest provocation. With others it is the green-eyed monster of envy, which fills one with spite over the good fortune or happiness of others.

With not a few it is gluttony, the excessive indulgence in food or drink. The mounting number of alcoholics and near-alcoholics, who degrade themselves to the level of beasts, is disturbingly large. Perhaps equally large is the number of people who eat to such excess as to injure their health and bring themselves to an early grave. Doctors tell us that in America the real battlefield today is the dining room and the most lethal weapons are knives and forks. Obesity is the distinctive malaise of our day.

One of my former students, a varsity football player, came back to the campus five years after graduation to be married in Notre Dame's famed log chapel.

"Why, Joe," I said, "I'd hardly know you. When you were on the team you weighed about 220 pounds. Now you must be 280. You're losing the battle of the bulge, and you won't be long for this world if you don't take off that barrel of fat."

"It will be different," he grinned sheepishly, "after I'm married. Jean will help me watch the calories. I'll look a lot different when you next see me."

"Yes," Jean said, "I'll put him on a regular diet that will enable him to lose two pounds a week. I'll call the signals and Joe has agreed to follow them."

"That's wise strategy," I said. "Hold fast to it, and you'll get results."

Through pride the angels fell, and it is still claiming its victims among men. Overweening self-esteem, conceit and vanity bite into one's moral character like cancer, and fill him with an exaggerated sense of his own importance and worth. Covetousness, greed, sloth and utter indolence cripple not a few.

The most common weakness of human nature, however, is lust, the weakness of the flesh. Every child of Adam can testify to its pull upon him. With the Apostle Paul he can cry out: "There was given me a sting of my flesh, an angel of Satan, to buffet me." Universally present in human nature, lust is probably the predominant passion of most people and the weakness against which they have to struggle with the greatest frequency and persistence.

Look frankly then into your own spiritual life and determine your besetting weakness, your predominant fault, the inclination against which you have to contend forever and a day. When you have done this, you are in a position to work out an intelligent plan of campaign. Like a thoroughly informed military leader, you are able to direct your heaviest guns upon the strongest fortifications of the enemy. Once these are leveled, the mopping-up action—the conquest of the minor ones—will be a comparatively easy affair.

It is well to supplement one's own efforts to determine his chief weakness by earnest prayer. Often we are quick to notice the shortcomings of others but slow to recognize our own. Hence we should all beg of God the light to discern our besetting fault and the strength to overcome it. Helpful is the simple little prayer: "O God, the infinite source of all light, knowledge and truth, open my eyes that I may see myself as I really am. Help me to discern the chief rebel in the citadel of my soul and grant me the power to crush it that I may enjoy the peace and happiness which come from the keeping of Thy commandments and from conformity to Thy holy will."

The plan of campaign or strategy that each must work out will differ in accordance with what each one finds to be his predominant weakness. Upon that he will concentrate his greatest efforts. There are, however, certain basic stratagems that are common to all effective plans.

Avoid
Near Occasion

The first of these is: *Avoid the near occasion of the sin*: the person, place, thing or other particular circumstance that leads to it. Indeed one is *obliged* in conscience to avoid not only the sin, but also the circumstances occasioning it. If some unusual circumstance should force one into such an approximate occasion of sin, he must have instant recourse to prayer and exercise the utmost vigilance against falling into the trap.

Our safety lies not in stalking the enemy but in avoiding it. "He that loveth danger," warns Ecclesiasticus, "shall perish in it." The sacred writer regards this warning as of such importance that he sounds it again: "He that toucheth pitch, shall be defiled with it." He who plays with fire will sooner or later be burned.

In the Sermon on the Mount our Lord stresses the importance of avoiding the occasions of sin. "If thy right eye is an occasion of sin to thee, pluck it out and cast it from thee . . . If thy right hand is an occasion of sin to thee, cut it off and cast it from thee; for it is better for thee that one of thy members should be lost than that thy whole body should go into hell." "Right eye" and "right hand" mean all that we hold most dear. If these treasures are a trap on the moral path and hence an occasion of sin for us, they are to be cast away. Such then are the warnings of almighty God: such too are the dictates of common sense.

I shall cite three cases illustrating different types of the near occasion of sin and show the necessity of avoiding them.

A businessman, nervous and worried looking, came to my office.

"I feel," he began, "that drink is beginning to get the upper hand. I know the moral and spiritual ruin it causes. I've come to you for help before it gets too firm a hold on me."

"What's the occasion," I asked, "of your excessive drinking?"

"About five months ago," he replied, "I joined a poker club that meets biweekly. Each session ends with sandwiches and drinks. It's a convivial group, and I try to hold my own with the others. But it's getting the better of me, and unless something is done, I'll be a real toper."

"You've pinpointed the occasion of your drinking," I pointed out, "and it's clear that you will have to drop out of that club at once. Play it safe by abstaining completely from liquor until you feel you're out of all danger."

A few months later he dropped into my office—a different-looking man. Gone were his worried look, his nervousness and his brooding anxiety. He was the picture of a self-confident man who had things well under control.

"I've decided," he remarked, "to play it safe by staying on the wagon for good. It's a lot easier that way."

"I heartily agree," I said. "There's no sense in playing with fire or firewater."

"Yes," he chuckled, "it's hard to say which is the more dangerous."

Stay Away from Danger

So prone to weakness is human nature that danger, like lightning, strikes from all directions. A middle-aged man, apprehensive and downcast, came with a different problem.

"I've got a good reputation," he said, "and I don't want to lose it. But I've incurred some gambling debts and the gamblers are breathing down my back, threatening to kill me if I don't come across. I have access to the funds of the firm where I work, and I wonder if under the circumstances I might take some money—as a loan. I know that I can cover it up on the books and pay it back in a year or two without anyone being the wiser."

"No," I replied. "You would only compound the blunder. You never escape from one mistake by committing another. Since the occasion of your getting into this trouble is gambling, there's only one thing to do: *stay away from the gamblers entirely*. Indeed since gambling has tempted you so seriously to embezzlement, you are *bound* in conscience to do so."

Fortunately, he was brave enough to do this. He was able to borrow some funds from the bank, settle his debts, and start with a clean slate.

Among the most difficult cases which have come to me over the years are those which married couples have brought. Because they involve such intangible and subjective factors as feelings and emotions, so unamenable to mere logic, they are often hard to straighten out. But if they can be gotten early, before the emotional involvement has become too great, they are easier to solve.

Here's one that was. A couple in their early thirties called. The wife was much upset and on the verge of tears. "Tom and I have been happily married for ten years," she began, "and have four children. I got the shock of my life when I chanced upon a letter in his desk. It's from a married woman in the office where he works. She says that she has fallen in love with him and suggests they both get divorces so they will be free to marry."

"I've done nothing more," explained Tom, "than drive her home a few nights when we both had to work late at the office. It was a shock to me when she wrote me that letter. I was merely courteous and just a bit affectionate. Hence I was bewildered when Betty chanced upon that silly letter which I should have destroyed."

"That's good to hear," I said. "But there are elements of danger in that situation—if not for you, at least for her. She evidently is reading more into your little expressions of affection than you had realized. Don't prolong the danger. Arrange quietly to get transferred to another division"—it was a large company—"where you will have nothing further to do with her. You will thereby safeguard her marriage as well as your own."

Tom was able to do this, and what threatened, if it continued, to disrupt two homes, was nipped in the bud.

These three cases were solved by the simple expedient of avoiding the near occasion of the danger or the sin, regardless of whether it was a person, a place, a thing or a combination of them. My files are bulging with similar cases, but these will suffice to emphasize the paramount importance of this first principle of an intelligent and effective spiritual strategy.

The Need
for Vigilance

The second is this: *Exercise the utmost vigilance in guarding against the danger or temptation.* Eternal vigilance is the price of liberty. In wartime sentries are stationed around every camp; they parade the deck of every vessel, day and night. Because even brief lapses are fraught with such grave consequences, they entail the severest penalties, even death itself. What a world of wisdom and of warning is contained in the memorable words which Christ addressed to Peter, James and John on the eve of His Passion: "Watch and pray that you enter not into temptation."

For momentary lapses in watchfulness individuals and nations have paid dearly. Before securing a match with Floyd Patterson, the heavyweight champion, Charles Liston, had won with ease 33 of his 34 professional fights. How did he come to lose that solitary one?

"He was hollerin' and going on," said Liston, "and I knocked him down. He got up and I was laughing. He caught me with my mouth open and broke my jaw."

Invincible with his guard up, this hulking giant was an easy target with his hands at his side and his mouth wide open.

The outstanding instance of lack of vigilance in World War II was the failure to blow up the bridge spanning the Rhine at Remagen. When the American soldiers came within sight of the bridge and saw it still standing, they could scarcely believe their eyes. Suspecting that it might be some kind of a trap, they advanced over it cautiously and warily, fearful that it might explode at any moment. But it held firmly and no gunfire met them from the other side. The amazing news spread from division to division and soon men, tanks, trucks and guns were speeding across it without hindrance, to plunge deep into enemy territory.

What had happened? The officer in charge of the bridge's demolition claimed that the explosive mechanism was faulty. But this could and should have been carefully checked ahead of time. Moreover with the advance knowledge that the American forces were nearing that area, it should have been blown up several days before. The lack of vigilance was as clear and unmistakable as it was monumental and costly.

Wild with rage, Hitler ordered the officer's immediate execution. But the damage was already done, and it was irreparable. The German Third Reich, which Hitler had boasted would last a thousand years, was mortally wounded and its days were numbered.

Alfred Henley in Gibsonton, Florida, had a small zoo which attracted passing motorists. On March 16, 1961, he fed the animals as usual but failed to lock the cage of his 22-foot long, 210-pound python. With surprising speed and stealth the huge snake slipped out and coiled around Henley's body. It pinned his arms helplessly at his side and crushed him to death. A momentary lapse of alertness cost him his life. That serpent is an apt symbol of any passion which, if allowed to get a grip on one, holds him as in a steel vise and slowly crushes him to death.

Lapse of Alertness
Costly

In the spiritual domain a lapse of vigilance is still more costly. Peter ignored Christ's warning to "watch and pray," and fell asleep. What a penalty he paid! Soon the Apostle who had boasted, "though I should die with thee, I will not deny Thee," was denying the Master not once but thrice. What bitter tears he shed over the remembrance of that tragic defection. But they could not erase the horrible reality: the record will stand not merely till the crack of doom but through all eternity.

How apt are the words of Omar Khayyám:

> The moving finger writes, and having writ,
> Moves on: nor all your piety nor wit
> Shall lure it back to cancel half a line
> Nor all your tears wash out a word of it.

If one could but read the record of man's moral stumbling, how many instances he would find that were traceable to momentary slips in watchfulness. A whole menagerie of latent passions is lurking in the cage of our lower nature, ready to spring upon us the moment we relax our vigilance.

Look into your own conscience and recall how many slips from virtue are traceable to a failure to keep up your guard. It is such failures that transform neutral circumstances—persons, places, things—into occasions of sin. The more numerous such pitfalls, the more hazardous becomes our journey through life.

On the highways of this country we are slaughtering more than 40,000 persons a year and injuring more than a million. While the causes are numerous, it is probable that the chief one is lack of vigilance: failure to notice the traffic light, the pedestrian, the oncoming car, the speed limit, the speedometer reading, the railroad crossing signal and the other traffic signs warning of various dangers. What a ghastly toll we pay for lack of alertness on our highways! Much more costly, however, is the toll we pay for the same slips on the moral highways of life.

Guard the Senses

A third rule to be incorporated into one's spiritual strategy is: *Guard the senses, particularly the eyes and ears.* The senses are the gateways to the mind. To keep our minds clean and pure we must guard these entrances with special care. If inflammatory material is smuggled in through any of these channels, it will kindle a flame that will do some damage and may even set our whole spiritual house on fire.

Failure to observe custody of the senses is the fertile cause of many moral lapses. The suggestive story or the smutty joke may start a train of thought that will be hard to head off. The lewd picture, the salacious movie, the prurient paperback and the lascivious floor show penetrate beyond the retina of the eye to paint their incendiary images upon the mind. The eye is not satisfied with seeing, however, nor the ear with hearing. They kindle desires and inflame passions which are not easily choked or extinguished. Even when they do not lead at once to their satisfaction, they plant the seeds of future action. They are like the time the Nazis dropped bombs on England early in the war.

I was doing research at Oxford when a bomb, dropped from a German plane, fell in the nearby countryside. As it hadn't exploded, people thought it was a dud and gathered around it, curious to see the strange object. Some minutes later when the crowd had reached its peak, the bomb suddenly went off, killing several and maiming more. Inside the mechanism was a device which delayed its explosion so that its destructive fury would reach the greatest number. Such are the time bombs stored in the mind by incendiary images.

Of all the senses, sight is the one which presents perhaps the greatest danger. Custody of this sense is consequently of the utmost importance. It is not so much what one sees, but what one *looks at*, that matters. The following up of the visual stimulus with attention, eagerness and a direction of the thought, is what inflames the emotion and leads to the lustful act.

Images etched deeply into the memory frequently serve as the hidden stimuli of repeated acts, and thus carry on indefinitely their train of evil consequences. One who really wants to keep his soul unsullied will guard the portal of the eye with unrelenting care. Through that portal the enemy usually seeks to gain entrance to the mind. With what penetrating discernment does Shakespeare say:

> Where, or when is fancy bred?
> Or in the heart, or in the head?
> How begot? how nourished?
> Reply, reply,
> It is engendered in the eyes,
> By gazing fed; fancy dies
> In the cradle where it lies.

Poisoning
the Wells

One of the stratagems of warfare in ancient times was to poison the wells. From those sources the infection would spread to hundreds of thousands. The wells today are the printing press, cinema, television, radio and theatre. They paint their images, for good or for evil, upon the retinas, eardrums and the minds of millions, young and old alike.

That is why society cannot be indifferent as to the material carried by these mass media. If pure food laws are necessary to protect our physical health, similar legislation is not less necessary to safeguard our moral and spiritual health. The sections of our large cities, where indecent shows are permitted, are the areas where vice and crime are rampant, where anyone who ventures out at night takes his life in his hands.

Some time ago a man was convicted because of criminal attacks and sexual perversions which shocked the nation.

"What," asked a news reporter, "led you to be such a pervert?"

"Pervert?" replied the criminal. "That word makes me laugh. I'm no different from anybody else. I can see now what made me what I am. It didn't come from inside me but from outside. From those filthy magazines and paperbacks that you nice people allow to be plastered all over your newsstands. From the filthy floor shows and striptease joints 'where everything goes.'"

Yes, these are the time bombs with the delayed fuse, which spread death and destruction in thousands of communities today. They do it through the dynamite which they store in their victims and which explode only when the latter can kill, rape or maim others.

Custody of the eyes was a point frequently stressed by St. Francis of Assisi in his conferences to his brethren.

"Father, come with me," he said to a fellow religious, "and we shall go to Assisi and preach a sermon."

They walked in silent prayer into the city and through its main streets without a pause. The priest was beginning to wonder where the saint was to preach. Then to his astonishment, they returned to the monastery.

"Brother Francis," he asked, "why didn't you preach that sermon?"

"Father," replied the saint, "we preached all the time we walked through the streets of Assisi, for we observed custody of the eyes. That is a sermon in itself."

Guard
Your Thoughts

The fourth rule is: Guard your thoughts. All action begins in thought. By guarding our thoughts we control our conduct. By suppressing instantly any evil thought, imagination or desire, we nip in the bud any evil action. By directing our attention to wholesome, uplifting and inspiring truths, ideals, topics and considerations we deepen their appeal, we weave the truths into the very texture of our minds, we make the ideals our own and we grow in uprightness and nobility of character.

The importance of guarding our thoughts is stressed in the Old Testament and the New. "Evil thoughts," warns Proverbs, "are an abomination to the Lord." "Perverse thoughts," says Wisdom, "separate us from God." God "searched out the deep," says Ecclesiasticus, "and the heart of men and considered their crafty devices . . . No thought escapeth him."

Jesus shifted the emphasis from the distinction between so-called clean and unclean food to purity of heart and mind. "Out of the heart," He says, "come evil thoughts, murders, adulteries, immorality, thefts, false witness, blasphemies. These are the things that defile a man." When a matter is brought to that tribunal, however, we can strengthen the will to decide in accordance with one's conscience by the proper direction of our thoughts.

This is illustrated by an incident in the life of St. Thomas More. As Lord Chancellor of England he had brought fame to English courts by his able and fearless administration of justice. When ordered to acknowledge his monarch, Henry VIII, as the "Supreme Head of the Church of England," More refused. He was imprisoned in the Tower of London where he languished for fifteen months, strengthening his will to resist to the end. This he did by directing his thoughts to God in prolonged meditation and prayer, as revealed in his book, *Dialogue of Comfort Against Tribulation*, written in his prison cell.

He was visited by his wife Alice who urged him to yield, and thus get out of the filthy prison with its mice and rats, come back to his manor house and enjoy the comforts of his home and family.

"I pray thee, good Mistress Alice," said More, "tell me one thing!"

"What is that?" she asked.

"Is not this house," he said, "as near to heaven as my own?"

"Tylle valle, Tylle valle!" was all she could say.

Thus had More steeled himself by the focusing of his thoughts upon God and eternity to resist all entreaties to save his life.

The shepherding of our thoughts is an effective strategy of defense in all temptations and dangers. "As a man thinketh in his heart," runs the proverb, "so is he." No wolf can ravage the flock of our thoughts when the shepherdess is at her post of duty. Aptly does Alice Meynell say:

> She walks—the lady of my delight—
>   A shepherdess of sheep.
> Her flocks are thoughts. She keeps them white;
>   She guards them from the steep;
> She feeds them on the fragrant height,
>   And folds them in for sleep.

Guilt is incurred by the *willing* of a deed, whether it be done or not. We shall best protect the will from such a decision by guarding our thoughts and thereby preventing such a proposal from even reaching the high tribunal of the human will.

Resist
the Beginnings

The fifth rule is: *Resist the beginnings of an evil deed.* This is a basic principle of the spiritual life. In his great work, *The Imitation of Christ*, second only to the Bible in its inspirational and spiritual value, Thomas à Kempis says: "We must watch, especially in the beginning of temptation; for then the enemy is more easily overcome if he be not suffered to enter the door of the mind, but is withstood upon the threshold the very moment that he knocketh. Whence a certain one hath said: 'Resist beginnings: all too late the cure / When ills have gathered strength by long delay.'"

The psychological sequence in temptation is clear to everyone who has examined his conscience. First there is the simple thought. If not instantly banished, it kindles the imagination and holds forth the prospect of great delight. Then it begins to excite sexual pleasure and under that pressure the will caves in. Such is the stealthy and treacherous manner in which the malignant foe gains the upper hand when he is not resisted at the threshold.

Defend
the Scrimmage Line

A crucial period in a football game is when a team brings the ball within the ten-yard line of the opponents' goal. Then the defenders must fight with redoubled fury, for here the slightest lapse of vigilance or skill may spell defeat. The wise coach will drill his players in the tactics of defense not only at that crucial period but also on how to keep the foe from getting to that danger zone.

In 1924 Notre Dame had one of its great football teams. Grantland Rice had named its backs the "Four Horsemen" and Rockne had humorously dubbed its linemen the "Seven Mules." With its backs averaging less than 175 pounds it was one of the lightest teams in the school's history. The players made up in speed, grit and skill, however, what they lacked in weight. Only Stanford, their Rose Bowl opponent, stood between them and the national championship, but it was a powerful team and out-weighed Notre Dame 12 pounds to the man. When Ernie Nevers and his teammates came charging out on the field, their muscles bulging, one of the Notre Dame linemen turned to Rockne.

"Coach," he said, "how in the world are we ever going to keep those giants from scoring on us?"

"It's very simple," grinned the famous coach. "Don't let them cross the *scrimmage* line. Then you won't have to worry about the *goal* line."

The tactic outlined by Rockne, generally acclaimed the wiliest strategist in football history, is effective not only in the rugged sport of the gridiron but also in the grim warfare which we all must wage, the unrelenting battle of the spirit against the flesh. Here the possibilities of slips are vastly greater and the stakes infinitely higher.

The First
False Step

How many an addict looks back with regret upon the first false step: the taking of the first "shot." Before that he was his own master, with his freedom unimpaired. But the first shot soon led to the second, and that to a third. Before he could realize what was happening, he found himself an abject slave to the habit. Wanting desperately then to stop, he found to his horror that he couldn't. What is more tragic than the spectacle of a man, cowering like a slave, under the galling tyranny of the narcotic, the bottle or the cigarette!

I was once called in the middle of the night to minister to a man dying in a cheap hotel in a slum section. He was a college graduate, only in his forties. His hair was prematurely gray, his eyes bleary, his face stamped with the unmistakable marks of the habitual drunkard. He had been on one binge too many and his hours were numbered.

He told me of the wife and children he had left in the East, no longer wanting to add to their shame with the spectacle he was making of himself. He asked me to write and tell them that his last thoughts were of them and of his sorrow for the humiliation and suffering he had caused them.

"Father," he said as I was leaving, "there isn't anything I wouldn't give, do or suffer if I could only start again. How I would push back in scorn that first fateful drink!"

What a world of poignant regret and sorrow there was in those anguished words! They have haunted my memory for forty years, and I find them trooping out whenever I see anyone starting on a path that can lead only to empty frustration, ruin and tragedy. The crucial period is the beginning. Don't take the first step down the slippery path of vice, and there will be no second and hence no final tumble headlong into the pit of darkness and of slavery. Better than a ton of remedies is an ounce of prevention. This applies not only to addiction to narcotics and liquor but also to all the actions which lead one to surrender his freedom to the tyranny of any undesirable habit or vice. Such are the principles, rules and tactics of an effectively integrated strategy of spiritual defense.

Strategy of Offense

Victory in any struggle requires, however, not only a carefully planned defense but also a strong and vigorous offense. The importance of the latter is reflected in the adage, "The best defense is a strong offense." In the spiritual domain this means that we must not only resist temptation but must also advance in virtue and holiness of life. The tactics and rules for such an advance can be stated briefly and need little, if any, development.

The sixth rule in spiritual strategy is: *Have instant recourse to prayer.* God is the infinite source of all spiritual power and strength. Prayer taps that source and channels the power to the individual soul. Prayer is both armor and ammunition. Without prayer our bows have no arrows and our guns no bullets. Without God, nothing is possible: with Him, all things are possible. Faith moves mountains and faith expresses itself through prayer. In his affliction the Apostle Paul turned to God for help and received the comforting assurance: "My grace is sufficient for thee, for strength is made perfect in weakness."

"I've got an ungovernable temper and blow my top with little or no provocation," related a man whose marriage was on the brink of disaster. "I'm sorry for it afterwards, but the damage is done then. My wife is fed up with it, and has threatened to call it quits the next time it happens. What can I do?"

"When you find yourself getting angry," I suggested, "say a few Our Fathers for the grace of patience before you venture to speak aloud. Think, too, of Christ enduring the excruciating pains of the cross. Not only did He utter no angry word but He prayed for the forgiveness of His executioners. After the Our Fathers say, 'My crucified Savior, help me to be meek and humble of heart like Thee. Give me the grace of unfailing patience in times of trial.' "

Six months later the man came into my office.

"The remedy you suggested," he said, "was a simple one. But it has worked like a charm. That minute of silent prayer chokes off my anger and enables me to use my brains instead of my lungs and mouth in dealing with provocations that formerly upset me."

In all the crises of life the first thing to do is to pray. It brings to us the power not only to resist the temptation but also to do the right and virtuous deed. Face to the light and walk in that direction; then you find the shadows are falling behind you. In all times of danger and temptation, when the burden seems heavy and the way boulder-strewn, when the challenge is awesome and the odds are piled high against us, God's hand is stretched out not only to defend us but also to help us to move forward in the right direction.

The seventh rule is: *Plunge with vigor and determination into the struggle to achieve the highest holiness.* In this domain, as in all others, victory is achieved not by the faint-hearted and the irresolute but by those who put forth resolute and determined efforts.

The amazing success achieved by Germany in the early months of World War II was due to the vigor and speed with which it launched co-ordinated offensives by tanks, infantry and bombing planes. Before neighboring nations realized what was really going on, they found the invaders deep within their territory. They did this with such frequency and in such a spectacular and stunning manner that they brought two new words into our language—blitz and blitzkrieg—a lightning offensive and a lightning war.

In the spiritual domain one must burn the bridges with a sinful past; he must turn over a new leaf not hesitantly but with decisiveness and speed.

"When I decided to go on the water wagon for good," related a former alcoholic, "I gave away all my liquor, discontinued my membership in a poker club that served drinks between games, and bade a permanent adieu to the tavern I had long frequented. It provided the momentum needed to carry me through the difficult early stages, and it paid off handsomely."

Invincible
with God

The eighth rule is: *Keep ever in mind your goal.* This will help you form a proper hierarchy—or order of values, in which the top ones are spiritual. It was to emphasize the primacy of spiritual values and to help His followers keep them uppermost in their minds that Christ said: "What shall it profit a man if he gain the whole world and lose his own soul?" By keeping ever in mind your eternal salvation, you will be enabled to appraise things at their true worth and not be misled by mere outward appearances.

St. Bernard established a Cistercian monastery in the wilderness of Clairvaux so that he and his fellow monks might be cut off from the world as completely as possible and devote themselves to prayer, meditation and other spiritual works. Often he would remind himself of this purpose by asking: "Bernard, for what purpose did you come hither?"

That is the question which might well be asked not only by the thousands who go to secluded monasteries to make a spiritual retreat but also by every one of us. We have a goal, and the more frequently we recall it to mind, the more powerful will be its influence in our lives.

"Where will you spend eternity?" This was the question which not a few saints had framed and placed in a prominent place in their rooms. It helped them to keep ever in mind the purpose for which they had been created: the achievement of their salvation and union with God for all eternity. There is but one supreme success in life and that is the achievement of genuine virtue and sanctity. Similarly there is but one unrelieved tragedy and this is the failure to do so.

The ninth rule is: *Deepen your appreciation of spiritual values by frequent and even daily meditation.* The more we meditate upon spiritual values, the greater becomes their appeal to us. This means that our motivation to achieve those values is multiplied manifold.

Coming into the courtyard of the Sorbonne, the University of Paris, the visitor sees an old sundial, made by the famous mathematician Picard in 1676. On it is inscribed: *Sicut Umbra Dies Nostri*—Our days are like shadows. It reflects the fugitiveness of human fame and the transience of wealth and worldly glory.

This is the lesson which the Church seeks to impress upon her members on Ash Wednesday, the first day of Lent, when her minister places ashes upon the forehead of each and says: "Remember man that thou art but dust, and unto dust thou shalt return." How important it is for the Christian to meditate upon this truth and thus deepen his appreciation of spiritual values.

The tenth rule is: *Remember that God and one constitute a majority*. If you have God on your side, you are invincible. Nothing can long impede your advance in holiness if you strive each day to grow in the love of God and of your neighbor. God then dwells in your heart and nothing can keep you from achieving the only lasting victory: eternal union with God and everlasting happiness.

When Frederick B. Snite, Jr., a young Notre Dame graduate, was traveling with his parents in China, he was stricken with infantile paralysis. The doctors gave him about a week to live. They didn't realize, however, the sustaining power of a deep faith. He lived for years and was able to marry and have a family. Many of those years were spent encased within the walls of a huge iron lung. The malady had paralyzed the respiratory muscles and for months he was unable to utter even a word. When at last he regained the partial use of his voice, he uttered slowly the single word "God." Years later I visited him at his home in Florida.

"The one thing that sustained me," he related, "during that trying period when I was unable to breathe or to speak was my faith in God. I knew that He was with me and that He could hear my silent prayers. If a person has God with him, he has nothing to fear."

What sustained Joan of Arc when she was being burned at the stake in Orleans? It was the consciousness that God was with her. As the flames leaped higher and higher about her, she called out continuously, "Jesus! Jesus!" until she was no longer able to speak.

It is the consciousness that God and one constitute a majority and with Him on one's side there is nothing to fear, that has sustained not only all the saints and martyrs but also all the noble souls who have fought against overwhelming odds for truth, right, justice and freedom.

Such are the important principles, rules and tactics which constitute an effective strategy for the winning of the spiritual war which we all must wage.

POINTS TO REMEMBER

1. A wise strategy helps in winning every battle. As the spiritual life is a warfare of the spirit against the flesh, an effective strategy is of the utmost importance here.

2. One of the important exercises in the spiritual life is the daily examination of conscience.

3. It is well to determine early in life your chief fault or predominant passion.

4. Part of any wise spiritual strategy is the avoidance of the near occasions of sin.

5. Guard the senses, particularly the eyes and ears, for they are the gateways to the mind.

6. As all action begins in thought, it is important to exercise vigilance over your thoughts and imagination.

7. A basic principle of the spiritual life is to resist temptation in its very beginnings.

8. God is the infinite source of all spiritual power and strength. Prayer taps that source and channels the power to the individual soul.

9. Plunge with vigor and determination into the struggle to achieve the highest holiness.

10. Keep ever in mind your goal. This will help you form a proper sense of values.

11. Remember that God and one constitute a majority. If you have God on your side, you are invincible.

8.

MEDITATION:
OUR LADDER TO HEAVEN

"With desolation is all the land made desolate
because there is none that considereth in the
heart"—*Jeremias*

"Come unto me, all you who labor and are burdened, and I will give you rest."—*Jesus* (*Matthew*
11:28)

John K. Lagemann, a writer, tells of a time when he faced
a difficult decision: whether or not to accept a job that would
entail moving to another city and changing his whole mode of
living. Progress on the manuscript on which he had been working came to a complete standstill. After agonizing uncertainty he
was on the way to accept, when impulsively he dropped into a
barber shop for a haircut.

By the time he arose from the chair, he was dead sure of
exactly what he wanted to do. He turned down the job, was at
complete peace with himself, returned home and finished his
manuscript in a jiffy. Subsequent years amply proved the wisdom
of his decision.

The quiet uninterrupted time spent in that chair had filled a
desperate need in his life: the need to be alone with himself, to
meditate, to turn inward. "In those moments of self-awareness,"
he relates, "I gained a deeper understanding of the problems
that had come up in my life and tapped unsuspected stores of
energy." It started him on the practice of meditating, which has
enabled him to make excellent use of periods of time which
previously had been largely wasted.

The practice of meditation adds a new dimension to all human life. It sends the drill point down below the layers of ordinary consciousness and thus draws upon hidden reserves of energy and insight. Only one-eighth of the mass of an iceberg appears above the surface: what makes it an object of such dread to mariners is its tremendous hidden bulk, capable of smashing a vessel like a toothpick.

We too are like an iceberg in the sense that we use only about one-eighth of our intellectual potential, letting its bulk go to waste. Meditation is the means of harnessing that intellectual and spiritual Niagara to the important enterprise of living deeper and richer lives. "The more self-awareness a person has," the psychiatrist Rollo May points out, "the more alive he is." Over the years the psychiatrists with whom I have collaborated in marriage counseling have often remarked that the malady afflicting most of their patients is that they have lost contact with themselves.

A Novelist
Finds Himself

When A. J. Cronin was 33, he developed a gastric ulcer from ministering to his patients all day and half the night in the West End of London. A fellow doctor ordered him to take a six months' complete rest in the country on a milk diet. At a lonely farm by a rain-drenched lake in the Scottish Highlands, the young doctor began to get acquainted with himself. Upon boring deeply into his inner self, he perceived among his long buried hopes and dreams the aspiration to write a novel. In "The Turning Point of My Career" in *The Reader's Digest* he tells the whole fascinating story. Here in condensed form are its highlights.

"By Heavens!" he exclaimed. "This is my opportunity. Gastric ulcer or no gastric ulcer, I *will* write a novel." Buying two dozen penny exercise books at the village store, he set to work. He was woefully unprepared: he had never seen a thesaurus; he had no knowledge of style or form and no training in composition. He corrected and recorrected until the page looked like a spider's web. Tearing it up, he would start again, averaging a mere 800 words all day.

When he was halfway through, discouragement and desolation struck him with the fury of a sudden avalanche. Abruptly, furiously, he seized the manuscript and threw it in the ashcan. Walking out in the drizzling rain, he came upon Angus, his landlord, patiently, persistently, stubbornly digging a ditch in the bogged and peaty heath which made up most of his hard-won acreage. When Angus heard what his guest had done with the manuscript, he was silent. A look of disappointment, mingled with contempt, came over his weathered countenance.

"My father," he remarked, "ditched this bog all his days and never made a pasture. But pasture or no pasture," resuming his digging, "I canna help but dig. My father knew and I know that if you only dig enough, a pasture can be made here."

The words sank home. They kindled a flame of stubborn determination to complete the job. Retrieving the soggy bundle from the ashcan, Cronin flung himself with a ferocity of purpose and unremitting industry at his unfinished manuscript. At the end of the third month, he wrote finis. He had written a novel. Whether it was good, bad or indifferent, he knew not.

Sending the manuscript to a publisher, chosen at random from a catalogue, he promptly forgot about it. The novel, Hatter's Castle, was chosen by the Book Society, dramatized, serialized, translated into 19 languages, cinematized by Hollywood and long ago passed the three million mark. There followed many other novels, including the memorable The Keys of the Kingdom, bringing pleasure, enchantment and inspiration to uncounted millions.

It was through prolonged meditation on that isolated farm that Cronin found himself and put his long-buried talent to work. It was there too that he learned a twofold lesson of paramount importance to us all: 1. The way to overcome discouragement and despair is to stick resolutely at the job until it is finished. 2. The greatest of all victories is the victory over oneself: he who wins this triumph can never know defeat.

The Power
of Patient Thought

When Isaac Newton was struggling to formulate the law which would explain the attraction of bodies in relation to their masses and distances, he discovered the indispensable necessity of having long periods of unbroken time to mull over the bewildering mass of data before him, analyzing and studying it from every angle. Accordingly he had a small opening cut in the door of his study. Through it the servant would silently insert the trays containing the scientist's meals.

Imagine the servant's surprise and awe when he would bring the evening meal only to discover the previous tray still untouched. Time and bodily needs seemed suspended as the great scientist, with concentration sharpened to the point of a gimlet, bore through the mass of mathematical calculations till he reached the underlying principle which explained the mystifying phenomena—the law of gravitation, which forms the foundation of a great portion of physical science.

As a magnifying glass can focus the gentle rays of the sun upon a single point and thus raise them to an intensity that will kindle a fire, so sustained meditation can give thought a penetrating quality that enables it to plumb new depths and thus discover long-buried truths. It is through the heightened awareness that comes from prolonged concentration and meditation that we have come into possession of all the laws of science and the truths of philosophy. "If I have done the public any service," wrote Newton toward the end of his life, "it is due to patient thought."

The experiences of Lagemann, Cronin and Newton, among hundreds of others, dramatize the importance and the fruitfulness of meditation in the sense of prolonged and concentrated thought and reflection. It is well for all of us to cultivate this faculty to the full extent of our respective talents. This is the endowment which distinguishes man from the brute and in its use he finds his greatest satisfaction and joy.

Valuable as are the fruits of meditation in the general sense of concentrated thought on any subject, they are even more precious when the meditation is directed upon spiritual themes: God, the human soul, our relations with God, the meaning of human life and the destiny of man. These are the mighty themes which confront every man and woman. Indeed they cannot be ignored if life is to have any meaning and not be simply a game of blindman's buff.

The Meaning of Meditation

Meditation in the religious sense is closely akin to mental prayer and may even be considered a form of it. Meditation consists in the application of the intellect, imagination, memory and will to the consideration of some spiritual principle, truth or ideal in order to stimulate the appropriate spiritual emotions and thus resolve on some act or course of conduct regarded as God's will or as a means of achieving union with Him. Meditation differs from spiritual reading: the object of the latter is to enlighten the mind, while the purpose of the former is to move the will so as to improve one's conduct. Spiritual reading makes one *wiser*; meditation makes one *better*.

Like prayer, it enables the individual to make contact with God. It is a bridge which stretches from the heart of man to the heart of God. It is the unseen bridge thus depicted by Gilbert Thomas:

> There is a bridge, whereof the span
> Is rooted in the heart of man,

> And reaches, without pile or rod,
> Unto the Great White Throne of God.

Meditation has always been practiced by holy people, from whose minds God and eternity are never far distant. The Old Testament and the New are replete with testimony concerning the practice of meditation and its fruitfulness.

David the Psalmist bears eloquent witness to this. "I set the Lord," he says, "always in my sight: for He is at my right hand that I be not moved . . . I will meditate on Thy commandments: and I will consider Thy ways. I will think of Thy justifications: I will not forget Thy words." "Blessed is the man," says Ecclesiasticus, "that shall continue in wisdom, and that shall meditate in His justice, and in his mind shall think of the all-seeing eye of God." Yes, meditation makes us aware that we are always in God's presence.

Giving detailed instructions on what to meditate, Ecclesiasticus says: "Seek not the things that are too high for thee, and search not into things above thy ability: but the things that God hath commanded thee, think on them always . . . Meditate continually on His commandments: and He will give thee a heart, and the desire of wisdom shall be given to thee."

The Example
of Jesus

Jesus Himself stresses the importance of prayer and meditation. On the eve of His Passion He went into the Garden of Gethsemane, taking with Him Peter, James and John. He bade them watch, meditate and pray, while He went forward a little way. Later, when He returned, He found them sleeping.

"Could you not then watch one hour with me?" He asked. "Watch and pray that you may not enter into temptation. The spirit indeed is willing, but the flesh is weak."

How different might have been their conduct during the terrible ordeal that was about to begin, if they had allowed the power of God to enter their souls through absorbing meditation during that crucial hour!

Echoing the teaching of his Master, the Apostle Paul stressed the importance of meditating upon the truths and precepts of the Gospel. "For the rest, brethren," he said, "whatever things are true, whatever honorable, whatever just, whatever holy . . . *think* upon these things. And what you have learned and received and heard and seen in me, these things *practice*. And the God of peace will be with you." To his young disciple, Timothy, he wrote: "*Meditate* on these things, give thyself entirely to them that thy progress may be manifest to all." Yes, progress in holiness and peace of mind is conspicuous among the precious fruits of meditation.

In accordance with the injunctions of almighty God speaking through the Scriptures, meditation plays a central role in the spiritual life of the religious. In virtually every religious community the day begins with a meditation of at least a half hour. Periods of recollection and examination of conscience occur also at noon and in the evening. It is during these periods of meditation that the religious derives the strength and fervor to fulfill the exacting duties of his state in life.

John Wesley was accustomed to spend two hours each day in meditation and prayer. This meant that he usually had to arise very early to get in his devotions because of his strenuous work and journeying. One evening when he was preparing for an unusually busy schedule on the morrow, a friend advised him to sleep longer and curtail his spiritual exercises.

"It is precisely because I will be so heavily burdened tomorrow," replied Wesley, "that I will need those hours of meditation and prayer. I couldn't possibly get through that schedule with less time spent with God."

Without periods of strength-absorbing union with God, one's spiritual life will wane and ultimately collapse. Spiritual writers of all faiths are unanimous in warning that, no matter how engrossed in praiseworthy activities a person may be, he must not neglect prayer and meditation. Otherwise he becomes an empty channel, a dried-up spring, a broken vessel, a lamp whose flame has flickered out.

St. Bernard of Clairvaux, a humble Cistercian monk, once pointed this out in somewhat blunt language to Pope Eugenius III.

"Your Holiness," said Bernard, "I note that you have become engrossed in the many duties of your office, your many audiences and meetings. These are perhaps unescapable. But they must be curtailed if they infringe upon your periods of prayer and meditation.

"Business can be shortened or delegated to others, but prayer and meditation can neither be delegated nor abbreviated. These must take precedence over all other matters."

"Thank you, Father Bernard," replied the Pope. "We all need to be reminded of that great truth, especially those of us engrossed in administrative tasks. Our spiritual exercises come first, for they keep us in vital contact with the Source of all graces and blessings. I appreciate your timely admonition."

Meditation Necessary
for All

Meditation is necessary for all who seek to grow in spiritual stature, power and godliness. The gentle Christ was speaking to all when He said: "Love your enemies, do good to those who hate you, and pray for those who persecute and calumniate you . . . You therefore are to be perfect, even as your heavenly Father is perfect." It is impossible to fulfill any of these precepts, especially to achieve perfection, unless one comes frequently in meditation to the Infinite Source of all grace, holiness, power and perfection.

This is particularly true today when life is full of so many distractions, fears and anxieties which shatter our peace of mind and whirl our thoughts like a windmill. The frantic pace of modern life, newspapers with headlines screaming new threats of global war, blaring radios and television sets assailing our ears from morn till night and speeding cars menacing our limbs and lives on every highway are throwing us into tension, shock and panic. How are we to keep our perspective, our sense of direction and our supreme and ultimate destiny before us unless we withdraw at times from the tumult, the shouting and the frenzy of the world?

Applicable with redoubled force to the world today are the memorable words of Wordsworth:

> The world is too much with us; late and soon,
> Getting and spending, we lay waste our powers.
> Little we see in nature that is ours;
> We have given our hearts away, a sordid boon!

How to Meditate?

"How does a person meditate?" This is a question I've often been asked. There's no particular mystery about it; no one special technique is necessary. One meditates simply by directing his attention to God, to His commandments and counsels of perfection, to some great spiritual truth or to a consideration of his own spiritual state. It might be described as a *silent conversation* with God. The object is to increase our love of God and to strengthen our resolution to serve Him with greater loyalty and generosity.

In meditating it is better to speak naturally and spontaneously to God than to use borrowed phrases and stilted language. When you are having a heart-to-heart chat with a friend you don't read an address to him. You talk to him from the fullness of your heart: you say what is on your mind.

The television star, Red Skelton, and his family had a visit with Pope Pius XII a few days after the newspapers reported the pontiff had received some dental treatment. When presented to the Pope, Skelton's young son opened the conversation in a natural, down-to-earth way.

"How's your tooth, Pope?" he asked.

Chuckling heartily, the Pope reported the happy outcome of his visit to an office into which most youngsters enter with something short of ecstasy. In saying spontaneously what was uppermost in his mind, the child got the conversation off to a running start.

"What could be more boring to God or man," asks Gilbert Roxbury, O.P., in a treatise on meditation, "than to open up one's soul, invite God in, and read an address to Him in stilted language as though He were a visiting potentate? We too often treat God like a wealthy great-aunt on her yearly visitation of the family—someone to be treated with great deference, placated by a few muttered formulas of humility and respect, and waved goodbye to with sighs of relief that an ordeal is past."

An Example
of Meditating

Suppose, for example, we are meditating upon the memorable words of our Divine Savior: "What does it profit a man, if he gain the whole world, but suffer the loss of his own soul? Or what will a man give in exchange for his soul?"

We begin by placing ourselves in the presence of God and asking His help to focus our thoughts upon the subject of our meditation. We then visualize the most costly mansions, castles, estates and riches of kings and millionaires. We think of their retinue of servants, their automobiles, yachts and tables groaning with the choicest foods.

We then recall people who achieved great popularity and fame—generals, statesmen, artists, singers, writers and actors. Their names, pictures and deeds were featured in newspapers, magazines and television. We recall persons famous for their beauty and admired by millions.

Let us place all these worldly things—wealth, fame, popularity, beauty—on one side of the scales. On the other side we place the soul of a humble peasant or of a ragged beggar. We see how that soul outweighs all the treasures which the world values so highly. They are but dust and ashes compared with a soul destined by God for everlasting happiness.

Let us visualize on their deathbeds individuals who once possessed great earthly treasures. They can take none of these things with them. Into the world naked they came, out of it naked they go. The record of their deeds precedes them. What a tragic bargain they shall have made, if they have sold their souls for the transient things of earth. How infinitely wiser is the individual who has kept God's holy commandments, loved his God and his neighbor, walked with honor, humility and kindness among his fellows and has stored up treasures in heaven. "Eye has not seen," we remember St. Paul saying, "nor ear heard, nor has it entered into the heart of man, what things God has prepared for those who love him."

We then arouse in our hearts the love of God who endowed us with an immortal soul, thank Our Lord for redeeming us upon the cross, and resolve to keep ourselves always in God's friendship by living blameless lives. Here each can particularize his resolution by focusing his attention upon specific faults to avoid and definite virtues to practice. After formulating a definite resolution we end by begging God's grace to keep it and thus to grow each day in holiness.

Learn
by Doing

St. Ignatius Loyola, whose method of meditation is probably the one most widely followed among the religious, recommends the use of the imagination to construct the scene as vividly as possible. This helps to keep it in the focus of attention and to stir the appropriate emotions. The contemplation may be interrupted occasionally with brief and ardent prayers, called colloquies. After each such prayer it is advisable to pause and listen to what God is whispering in the ear of our conscience.

To retain the gist of our meditation and resolution it is helpful to twine both around some text of Scripture, *The Imitation of Christ*, or from the work of some other spiritual writer. The recollection of such a text will help to perpetuate and consolidate the fruits of the meditation. "Keep present before you all day," counsels St. Theresa of Avila, "what you meditate upon in the morning, and use much diligence on this point, for it will be of great benefit to you. Observe carefully the thoughts with which Our Lord may inspire you, and execute the desires which He shall give you in prayer."

One learns to do a thing by *doing* it. So one learns to meditate by *meditating*. As every golfer knows, what matters in putting is not the method, but getting the ball in the hole. So too in meditating, each individual can work out the method which best suits his temperament, conditions and needs. The important thing is to concentrate on some great spiritual truth until it becomes so woven into our minds, hearts, souls and wills that it is now an integral part of our whole being. It must be gotten into our spiritual bloodstream so that it permeates our character, personality and shapes our sense of values.

Opportunities for Meditation

How much time is required to make a meditation? It may range from half an hour to a few minutes. The individual who averages fifteen minutes a day will find it of immense benefit. Even briefer periods, which otherwise would be wasted, can be pressed into service with fruitful results. We all do some things almost automatically, so that while doing them we can meditate upon timely spiritual truths.

"I have been shaving so long," remarked a friend, "that I find

I can do it effectively while making a ten-minute meditation—
and a good one at that." What a splendid way to start the day!
"While washing the dishes," a housewife said, "I meditate on
the truths in the chapter of the Bible which I read each day. It
takes the drudgery out of that daily chore and pays rich spiritual
dividends."

"I used to fume and fuss," said a Chicago businessman, "when,
in driving home, I would be held up by a long line of traffic. I
would be a bundle of nerves by the time I arrived home, and
likely to blow my top at the least provocation. Now I've learned
to relax, make a brief meditation during those delays, and see
what fault I can correct or what virtue I should acquire in
greater measure.

"When I reach home, I radiate peace and joy. Those little
delays which formerly irritated me so much have now become
little havens for quiet meditation. They've made me a different
man."

Amidst the hustle and bustle of a city's crowded traffic he
learned the truth of the words penned in the second century by
Marcus Aurelius: "Nowhere does a man retire with more quiet
or freedom than into his own soul." It is, moreover, one of the
few temples where the doors are always open and admission is
always free.

Spiritual
Bomb Shelters

Do you get upset when you miss the bus, the elevator or the
green traffic light, when the waitress is slow in taking your order,
when the train or airplane is late, when your wife remains un-
duly long before the mirror, when a friend or client is late? If
so, you can transform these periods of strain and vexation into
restful sanctuaries for meditation on the timeless truths which
emancipate us from the tyranny of the transient and give us repose, refreshment, insight and wisdom. By withdrawing into

the inner temple of the soul we find ourselves in the audience-chamber of God.

When an oyster is irritated by a grain of sand that has gotten into its shell, the mollusk secretes a juice around it. It thereby transforms that irritation into the most beautiful thing an oyster can ever make—a shining pearl. Through the alchemy of meditation we can transform the irritating moments of waiting into the glorious pearls of spiritual growth, enrichment and achievement. We can store up for ourselves treasures in heaven.

Some families have built shelters in which they hope to find protection from the deadly fallout in case of nuclear war. Meditation provides similar shelters in which one can find a safeguard against the pressures, harassments and vexations which daily cast their lethal fallout upon his peace of mind. How desperately that shelter is needed is evident from the mounting number of patients crowding the offices of psychiatrists and filling our sanitariums and asylums.

It was not a divine but one of the world's greatest medical scientists, Dr. Alexis Carrel, who warned: "If it is to avoid a definite collapse into chaos and incoherence, civilized humanity must once again build cathedrals in the bleakly magnificent universe of the physicists and the astronomers." Fortunately it is within the power of each individual to build within the universe of his own soul a cathedral of majesty and beauty, in which he can commune with his Maker.

Clearer Perception
of Spiritual Truths

What are some of the chief benefits of meditation? First, *it helps one to perceive more clearly the purpose of life and one's ultimate destiny.* It enables him to answer the stupendous question which confronts everyone: "What does it profit a man if he gains the whole world and suffers the loss of his own soul?" It helps him also to put that answer into practice.

Ignatius Loyola was a soldier in the army of Ferdinand and Isabella in 1521, when the French laid siege to the citadel of Pampeluna, Spain. Severely wounded, he spent many weeks convalescing in a castle at Loyola. To help pass the weary hours he asked for some books of romance. None was available, but he was given the lives of Christ and of the saints. Each day he spent considerable time in meditating on what he had just read. Those hours of meditation marked the turning point in his life.

Instead of continuing in the service of an earthly monarch striving to win military victories, he decided to devote his life to the service of his God and seek to achieve spiritual victories whose fruits would be everlasting.

"Take, O Lord!" said Ignatius. "Take all—my liberty, my memory, my intellect, my will—all that I am and all that I have. You gave it all to me. I give it back again to You. All of me is Yours. Do with me whatever You will. Give me Your love and Your grace. That is enough for me."

Ignatius founded the Society of Jesus, which has given to the world so many saints and scholars. He wrote a little book, The Spiritual Exercises, which became a classic, and achieved such eminent holiness that he was declared a saint. Who can measure the extent of the far-reaching influence which St. Ignatius Loyola has exercised, and is still exercising, upon the lives of uncounted millions?

Uproots
Sinful Habits

Second, meditation helps one to conquer his vices, to uproot sinful habits and to rise to a high plane of virtue. For many years Augustine was enslaved in sensuality. These habits were so deeply rooted that they resisted his every effort to break them. Finally one day he was walking in a garden in Milan, when he heard a voice saying, "Take and read; take and read."

Startled, he opened the book of Epistles and read the first

verse which met his eyes: "Not in rioting and drunkenness, not in chambering and impurities, not in contention and envy, but put ye on the Lord Jesus Christ, and make not provision for the flesh in its concupiscences." Augustine read no more, nor was there any need for him to do so. Those words of the Apostle Paul penetrated like an electric current into the core of his being and singed the very marrow of his conscience.

They plunged Augustine into a meditation so profound and soul-stirring that it would seem to have some elements in common with Christ's agony in the Garden of Gethsemane. It changed the course of his life. A great sinner became a great saint. The fragrance of his exalted sanctity comes into the sex-saturated civilization of today like the sweet breath of spring.

Recalling the meditation that, with God's grace, led to his conversion, St. Augustine says: "Go not out! Turn *inwards* into yourself! Truth dwells within, in the inward man." Then he adds with an undertone of deep emotion: "I, Lord, went wandering like a strayed sheep, seeking Thee with anxious reasoning without, whilst Thou wast *within* me . . . I went around the streets of the City of this world, and I found Thee not, because in vain I sought without for Thee who wast within myself."

Sharpens Appreciation of Spiritual Values

Third, *meditation sharpens one's appreciation of spiritual values and opens one's eyes to realities hidden from the worldling.*

Louis IX, the holiest king ever to sit upon the throne of France, was walking one day with his crusaders along a road in Palestine. At his side was his close friend, Sire de Joinville. Sprawled in the dust was a leper.

"I would prefer to be a leper," remarked the king, "than to commit one mortal sin."

Joinville shuddered at the sight of the ulcerous leper.

"Not I, Your Majesty!" he blurted out. "I would rather have thirty mortal sins on my soul than leprosy in my body."

"Joinville," replied the king, "you are wrong. Nothing is worse, absolutely nothing, than to lose Christ's life within you by one mortal sin."

Commenting on this in his stimulating book of meditations, *God Speaks*, Charles Peguy depicts God as saying:

"Joinville loves me in the ordinary way. St. Louis loves me thirty times more than the ordinary."

What was the secret of the king's appreciation of spiritual values? It was the habit of making a daily meditation, which he had learned from his sainted mother, Queen Blanche. She had instilled in his mind the horror of mortal sin. When he was a child of twelve, she had a little talk with him, in which she sought to prepare him for the temptations which surround every throne.

"Louis, my son," she said, "I love you with all my heart. But much as I love you, I would rather see you a corpse at my feet than to have you stain your soul with one mortal sin."

Often the young son pondered on these words and the fruit of those many meditations became evident that day in Palestine.

Increases Awareness of God's Presence

Fourth, *meditation increases the consciousness of God's presence, awakens us to the realization that He is ever at our side, ever ready to help us if we but call upon Him.* When Christ was carrying His Cross to Calvary, an ancient tradition relates, a woman, known to us only as Veronica, was moved with compassion at the sight of the bleeding Savior. Rushing to Him, she extended a towel. Jesus pressed it to His face and left on it the impression of His holy countenance.

Upon the heart and mind of the person who daily meditates upon the life, sufferings and death of Our Divine Redeemer, there is likewise imprinted the face of Christ. In a special manner Jesus dwells in the soul of that person so that his heart loves what Christ loves and his mind thinks the thoughts of Christ.

To a humble lay brother, known in religion as Brother Lawrence, we owe the form of meditation or recollection, called "the practice of the presence of God." Living in a monastery in France in the seventeenth century, this humble religious tells us how God was just as real to him in the kitchen as in his cell. While cooking or washing the dishes, Brother Lawrence was able to commune with his God. Among all the brethren in the monastery, Brother Lawrence was noted for his spirit of recollection, his keen awareness of God's presence and his constant serenity.

All actions have their roots in thoughts. If our thoughts are upright, pure and Christlike, so will our actions be. The best way to improve our conduct is to guard our thoughts, barring from the soul's entrance whatever would defile it. "He that looketh after a woman to lust after her," warns Jesus, "hath already committed adultery in his heart." By squelching the thought, one nips temptation in the bud.

What a volume of educational psychology is contained in the brief utterance of the author of the Book of Proverbs: "As he thinketh in his heart, so is he." What better way of learning to think only upright, pure and holy thoughts than to remain through meditation in the presence of the Source of all holiness, God Himself?

Deepens Faith
Increases Courage

Fifth, *meditation deepens one's faith, inspires him to put his unfaltering trust in God, and thus gives him the courage to face any task, difficulty, danger or ordeal.* Probably no statesman in modern times was so devoted to the practice of daily meditation as the late Mahatma Gandhi of India. A genuinely holy man, he found in prayer and particularly in his long hours of meditation the strength and the courage to face, without an army or navy, a mighty empire and demand independence for his people.

Relying simply upon the moral strength of his cause, he inspired the strategy of passive or nonviolent resistance. Even when engaged in a week of conferences with rulers and statesmen, Gandhi would follow his schedule of prayer and meditation, sometimes absenting himself from the meetings for an entire day. More vital and important than his contact with statesmen, he realized, was his contact with God, the Infinite Source of strength and power. Thus was this frail man, weighing but ninety pounds, able to lift his people from serfdom to independence and freedom.

What has enabled the martyrs in all ages to face the executioner's sword, the gallows, the wild lions in the Roman arena, the firing line, the bonfire and the stake? It was a profound and unshakeable faith in God as the eternal Vindicator of right. But such a faith can be sustained only by prayer and meditation, the channels through which spiritual power, strength and courage come to all human beings.

Think of the Apostle Peter when he was led out from his prison in Rome to be crucified. Did he quail or quiver at the sight of the cross on which he was about to be nailed? On the contrary, he gazed fearlessly into the faces of the Roman soldiers.

"I am not worthy," he said, "to be crucified in the manner of my Savior Jesus Christ. Nail me to the cross with my head downward."

Safeguards
Against Self-Deception

Sixth, *meditation safeguards us against self-deception and enables us to see ourselves as God sees us.* When Michelangelo was laboring on one of his great sculptures or paintings, he wore on his cap a small torch so that no shadow of himself would fall upon his work. What care we all need to take to prevent the shadows of our pride, ambition, and self-seeking to fall upon our thinking and our actions, distorting them and deceiving us.

"Meditation," observes my old schoolmate, Bishop Fulton J. Sheen, "enables us to hold the mirror up to our souls, to perceive the fatal diseases of self-love in the blinding light of the Radiant Christ . . . As there is no egotist who is not also a self-deceiver, so no one accustomed to meditate has any illusions as to his own grandeur. The clearer we see our souls in relation to God, the less egocentric we become."

Meditation guards us against the tongues of flatterers and eradicates the itch for praise. It keeps before us the image of the gentle Christ, spat upon, buffeted, mocked, ridiculed, scourged, crowned with thorns and crucified. Though He was innocence personified and love incarnate, He was sent to Calvary, while the brigand and murderer Barabbas was preferred to him and released from prison. In the light of these truths, burnt into one's mind by daily meditation, how can he hanker for praise and find delight in the tongues of flatterers?

See Christ in Others

Seventh, *meditation enables us to see the Christ in others, to realize that we are all brothers, children of the same Heavenly Father, and thus fosters love for God and man.* "God is love," the beloved Disciple tells us. Hence the more we love, the better we know God and the more Godlike do we become. Love then is one of the highest forms of prayer and meditation. Samuel T. Coleridge expresses a great spiritual truth when he says:

> He prayeth well who loveth well
> Both man and bird and beast.
> He prayeth best who loveth best
> All things both great and small;
> For the dear God who loveth us,
> He made and loveth all.

Albert Schweitzer was a distinguished philosopher, linguist, Scriptural scholar, theologian and organist when he learned of the sad plight of the natives in the Lambarene district of French Equatorial Africa. There wasn't a *single* physician to minister to their many needs!

He resigned his chair at Strassburg University, studied medicine, specializing in tropical diseases, and set off for Africa. For many decades he has labored at his jungle hospital, easing the pains of the afflicted and saving many lives. His motivation? His daily meditation upon Christ and His commandment: "Thou shalt love thy neighbor as thyself."

"The essential element in Christianity," says Schweitzer, "as it was preached by Jesus . . . is this, that it is only through *love* that we can attain to communion with God." Through a life of sacrificial service for some of the most neglected of God's children, Albert Schweitzer has put that ideal into daily practice and has won the admiration of the whole world.

Frederick Ozanam ministering to the poor in Paris, Toyohiko Kagawa devoting his life to the underprivileged and downtrodden in Japan, Florence Nightingale caring for the wounded and dying in the Crimean War and Father Damien ministering to the lepers of Molokai are other examples of men and women who saw Christ in others. In loving and caring for them, they offered their homage and love to the God who is the Father of us all. A study of the lives of all these disclose that they drew their vision, inspiration, power and strength from their union with God through frequent prayer and meditation.

Have a Regular
Time and Place

Many other fruits of meditation might be cited. But the ones mentioned are sufficient to show the enormous fruitfulness of this practice. Meditation is the golden key that unlocks the treasure of Heaven, the mighty channel through which flows to us the vision, knowledge, insight, power, strength, courage, compassion, understanding and love of the Infinite Creator. Without meditation, man walks in a daze; life becomes a weary treadmill, an empty shadow, "full of sound and fury, signifying nothing."

Only through meditation do we become really *acquainted* with God. How immensely sad is the lot of those who go through life, like spiritual wallflowers, never entering the royal audience chamber and never really becoming acquainted with the God who made them, redeemed them and loves them with a love that surpasses that of any earthly father.

While one may meditate anywhere and at any time, and thus fill in periods of waiting, of traveling and of doing things automatically, it is, of course, far better to have a suitable place and a set time. Perhaps families which have the custom of reading a chapter of the Bible and saying a few prayers after the evening meal, would find that an ideal time for a brief meditation which might well include a review of the day and an examination of conscience.

Whatever time and place are chosen, however, it is advisable to keep that appointment with unfailing regularity. This will enable the law of habit formation to operate most effectively. Soon the practice will then be an integral part of your life, a second nature. At the beginning you may experience a bit of difficulty, as is true of all habits, but perseverance will take you successfully over all hurdles and crystallize what will be one of the most wholesome, fruitful and blessed habits of your life. Before long you will experience the peace and happiness aptly described by Paul Hamilton Hayne:

> Happy the heart that keeps its twilight hour
> And, in the depths of heavenly peace reclined,
> Loves to commune with thoughts of tender power,
> Thoughts that ascend, like angels beautiful,
> A shining Jacob's-ladder of the mind.

Yes, that's what meditation is—a ladder leading us to God and Heaven.

POINTS TO REMEMBER

1. The practice of meditation sends the drill point down below the layers of ordinary consciousness and thus draws upon hidden reserves of energy and insight.

2. Meditation is the application of the intellect, imagination, memory and will to the consideration of some spiritual principle, truth or ideal in order to stimulate the appropriate spiritual emotions and thus resolve on some act or course of conduct regarded as God's will or as a means of achieving union with Him.

3. Jesus stresses the importance of meditation and practiced it Himself, notably in the Garden of Gethsemane.

4. In meditating it is better to speak naturally and spontaneously to God than to use borrowed phrases and stilted language. Talk to Him out of the fullness of your heart and say what is on your mind.

5. As one learns to do a thing by *doing* it, so one learns to meditate by *meditating*. Perfection is achieved only through constant practice.

6. You can transform periods of waiting and vexation into restful sanctuaries for meditation on timeless truths which will give you repose, refreshment, insight and wisdom.

7. Meditation helps one to preserve more clearly the purpose of life and one's ultimate destiny.

8. Through meditation one secures the strength to uproot sinful habits and rise to a high plane of virtue.

9. Meditation sharpens one's appreciation of spiritual values and opens one's eyes to realities hidden from the worldling.

10. Meditation increases the consciousness of God's presence and awakens us to the realization that He is ever ready to help us, if we but call upon Him.

11. Meditation deepens faith and gives one the courage to face any task, danger or ordeal.

12. Through meditation we are safeguarded against self-deception and are enabled to see ourselves as God sees us.

13. Meditation enables us to see the Christ in others and to realize that we are all brothers.

14. It is advisable to have a regular time and place for meditating and to keep that appointment with unfailing regularity.

9.

LOVING GOD:

OUR WAY TO HEAVEN

"We know that for those who love God all things work together unto good."—*St. Paul, Apostle to the Gentiles*

"God is love, and he who abides in love abides in God, and God in him."—*St. John, the Beloved Disciple*

One of the most significant scenes in the life of Christ was enacted in Jerusalem when the Pharisees gathered around Jesus, and one of them, a doctor of the Law, confronted Him with a question often debated among them.

"Master," he asked, "which is the great commandment in the Law?"

The question looks innocent enough, but is really loaded. The rabbinical commentators had teased out of the Mosaic law no less than 613 ceremonial and moral precepts. Some of these were considered *light* and others *grave*, and bitter controversies raged as to which was the most important.

Slashing like a scythe through the massive weeds, Jesus cut through the tangled mass of casuistic controversy with an answer as unqualified as it was direct and unequivocal.

"Thou shalt love the Lord thy God," He replied, "with thy whole heart and with thy whole soul and with all thy mind."

Then He added, "This is the greatest and the first commandment. And the second is like it, 'Thou shalt love thy neighbor as thyself.' On these two commandments depend the whole Law and the Prophets."

What is of special significance in the Savior's answer is that He immediately joins to the duty of loving God the obligation to love one's neighbor. The fact that He disclosed the second commandment without being asked shows His unwillingness to separate the two. Love of God and love of neighbor are parent and child: love of neighbor is but an overflow of the love of God.

This is evidenced in the various religious orders which were founded to ransom Christian captives from slavery. In 1180 the order of Montjore was founded in Spain to rescue Christian crusaders who had fallen into the hands of Moslems; in the thirteenth century St. Peter Nolasco established the Order of Our Lady of Mercy, commonly called Merdecarians, for a similar purpose. Toward the end of the twelfth century the Trinitarians, founded for the liberation of Christian captives by St. John of Matha, a doctor of the University of Paris, had 250 houses throughout Christendom.

The members of these communities not only raised funds for the ransoming of captives but, when funds were not available, offered themselves in exchange for the prisoners. The liberators were motivated solely by the love of God, and were not even acquainted with the captives for whose freedom they spent the rest of their lives in slavery. What striking instances of the love of God flowing over into the love of neighbor!

The Fulfillment
of the Law

As Jesus was the first to join the two commandments of love, so was He also the first to give the widest meaning to the word "neighbor." The purpose of "the whole Law and the Prophets" is to secure the fulfillment of this twofold commandment: love God and your fellow man. What a beautiful and penetrating exposition of the primacy of love in human life! In the light of this memorable scene, observes the noted Scriptural scholar M. J. Lagrange, "we now understand what this divine system was that

Jesus had come, not to destroy, but to bring to perfection: it was essentially the law of love." The love of God above all things was thus made the cornerstone of mystical and ascetical theology and the love of neighbor was made the basis of Christian ethics.

What can be of greater importance for progress in the moral and spiritual life than the proper understanding of this twofold law and the methods of its fulfillment? In its observance, the Savior tells us, we are *fulfilling all the commandments*. If we love God, we will keep His commandments: if we love our neighbor, we will respect his rights. The first three commandments of the decalogue are concerned with our duties to God and the following seven with our obligations to our neighbor. All of them are designed to help us fulfill the twofold commandment to love God and our fellow man.

The Meaning
of Love

In this chapter we shall consider the first of these: the duty to love God with our whole hearts, souls and minds. Here we are speaking of love not as a mere instinct, an expression of the sensual appetite or an emotional reaction to stimuli of the senses, but as one of the three great virtues, of which the other two are faith and hope. In this sense love is a virtue inclining the will to cherish God for His own sake above all things, and man for the sake of God. It is the virtue which joins us to God in the bonds of the highest friendship so that our will is intimately united with His.

"God is love," says St. John, "and he who abides in love abides in God, and God in him." This union, begun in this life, finds its completion through the Beatific Vision in heaven. This is the chief joy of heaven and its very essence. Since God has destined our hearts for union with Him, they shall be as restless as the sea until they rest in Him. Deep in our souls is a God-ache which can be appeased only by God.

Only the person whose heart is filled with the love of God is truly rich. That love comforts him in adversity, enables him to succor the needy and endows him with inexhaustible wealth. Such a one is aptly described by the Apostle Paul, "as sorrowful yet always rejoicing, as poor yet enriching many, as having nothing yet possessing all things."

We are indebted not to any movement of the sensible appetite but to God for this divine gift. "The charity of Christ," St. Paul tells us, "is poured forth in our hearts by the Holy Spirit who has been given to us." It is infused along with sanctifying grace to which it is closely related. Its seat is not in the *emotions* but in the rational *will*, thus enabling us to direct it to a person regardless of the reactions of the senses—i.e., whether he appeals to us as attractive or not.

Great as are faith and hope, love towers above them. Faith is concerned with things not seen, hope with things not yet in our possession, and love with the person already possessed. Speaking of these three virtues, St. Paul says, "the greatest of these is charity." In his letter to the Colossians the Apostle calls charity "the bond of perfection."

In similar vein Cardinal Wiseman remarks: "The other two virtues, faith and hope, dwell in the porch of God's house; they are as the lamp and the perfume of the outer sanctuary." Love, however, takes us into the inner sanctuary, where dwells the Holy of Holies, God Himself. The essence of love is union: in the union of our will with God's will we find our peace and happiness.

Thus a lover yearns to be with his beloved: in her presence he finds joy and ecstasy. Even when bodily presence is denied, love transcends space and time and produces a spiritual nearness. So too the love of God brings Him into the sanctuary of the human soul and fills that soul with radiance, peace and joy. In the Beatific Vision one experiences a joy, of which St. Paul says: "Eye has not seen nor ear heard nor has it entered into the heart of man, what things God has prepared for those who love him."

In short, where love is, there is God; where God is, there is heaven; where God is not, there is hell.

Jesus Visits
the Cobbler

In his story, *Where Love Is, God Is*, Tolstoy tells of an old cobbler Martin, who lived alone, read the Gospels, and endeavored to please God. Reading of the poor welcome accorded Jesus in the house of the rich Pharisee, Martin prayed that the Lord would visit him. One night in his sleep he heard a voice.

"Martin, Martin," said the Voice, "look out of the window tomorrow, for I shall come."

Next day Martin waited for his visitor, but no one came. But outside he saw a poor old man sweeping snow. Martin called him in and gave him some hot tea, while he kept his lookout at the window.

"Are you expecting someone?" asked the old man. Martin told him about the Voice, and spoke of our Lord till the elderly man wept.

Sometime later Martin saw a shivering mother with her crying baby. He brought them in, gave them some warm soup, and an old cloak to shield both from the cold. He told the woman about the Voice and she cried with joy.

"Who knows?" she said. "All things are possible. Farewell, and thank you."

It was dusk now, and still the Savior hadn't come. Looking out the window, Martin saw an apple-woman scolding a boy who had stolen an apple. Going outside, Martin made peace, paid for the apple, persuaded the woman to forgive, and made the boy so ashamed that he went off with the woman, carrying the basket for her.

That night Martin opened his Bible again.

"Martin, Martin," said the Voice, "don't you know me?"

"Who is it?" asked Martin.

"It is I," answered the Voice, and there for a moment was the old snow-sweeper.

"It is I," and there stood the mother with the baby.

"It is I," and there smiled the apple-woman and the boy. Then they all vanished.

Then Martin realized that Christ had visited him that day after all, and his heart felt strangely warm.

Thus does Tolstoy bring out the important truth that where love is, God is; and our love of God flows over to our neighbors. In short, it's impossible really to love God and hate His children.

Three Elements in Love

In love we can usually discern three elements: (1) emotion— a feeling of affection for a person and a desire for his companion- ship; (2) volition—a well-wishing or solicitude for his welfare; (3) action—an effort to express that concern, to assist him in his needs and to make him happy, even though it entails sacrifice. In our love of God, volition manifests itself in our eager solicitude for His honor and glory, while action consists in fulfilling His commandments. The best and most reliable test of our love is that given by our Lord Himself: "If you love me, keep my com- mandments."

Unlike, for example, the lustful love of Antony for Cleopatra, our love of God is a rational, disciplined and holy love. The amount of emotion varies with the temperament of the indi- vidual, but the important elements of volition and action, ema- nating from the will, are always present.

In some saints the emotional element manifested itself in a deep stirring of the heart and even in tears, as in the repentant tears of the Apostle Peter and of Mary Magdalen. The absence of any such external manifestation need not, however, disturb us, as God reads our hearts and minds and finds in our cheerful and devoted obedience to His will the true, authentic and un- failing expression of our love.

Love God
for His Own Sake

The story is told of a mystic who had a vision in which he saw
an angel carrying a torch in one hand and a vessel of water in the
other. He was mystified.

"Why," he asked, "are you carrying such things?"

"I am carrying the torch," replied the angel, "to set fire to
heaven and the water to extinguish the fire of hell so that God
would be loved *solely* for Himself."

Whether legendary or true, the story illustrates an important
truth. God is a being of such infinite perfection that He deserves
to be loved for His own self. Our love is perfect when we love
God not because of fear of punishment or hope of reward but
because He is infinite beauty, truth, goodness, mercy and love,
and hence is infinitely worthy of our love.

It is not difficult to achieve such love. Think of all the blessings
and favors which God has showered upon you: life, health of
body, sanity of mind, the beauty of nature and its immeasurable
bounty. Consider the love which prompted Him to bring you
through His divine Providence into existence.

Think of the love with which He pursues you every moment
of the day and night. Reflect upon the love which prompted
God to come in the form of your divine Savior, the Word Incarnate, to redeem you from the effects of your own sins. Keep
ever in mind the reward promised to those who love God. "Eye
has not seen nor ear heard," says St. Paul, "nor has it entered into
the heart of man, what things God has prepared for those who
love him."

God's Love
Is Greater

In a remote mountain district in Japan there is a village called
"The Place to Leave Your Mother." In the ancient feudal days
those who had reached seventy were brought there to die. While

a man was escorting his elderly mother up the mountain to leave her there, the villagers relate, he noticed she was constantly breaking twigs as she went along.

"Mother," he asked, "why are you breaking all those twigs?"

"Because, my son," she replied, "I don't want you to lose your way in returning home."

Deeply touched, the son burst into tears. Taking his mother in his arms, he carried her home. His action brought an end to that custom.

How vastly greater is God's love for us! Our Savior permitted Himself to be mocked, buffeted, spat upon, scourged and crucified for love of us. "Greater love than this," says Jesus, "no man hath, that one lay down his life for his friends." While the executioners are casting lots for His one possession, His seamless garment, and the others are mocking and jeering Him, Jesus lifts His eyes to the heavens and says, "Father, forgive them for they know not what they do."

How much does God love us? Jesus Himself supplies the answer: "As the Father has loved me, I also have loved you." As the love between the Father and Son is an infinite love, it is evident that God's love for us is likewise infinite. This love is not only for humanity as a whole but also for each one of us. "God looks on me individually," says Cardinal Newman. "He calls me by my name."

We think of the love of a mother for her child as perhaps the most intense of human love. Yet that love pales into insignificance in comparison with God's love for us. Speaking through the prophet Isaiah, God says: "Can a mother forget her child, so as not to have pity on the son of her womb? And if she should forget, yet will I not forget thee."

*Perfect Love
and Contrition*

Such considerations will, with God's grace, kindle in our hearts a deep and perfect love of God because of His own infinite perfections and particularly because of His infinite love for each of

us. The eliciting of such love is the most meritorious act one
can perform. In it there is implicit perfect contrition or sorrow
for sin, and hence it washes away the guilt of sin and restores the
soul to the immediate friendship and love of God.

"If any one love me," says Jesus, "he will keep my word, and
my Father will love him, and we will come to him, and will make
our abode with him." Since God is infinite holiness and perfection, no sin can exist in that soul in which He is present. Echoing the teaching of the divine Master, the Beloved Disciple St.
John says: "We have come to know, and have believed, the love
that God has in our behalf. *God is love, and he who abides in
love abides in God, and God in Him.*"

Make Frequent
Acts of Love

The making of this fervent act of perfect love and contrition
each day will deepen and intensify your union with God. It will
perpetuate His presence in your soul. It will fill your heart with
the love of God and man and wash out every trace of hatred and
malice. It will enable you to radiate God's presence to others and
make you a bearer of Christ, a Christopher, in the deepest sense
of that word. It will enable you not only to bear hardship and adversity but to do so with gladness and joy.

The constant presence of God in one's heart is the surest sign
of advancement in the spiritual life. Indeed it is an unfailing
harbinger of one's eternal union with God in heaven. "To love
God above all things," says the French spiritual writer, Le Camus,
"is to insure the sanctity of our whole life." It is both the principle and the goal of moral perfection.

Before Joyce Kilmer, the English poet, was killed on the battlefield of France in World War I, he wrote to a priest friend, asking prayers for his intention. If you were asked to guess what that
intention was, you would probably say: "He asked that his life
would be spared and that he would soon get back to his wife and
children."

But here's what he actually wrote: "Pray for me, my dear Father, that I may love God more and that I may be unceasingly conscious of Him. That is the intention for which I pray most ardently and for which I beg your prayers." Here was the love of God above all things, the love which washes out fear and floods the soul with the radiance of God.

Poets Depict
God's Love

Throughout the ages poets have vied with theologians and the writers of Holy Scripture in seeking to express the mighty truth that God is love and the unfailing source of our deepest happiness. This theme runs like a refrain particularly through the epistles of the Beloved Disciple. Theologians are agreed that an everlasting, all-embracing, benevolent and sacrificial love is of the very essence of God. Poets have used simpler language to express the same thought. Thus Robert Service says:

> Yes, if you're a tramp in tatters,
>   While the blue sky bends above
> You've got nearly all that matters—
>   You've got God and God is love.

Long before Service an unknown poet in ancient Chaldee sang the same refrain, rendered into English by Rabbi Mayir ben Isaac:

> Could we with ink the ocean fill,
>   And were the heavens of parchment made,
> Were every stalk on earth a quill,
>   And every man a scribe by trade,
> To write the love of God above
>   Would drain the ocean dry,
> Nor could the scroll contain the whole,
>   Though stretch'd from sky to sky.

Memorable too are the words of John Greenleaf Whittier, singing of God's boundless love:

> I know not where His islands left
> Their fronded palms in air
> I only know I cannot drift
> Beyond His love and care.

Love God
Above All Things

What is of great importance to remember is that God is our Creator, Redeemer and Sanctifier, our first Beginning and last End, the Alpha and Omega of our whole being. As such He asks to be loved with our whole heart, mind and soul and above all created things. Throughout the ages men, women and even children have obeyed this divine command even at the cost of life itself. This is illustrated in an incident that occurred during Diocletian's persecution of the early Christians. A little group of Christians was attending Mass in one of the catacombs. Suddenly a band of the emperor's secret police broke in upon them. Among the number seized were a father and his young son. Taken before the Roman tribune, the father was ordered to renounce his Christian faith or pay the penalty with his life.

"Not for you or all the riches of imperial Rome," he replied, "will I deny my Savior, Jesus Christ."

Whereupon he was beheaded. Seeing the fate meted out to his father, the little boy quailed.

"Be wiser than your father," admonished the tribune. "Deny this crucified Christ. Place a few grains of incense upon the fires burning before the gods of Rome and I will not only spare your life but give you anything you ask."

Relieved, the boy started toward the idols. He had taken about a dozen steps when suddenly he paused, as though spellbound. Echoing in his ear were the words of his martyred father. Quickly he walked over to the place where the sand was still crimson with his father's blood. Stooping, he clenched the moist sand in his hands.

"A few moments ago," he said, "I was weak and about to yield. But now I am strong with the blood of my father, and I too will die rather than deny my God."

Quickly the executioner did his job, and the blood of the son mingled with the blood of his father.

Like thousands of other Christian martyrs, they loved God with their whole hearts, souls and minds and above all things, even life itself. Nothing short of that must be our love for God.

The Greatest Incentive

St. Thomas Aquinas distinguishes three principal stages of growth in the love of God. The first is freedom from mortal sin by strenuous resistance to temptation. The second is the avoidance of deliberate venial sin by the diligent practice of virtue. The third stage is union with God through the frequent recurrence of acts of love. To these, ascetic writers such as St. Theresa and St. Francis de Sales add many more stages or degrees, thus anticipating even in this world the "many mansions in the Father's house."

The greatest incentive toward living a good life is the love of God. It makes the keeping of the commandments a pleasure and a joy. When motivated by love, all our actions, even those which are indifferent in themselves, are made meritorious, while the merit of good actions is further enhanced. God values the *love* of the giver more than the gift.

One day when Jesus was sitting in the Temple, He watched the people putting their gifts into the treasury. With much ostentation the rich were putting in large gifts. Then a poor widow came along and put in her two mites. The Savior turned to His disciples.

"Truly I say to you," He remarked, "this poor widow has put in more than all these. For all these out of their abundance have put in as gifts to God; but she out of her want has put in all that she had to live on."

The widow made the greater sacrifice because she *loved* more. "The greater is our love of God," says St. Francis de Sales, "the more meritorious are our actions. God does not regard the greatness of the work so much as the love wherewith it is performed." St. Paul admonishes that all gifts, no matter how great, and all good works and austerities are worthless without charity.

Lamps
Without Oil

Good works without the love of God are like lamps without oil. Just as some foods are tasteless and insipid without a condiment, so our works, devoid of charity, are without savor before God. He who loves God most will receive the greatest reward. This is illustrated in the incident of the sinful woman who, though uninvited, entered the home of Simon the Pharisee to wash and anoint the feet of Jesus. Simon was scandalized that the Savior permitted the woman to come near Him. Our Lord seized the occasion to teach the Pharisees a much needed lesson.

"Wherefore I say to thee," said Jesus, "her sins, many as they are, shall be forgiven her, because she has *loved* much." Then turning to the repentant woman, Jesus said, "Thy sins are forgiven thee."

Love Inspires
Sacrifice

Love of God, ardent and intense, is the most important factor in the two main phases of our spiritual life: justification and the acquisition of merit. It is the ladder on which we can climb from earth to the outstretched arms of our heavenly Father. It is the inspiration for the noblest deeds of self-sacrifice and self-surrender.

George Adams Smith tells of meeting a young priest while riding on a train in France. He learned that the young man had volunteered for missionary service in the Belgian Congo.

"I am on my way to Rouen," he said, "to see my mother for the last time."

"Why for the last time?" asked Smith.

"Because," replied the priest, "the average lifetime of a missionary in the Congo is two and a half years."

"But why are you going?" persisted Smith. "Why go to the Belgian Congo?"

The young priest replied, quoting the memorable words of St. Paul:

"The life that I now live in the flesh, I live in the faith of the Son of God, who *loved me and gave himself up for me.*"

One senses in the quiet words of the young priest the fire of a great love which inspired him with a willingness to sacrifice his life in the far-off mission fields for the Savior who had died for him and for all of us on Calvary's Cross. That death was the supreme expression of unselfish and sacrificial love which finds immemorial echo in the hearts of men. As deep calls unto deep, so love calls forth its timeless and unfailing response.

Commenting upon this incident, Joseph Fort Newton remarks: "That young priest had given his utmost to the highest in utter self-surrender, holding nothing back, going all the way, calmly, finally. Here lies the secret of such peace and happiness as we may know upon the earth. To the degree in which we give our whole selves wholly to what is the highest we know, to just that degree we find what life is and was meant to be."

God's Love
for the Repentant Sinner

Mortal sin alone can extinguish the love of God in our hearts. Such a sin involves serious or grievous matter, and is committed after sufficient reflection and with the full consent of the will. It is called "mortal" because it deprives the soul of the sanctifying grace which is its life. Hence it is to be avoided as the greatest evil which can befall one. Ours should be the determined resolution, so well expressed by St. Paul: "Neither death nor life, nor angels, nor principalities, nor powers, nor things present, nor things to come, nor any other creature, shall be able to separate us from the love of God."

If, however, one should unfortunately fall into sin, God does not turn His back on him forever. He stands ready to pardon if the sinner repents, and He even stretches out His hand to help him arise. This is brought out vividly and dramatically in the Parable of the Prodigal Son, one of the most touching stories of a father's mercy and forgiveness in all literature. How moving is the scene where the father, standing on a hill, sees in the distance his wayward son returning. He runs to him and embraces him.

"Father," cries the son, "I have sinned against heaven and before thee. I am no longer worthy to be called thy son."

"Fetch quickly," the father tells the servants, "the best robe and put it on him, and give him a ring for his finger and sandals for his feet; and bring out the fattened calf and kill it, and let us eat and make merry; because this my son was dead, and has come to life again; he was lost, and is found."

That scene, depicted by Jesus, discloses more clearly and vividly than many volumes of learned theologians the mercy, compassion and love of God, ever ready to pardon the penitent. Describing that compassionate love, Charles Keble says:

> The sun and every vassal star,
> All space, beyond the soar of angel wings,
> Wait on His word: and yet he stays His car
> For every sigh a contrite suppliant brings.

Keep Love
Burning Always

How easy and natural it is to say: "My God, Thou didst die for love of me on Calvary's Cross. I love Thee with my whole heart, soul and mind because Thou art infinitely worthy of my love. I shall be willing to die rather than to offend Thee by any grievous sin." The person who says that and means it makes an act of perfect contrition and love, most fruitful for his own spiritual life and most pleasing to God. It should be made often, even daily.

After Abraham Lincoln's death his body was taken back to his home in Illinois. On its journey the body lay in state in Cleveland. Long lines of people filed by the casket to pay their last respects to the great emancipator. Among the number were an elderly Negro woman and her little grandson. Reaching the casket, she paused and gazed with tear-dimmed eyes at the gaunt face. Then she lifted the little boy so he too could see.

"Take a long, long look, sonny," she said. "That man died for you."

When Christians see a cross they will do well to take a long and reverent look, for it is the symbol of God's undying love for man.

To keep the love of God burning in our hearts we should, of course, keep His commandments. "Love therefore," says St. Paul, "is the *fulfillment* of the law." That is the true test of the sincerity of our love. In addition, we should utter frequent short acts of love. Say often: "My God and my all, I love Thee." "O God, I love Thee with my whole heart and soul!" "O Lord, I offer Thee all my thoughts, words and deeds." "Grant, dear Jesus, that I may love Thee more and more!" "Come, Holy Spirit, fill my heart with the fire of Thy love!" "My God, I love Thee above all things. Keep me always in Thy love!"

These brief ejaculations, which can be made often throughout the day, will help to keep the love of God burning always in your heart. They will add depth and serenity to your life. They will protect you from the enervating and paganizing influence of a world that is too much with you. Like the Rock of Gibraltar, they will shield you against temptation and keep you always in the friendship and love of God. That is all that matters.

POINTS TO REMEMBER

1. The first and greatest commandment is to love God with your whole heart, soul and mind.

2. Love is a divinely infused habit inclining the will to cherish God for His own sake above all things, and man for the sake of God.

3. There are three elements in love: emotion, volition and action.

4. An act of perfect love and contrition is most pleasing to God and the most meritorious act one can perform.

5. The three principal stages of growth in the love of God are freedom from mortal sin, the avoidance of deliberate venial sin and union with Him through frequent acts of love.

6. The love of God makes the keeping of the commandments a pleasure and a joy.

7. Mortal sin alone can extinguish the love of God in our hearts.

8. Say often during the day: "O God, I love Thee with my whole heart and soul!"

10.

THE ACHIEVEMENT
OF SELF-CONTROL

"Self-reverence, self-knowledge, self-control
These three alone lead life to sovereign power."
—*Alfred Tennyson*

"A patient man is better than a warrior, and he
who rules his temper, than he who takes a city."
—*Proverbs 16:32*

For many years track fans wondered if any human would ever run the mile in less than four minutes. Then in 1954 there was a sensational breakthrough, with Roger Bannister of London leading the way. Herb Elliott of Australia then won world fame by accomplishing this feat in seventeen brilliant races. The secret? "Thrust against pain," replied his coach, "and be contemptuous of it."

Luxury-loving Americans aren't very conspicuous among the sub-four-minute milers, for they must be gluttons for pain and punishment. The most promising among them, little Jim Beatty, had to find a Hungarian coach, Mihaly Igloi, to show him how to do the trick.

"When I first reported to Mihaly," related Tiny Jim, "he looked at me and said, 'Ho, the fat boy!' I weighed 136 then. I weigh 127 now. I had to sacrifice. It was tough at times."

Mihaly promptly put him on a Spartan schedule: running *four hours a day every day*, except on the days he raced. Then he cut down to a stint of one-and-a-half hours. It paid off in February 1962 when Jim became the first man to break the four-minute indoors. Watching the little man forge ahead of the nation's best milers at the A.A.U. meet in New York, Ireland's great runner, Ron Delany, remarked philosophically: "Run. Run. Run. Run until you're insensible. It's a hard way to approach something that's supposed to be fun."

Yes, Ron is right. Back of the feat of every man who has run the grueling sub-four-minute mile is the story of endless hours of Spartan training and of punishing discipline. With every agonized nerve in his body screaming for rest, the runner drives himself on. Like a jockey whipping his steed to close the gap as he nears the tape, the miler lashes his body to eke out its last ounce of energy and gain the coveted prize. He is discipline incarnate: the triumph of the spirit over the flesh.

Test of Christ's Discipleship

Discipline, mortification and self-denial are necessary for the winning of races in the athletic arena; they are also necessary for the winning of the spiritual race in which we are all engaged. "Do you not know," says the Apostle Paul, "that those who run in a race, all indeed run, but one receives the prize? So run as to obtain it. And everyone in a contest abstains from all things—and they indeed to receive a perishable crown, but we an imperishable. I, therefore, so run as not without a purpose; I so fight as not beating the air; but I chastise my body and bring it into subjection, lest perhaps after preaching to others I myself should be rejected."

Here St. Paul brings out the important truth that the mastery of the body entails abstinence from the pleasures and indulgences which pamper the flesh and render it unruly. These privations must be supplemented by positive measures which strengthen and discipline it and make it the obedient servant of the spirit. Implicit here is his favorite theme: the struggle between the spirit and the flesh for the mastery of the human soul. To win this battle, discipline and self-denial are indispensable.

The Apostle is but echoing the teaching of his Master. "If anyone wishes to come after me," says Jesus, "let him deny himself and take up his cross daily and follow me. For he who would save his life will lose it; but he who loses his life for my sake will save it." Vivid in the minds of His listeners was the memory of the 2,000 Jews who only twenty years before had been crucified under the legate Varus for rebellion. Crucifixion was a penalty which had become so common in Judea that, as the Savior spoke, the figure of the cross loomed up ominiously before them.

Here then is one of the tests of Christ's discipleship: a willingness to deny oneself, carry one's cross daily and follow the Master. This is the stern test which separates the sheep from the goats. The consciousness that Jesus loves us to such a degree as to die for us upon Calvary's Cross has kindled our love not only for Him but also for the cross: the symbol of His sacrificial love for us.

The Cross:
Emblem of Divine Love

Once a symbol of shame and ignominy, the cross has been transformed into an emblem of love and devotion because Jesus died upon it. Many Christians show their love for their crucified Savior and their veneration for the cross by tracing the sign or figure of the cross upon themselves, while they say: "In the name of the Father and of the Son and of the Holy Ghost." In this brief but pregnant utterance and accompanying sign these Christians express their belief in the Blessed Trinity—one God in three divine Persons—and in their redemption through Christ's death on the cross.

The early Christians were accustomed to begin many of their actions by making upon themselves the sign of the cross. "At the beginning," says Tertulian, "and during the performance of all that we do, when we go in and out of the house, when we dress ourselves, when we lie down to rest, in fact in everything, we mark ourselves on the forehead with the sign of the cross." Fastened on a pole in the desert, the brazen serpent was an image of the cross of Christ and shielded all who gazed upon it from being bitten by the fiery serpents. Similarly the sign of the cross reminds us of the cross of Christ and protects us from the snares of the devil.

In 312 Constantine the Great was leading his army into battle when there appeared in the sky a cross on which were the words, "In this sign thou shalt conquer." Inspired thereby, he gained a decisive victory against the vastly larger army of Maxentius and became the first Christian Emperior of Rome. "Even to remember the cross of Christ," says St. Augustine, "puts the evil foe to flight and gives us strength to resist temptations."

Sacrifice, mortification and the daily carrying of the cross after the manner of our Lord constitute then the divinely revealed formula for our advance in holiness and the attainment of our salvation. The daily discipline of our bodies through self-denial is the sacrifice most pleasing to God. This is the refrain that runs through the teachings of Christ and the Apostles. "I exhort you therefore, brethren," says St. Paul, "by the mercy of God, to present your bodies as a sacrifice, living, holy, pleasing to God— your spiritual service."

Save for the inspired writers of Holy Scripture, probably no other writer has expressed so beautifully and so authentically the teaching of our divine Redeemer on this subject as has Thomas à Kempis in The Imitation of Christ. In the cross, he tells us, is salvation, life, protection from enemies, infusion of heavenly sweetness, strength of mind, joy of spirit, height of virtue and perfection of sanctity. "There is no other way to life," he says, "and to true interior peace, but the way of the holy cross and of daily mortification. Go where thou wilt, seek what thou wilt, thou shalt not find a higher way above, nor a safer way below, than the way of the holy cross."

Twofold Purpose
of Self-Denial

Self-denial, mortification and sacrifice serve a twofold purpose. First, they constitute penance and atonement for sin; they help to balance the scales of the moral universe thrown into disequilibrium by violations of God's holy commandments. They offer satisfaction for offenses committed. Since all have sinned, all are obliged to make reparation. "Unless you shall do penance," Jesus warns us, "you shall all likewise perish."

Second, mortification and self-denial serve to *discipline the will* so that it will be more capable of resisting temptation. The line of reasoning is clear and simple. By denying ourselves innocent pleasures we strengthen the will so that it shall be able to resist sinful ones. We thus make it more responsive to the voice of conscience.

Alex Morrison, one of my students at Illinois University, won the welterweight wrestling championship at the Olympics. Upon his return to the campus he received a great ovation from the students.

"Alex," I remarked, "I suppose that championship cost you a lot of practice."

"Yes," he said. "I spent more than an hour every day for the *last seven years* going through exercises to strengthen every muscle in my body. It was a long haul, but it finally paid off."

The Conquest
of Self

The supreme objective in the spiritual life is the achievement of eminent holiness. But this is attained, with the grace of God, chiefly through self-control. This is the ideal that every person has to keep ever before his mind. *The mastery of self is the greatest victory which anyone can achieve.* If he fails here, his failure is complete and irreparable. Victory over others is a miserable substitute. Man has to live with his own conscience, and the thunder of its scorn and condemnation drowns out the applause of all the world.

This truth has been perceived by the great minds of all ages. "I count him braver," says Aristotle, "who overcomes his desires than him who conquers his enemies; for the hardest victory is the victory over self." In his great treatise on *Laws*, Plato writes: "There is a victory and defeat—the first and best of victories, the lowest and worst of defeats—which each man gains or sustains at the hands not of another, but of himself." With pithy eloquence Seneca expresses the same truth: "To master oneself is the greatest mastery."

Extolling the bravery of those who conquer themselves, Shakespeare says:

> Brave conquerors—for so you are,
> That war against your own affections
> And the huge army of the world's desires.

A Being, infinitely wiser than all these, Almighty God Himself, confirms this truth. Speaking through the author of the Book of Proverbs the Almighty says: "A patient man is better than a warrior, and he who rules his temper, than he who takes a city."

Self-Knowledge:
First Step
to Self-Control

Self-knowledge, self-reverence, self-denial and self-discipline are the means of achieving self-control. Ascetical theology, the branch of divinity which deals with the achievement of sanctity, emphasizes the importance of all these means. They are so many steps on the path to moral perfection. Until one acquires a good knowledge of himself, his points of weakness and of strength, he is unable to plan an intelligent campaign. Quick to perceive the foibles and defects of others, we are usually blind to our own. Our predominant passion lurks, hidden in the soul's depths, a Fifth Column, a Trojan Horse, waiting to ambush us when it is least expected.

Dr. Marion Hilliard, chief of obstetrics and gynecology at Women's College Hospital, Toronto, has had long experience in ministering to unmarried women about to have babies. In "What Women Don't Know About Being Female" in *The Reader's Digest*, she reports that many of the falls are traceable to the failure of women to know their own weaknesses. They are ignorant, she says, of the "vicious power that can leap out of control without the slightest warning, when a man and woman merely share a companionable chuckle or happen to touch hands. The mechanism can be triggered unexpectedly by the low moan of a crooner, by a summer sky full of stars, even by fog collecting around a street light. . . .

"A woman's first protection against this betrayal," she continues, "is to appreciate that the speedup of her emotions is not only possible but natural and normal. Her best defense is to have no confidence at all in her ability to say nay at the appropriate moment. The belief that any woman can coolly halt lovemaking at some point before she is wholly committed is a tiger trap devised by romantics."

How often would a knowledge of the savage force of these hidden drives and libidoes have prevented a young couple from falling into the booby traps from which they emerge only with a horrible sense of guilt, their honor tarnished and their self-respect in shreds. Studies indicate that there is a disturbingly large percentage of marriages where the bride is already pregnant, and either one or the other feels caught in a trap. When provocations occur, the hidden resentment flares up. Soon the divorce mills will be grinding into dust and ashes their dreams of enduring love and happiness.

"Is It I, Lord?"

At the Last Supper Jesus surprised His disciples by saying: "Amen I say to you, one of you will betray me—one who is eating with me."

"Is it I?" asks each.

"It is one of the Twelve," replies Jesus, "who dips with me in the dish. The Son of Man indeed goes his way, as it is written of him: But woe to that man by whom the Son of Man is betrayed! It were better for that man if he had not been born."

The warning of Christ prompted each of the disciples, save the guilty one, to search his soul to see if treason lurked in its hidden depths. If only Judas had cast the spotlight on that treachery and recognized it for what it was, he could still have yanked it out and received the Master's pardon. His refusal to do so led to his doom. What a warning there is in this incident for everyone to look honestly into his own soul and come to grips with whatever enemy he discovers lying in ambush there.

The importance of self-knowledge has long been recognized. "Know thyself," said Thales, one of the seven wise men of ancient Greece. Such is the motto which the wise Greeks inscribed on the Temple of Apollo in Delphi thousands of years ago. "Nothing," says George Santayana, "requires a rarer intellectual heroism than willingness to see one's equation written out." Well does Matthew Arnold say:

> Once read thy own breast right,
> And thou hast done with fears!
> Man gets no other light,
> Search he a thousand years.

Self-Reverence and Self-Respect

A second means for the achievement of self-control is self-reverence and self-respect. Such reverence is best attained through the realization that one's body is the temple of the Holy Spirit and that God dwells within him. "Do you not know," asks the Apostle Paul, "that you are the temple of God and that the Spirit of God dwells in you? If anyone destroys the temple of God, him will God destroy; for holy is the temple of God, and this temple you are."

If men in all ages have reverenced the buildings of wood, brick or stone in which God is worshiped, how much greater should be our reverence for the living temple of the human body in which the Almighty abides? If it is a sacrilege to profane a material object dedicated to the worship of the Creator, how much greater is the sacrilege when the living body in which He dwells is used for sinful purposes?

This conclusion is further strengthened by the doctrine of the Mystical Body, so clearly taught by St. Paul. The Church is the body of Christ: He is the head, we are the members. "I rejoice now," says St. Paul, "in the sufferings I bear for your sake; and what is lacking of the sufferings of Christ I fill up in my flesh for His body, which is the Church." We are united with Christ's Mystical Body as living cells, and are nourished with His divine life. A sinful act brings pain not only to the other members of that body but also to Christ, its head.

In 1321 Douglas, the chief of the Scottish clans, was traveling with his soldiers to the Holy Land to bury there the heart of their fallen leader, Robert the Bruce. On their way they passed through Spain, which was then locked in a life and death struggle with the Moors. Douglas and his soldiers threw themselves into the battle in defense of Christian Spain. At a crucial moment, when the tide was going against his forces, Douglas raised aloft the golden locket containing the heart of Bruce. Then he hurled it into the ranks of the charging Moors.

"On, brave Scots," he cried, "and save the heart of Bruce!"

With fearless abandon the Scottish soldiers hurled themselves against the Saracens, fighting like madmen. Back, back, back they drove them till soon the Moors were fleeing in riot from the field. The tide had turned. Victory rested that evening upon the proud colors of Aragon and Castile. Removing the bodies from the heap where the fighting was the thickest, the Scots found at the very bottom the body of Douglas. In his clenched hands pressed tightly against his breast was the golden locket containing the heart of Bruce.

Lincoln's Reply

If men give their lives to rescue such a symbol—and many have given their lives to prevent their country's flag from falling into the hands of the enemy—with what greater valor should they not fight to keep their bodies, the temples of the Holy Spirit, from being dishonored! "The reverence of a man's self is," says Francis Bacon, "next religion, the chiefest bridle of all vices." In his famous *Meditations*, the Roman Emperior Marcus Aurelius remarks: "Never esteem anything of advantage to thee that shall make thee break thy word or lose thy self-resepct."

In 1864 the Missouri Committee of Seventy was pressuring Abraham Lincoln to pursue a course of conduct contrary to his convictions and conscience. He sent them the following memorable reply: "I desire so to conduct the affairs of this administration that if at the end, when I come to lay down the reins of power, I have lost every friend on earth, I shall at least have one friend left, and that friend shall be down inside of me." Thus admirably did he exemplify the truth of Longfellow's words:

> He that respects himself is safe from others;
> He wears a coat of mail that none can pierce.

Self-Denial Leads
to Self-Control

A third means of achieving the mastery of self is self-denial. We should deny ourselves those things which weaken us, decrease our resistance to temptation and frustrate the attainment of our goal. Hardship, sacrifice and suffering are not ends in themselves; they are means to ends. They do not spring from a Puritan aversion to pleasure, from the Manichean belief that matter is evil nor from the melancholy view that happiness is an offense against God. "I came," says Jesus, "that they may have life, and have it more abundantly." The religion of Christ is one of life and love and happiness.

The more detached one is from sinful gratification, the more abundant is his spiritual life, his freedom and his joy. "Men," points out St. Thomas, "must have pleasures. If they will not have the joys of the spirit, then they will degenerate into pleasure of the body." When one restrains himself from overindulgence in food or drink, he is not lessening his well-being but increasing it. This may entail a momentary slight hardship, but it yields a rich dividend in health and happiness.

A middle-aged man, short, double-chinned and rolling in fat, wobbled one afternoon into my office. He was out of breath and he looked really scared.

"I got the shock of my life today," he began. "Our company ordered its employees to undergo a physical examination. The doctor said that I have to trim down from 250 to 160—90 pounds —that I have high blood pressure and a serious heart condition. He said I was killing myself with a knife and fork. He put me on a rigid diet."

"I would scarcely think," I commented, "that you would need to do more than look in the mirror to discover what is wrong. Anyone carrying that amount of surplus weight is bound, sooner or later, to run into those troubles. The fifth commandment forbids not only murder but also suicide. You've been committing slow suicide. You'll have to pay the penalty now by going on that diet and sticking to it. Otherwise, your wife will soon be a widow and your children half-orphans."

"My friends kidded me so much," he explained, "that I thought it was just a laughing matter. I see now, however, that

it's a matter of life or death. I only hope the damage is not irreparable, that it's not too late."

How costly was the habit he had formed of overindulging a
bit every day. Slowly, stealthily, like a thief in the night, the layers of fat had accumulated over the years and now were beginning to strangle him slowly to death. His was but an extreme
case of the obesity which, in varying degrees, rests like a dead
weight upon such a disturbingly large proportion of the American people.

Walk in
the Spirit

What an apt illustration it offers of the rich dividends paid by
self-denial! What emancipation, health and happiness it offers
for reasonable restraint. This is true not only in the physical
domain but in the spiritual as well. "He who loses his life for
my sake," Jesus reminds us, "will save it."

The athlete of Christ must deny himself an indulgence in his
dominant passion. To be forewarned is to be forearmed. Accordingly he is on his guard against placing himself in the occasions of sin. He knows that the best technique of conquering his
chief passion is not to challenge it to a duel but to keep it
chained and let it die of atrophy. Echoing in his mind are the
warning words of the great Apostle Paul: "Walk in the Spirit,
and you will not fulfill the lusts of the flesh . . . And they who
belong to Christ have crucified their flesh with its passions and
desires."

This is the sacrifice, the self-denial which, like restraint at the
table, yields such rich returns in health, vigor, freedom and happiness. The cheerful embrace of such asceticism weans one from
his passions and enables him to share in the life of the Blessed
Trinity, which can best be attained by configuration with Christ
crucified.

The Conquest
of Pride

Self-denial and sacrifice must be applied not only to the flesh but also to the intellect. One of the great temptations to which it is exposed is pride: the sin by which the angels fell and by which no man can rise. Pride is the inordinate, excessive esteem of oneself and is a blend of vanity and conceit.

It is a kind of intellectual intoxication which fills one with strange fancies and leads him to talk in a conceited fashion and to do irrational things. The proud man is like the frog in the fable, that puffed itself out in the vain hope of appearing as large as the ox. "God," says the Apostle Peter, "resists the proud, but gives grace to the humble." Like the drop of gall that spoils the flavor of the most delicious wine, pride ruins virtue.

"When thou art invited," says Jesus, "go and recline in the last place; that when he who invited thee comes in, he may say to thee, 'Friend, go up higher!' Then thou wilt be honored in the presence of all at table with thee. For everyone who exalts himself shall be humbled, and *he who humbles himself* shall be exalted."

What a splendid example of overcoming the temptation to pride was given by John the Baptist! He was baptizing along the Jordan and great crowds were flocking to him. Not a few apparently considered him to be the long promised Messiah. Some of them complained to John that prospective followers were now being drawn away by Christ, and they were angry.

"I am not the Christ," replied the Baptist, "but have been sent before him. He who has the bride is the bridegroom; but the friend of the bridegroom, who stands and hears him, rejoices exceedingly at the voice of the bridegroom. This my joy, therefore, is made full. *He must increase, but I must decrease.*"

Here was the conquest of pride, the rejection of honor and glory that would readily have been accorded him if he had not humbly acknowledged himself to be but the precursor of the Lord, the strap of whose sandals he declared himself to be unworthy to loose. No wonder it was that Jesus said: "Amen I say to you, among those born of women there has not risen a greater than John the Baptist."

Ashen Cross
Traced on Brow

The nobility of self-denial and sacrifice has been recognized in all ages. "The more a man denies himself," says Horace, "so much the more will he receive from the gods." "Sacrifice," observes J. A. Froude, "is the first element of religion, and resolves itself in theological language into the love of God." Back in the second century Clement of Alexandria declared: "The sacrifice most acceptable to God is complete renunciation of the body and its passions."

Self-mastery is a theme to which one of the most eminent of contemporary philosophers, Jacques Maritain, devoted much thought and study. In his great work, *Freedom in the Modern World*, he reaches the following conclusion: "Man can become master of his nature by imposing on the world of his inner energies the law of reason, of reason assisted by grace. This work, which is the formation of oneself in love, requires that our *branches be cut in order that we may bear fruit*: which is *mortification*." To place our reliance upon machinery and technical processes for the achievement of self-mastery, he points out, is to become "irretrievably and literally lost."

While Christianity, like its founder, Jesus Christ, stresses the importance of self-denial and sacrifice in one's daily life, it redoubles this emphasis during the holy season of Lent. Beginning on Ash Wednesday and continuing till Easter, this period commemorates the forty days of fast, by which Jesus prepared for His public ministry. On Ash Wednesday the Church traces with ashes the sign of the cross on the forehead of its members, saying to each: "Remember, man, that thou art but dust and unto dust thou shalt return." This is the significant and colorful ceremony which inspired Lionel Johnson to write:

> Ashen cross traced on brow!
> Iron cross hid in breast!
> Have power, bring patience, now;
> Bid passion be at rest.

More prosaic but not less meaningful is the prayer recited in the Mass on that day: "Grant us, O Lord, to begin the service of our Christian warfare with holy fasting; that as we are about to fight against spiritual powers of wickedness, we may be fortified by the aid of self-denial." In short, one can make but little progress on the road to self-mastery unless he engages in frequent, if not daily, acts of self-denial and sacrifice.

Self-Discipline
Subordinates Lower Nature
to Higher

A fourth means of achieving self-control is self-discipline. It is closely akin to self-denial. There the stress is upon the negative aspect of restraint: rejecting and refraining from many pleasures and gratifications of the senses. Self-discipline embraces a larger field of action, and stresses the positive aspect of conduct: the doing of things which exercise the body, train the mind, strengthen the will, and fashion character.

At its heart lies the idea of subordinating the lower to the higher in obedience to the command of a superior or to the voice of conscience. Just as a well-disciplined army carries out in a prompt, determined and skillful manner the orders of its officers, so is a well-disciplined will the obedient servant of the conscience.

If there is any one quality which army officers seek to develop in raw recruits, it is discipline. Without that, the largest army will accomplish little. No amount of equipment or supplies can substitute for it. The Roman Legion in the ancient world and the French Foreign Legion in the modern became synonymous with discipline. As discipline multiplies the power of soldiers on the military battlefield, so it multiplies the strength of individuals on the spiritual battlefield where every man must wage a life-long war.

Candidates for the religious life—priests, brothers, nuns—go through a long period of training in novitiate and seminary to acquire the discipline that will enable them to live lives of restraint, abnegation and sacrifice. Candidates for officers in the army and navy spend four strenuous years at West Point and Annapolis undergoing daily discipline for their exacting posts of service.

On the day I write these lines, I see scores of young men in sweat suits, going through calisthenics, shadowboxing, running around Cartier Field and the campus lake in preparation for the annual Bengal Boxing Tournament. It is a strenuous discipline, seeking to strengthen every muscle in their bodies and to develop stamina, courage and grit. Foregoing pastries and sweets, they trim down to their best "fighting" weight. Gone is their carefree spirit, their easy-going ways. They have become young Spartans.

Developing Strength and Stamina

"Win or lose," said Dominic Napolitano the boxing coach, "this discipline proves valuable for these boys in every field of endeavor. It takes the softness out of them. It trains them to do hard things, to go against the grain, to stand up under blows as well as to give them. It disciplines them to put everything they've got into the job, and to develop reserves of strength and stamina that will stand them in good stead whenever the going gets tough."

We were standing in the Rockne Memorial gymnasium, watching the boys go through their strenuous exercises. Looking down upon us was the bronzed figure of Knute Rockne, whose memory is still an inspiration to Notre Dame men. It brought back to my mind the words spoken a generation ago before a group of eminent educators.

Rockne was denouncing the softness which even then was creeping into American life, sapping the virility of young men and turning out lounge lizards and tea hounds. He stressed the necessity of toughening the fiber of youth through vigorous physical, intellectual and moral discipline.

"If I have learned any one fact in my twenty years of work with young men," he said, "it's this: the most dangerous thing in American life today is that we're getting soft, inside and out! Youth today needs more of the iron of discipline in its blood and in its spine. No education is worthy of the name unless it disciplines the body, mind and will and thus lays the foundation for sturdy moral character."

To be most effective, discipline must begin early in life, and the earlier, the better. Actions soon form into habits and they, like plaster, quickly harden into a mold.

"When should I begin to train my child?" a young mother asked the famous doctor, Sir William Osler.

"How old is your child?" asked Osler.

"Two years."

"You are already too late," replied Osler.

Root Cause
of Juvenile Delinquency

The root cause of the juvenile delinquency mounting like a tidal wave in America is the failure of parents to discipline their children and to do it from their earliest years. "The spoiled child," said Alexis Carrel, "is America's heaviest crop. Nowhere else in the world are the young so systematically pampered and fatally handicapped by parents who have failed to teach them to work, earn and learn." Sharing this conviction was the late Will Rogers who epitomized in memorable words the thought of all who have studied this subject: "What the younger generation

needs is to chop more kindling wood and to cultivate a few in-
hibitions."

While the years before twenty are of crucial importance in the
formation of habits, discipline is needed not only then but also
throughout the whole of life. Lapses can and do occur at all
ages and hence unremitting discipline is necessary. "He who best
knows how to endure," says Thomas à Kempis, "will possess the
greater peace. Such a one is conqueror of himself and lord of the
world, the friend of Christ and an heir to heaven."

Mastery
of Self
Is Goal

The goal of self-knowledge, self-denial, self-reverence and self-
discipline is self-control, the mastery of self. This is the moral
perfection at which we all must aim. This is the distinctive at-
tribute of all the saints: it is the crowning perfection for which
they struggle all their lives.

As a young man St. Francis de Sales had to contend with a
choleric temperament, finding himself easily irritated. For twenty
years he labored so assiduously in conquering it that he became
a model of meekness.

"What was the secret of your success?" a friend asked.

"I made an agreement with my tongue," he replied, "never to
utter a word while my heart is excited."

Blessed Clement Hofbauer was collecting alms for the orphan
children of Warsaw. He approached a group of men at a card
table. One of the players spat in his face.

"That, sir, was for myself," he said, as he wiped his face. "Now
may I ask for something for my poor orphans?"

So overwhelmed was the man that he grabbed the stack of
bills before him and placed them in Clement's hands.

Jean de Brébeuf had come as a Jesuit missionary from France
to bring the light of the Christian faith to the Huron Indians in

the New World. On March 16, 1649 he was captured by the Iroquois when they attacked the mission at St. Louis and dragged him to St. Ignace. He was showered with stones, beaten with clubs, and then tied to the stake to be burnt to death.

The fire was lighted under him and his body slashed with knives. A collar of red-hot tomahawk heads was placed around his neck, and a red-hot iron thrust down his throat. To the amazement of the savages, Father Brébeuf displayed no anger, uttered no word of complaint, but died with the prayer, "Jesus, have mercy," on his lips.

Here was a self-control that matched that of the Apostles and the other early Christian martyrs. Indeed it was a self-mastery that approximated that of Christ who is holiness incarnate and the model of all who strive for self-control and moral perfection. See Him as His executioners scourge, buffet, mock and taunt Him, placing a crown of thorns upon His head. Gaze at Him as He carries His Cross to Calvary and hangs suspended upon it, bleeding from a hundred stripes and wounds.

While the rabble shout in derision, "If thou art the Son of God, come down from the Cross!", Jesus utters no word of rebuke. He pardons the repentant thief on the cross beside him, and says, "This day thou shalt be with me in paradise." Then as His strength ebbs away, He raises His eyes to heaven and prays for His executioners, saying, "Father, forgive them, for they know not what they are doing." Here is the one infinitely perfect life ever lived on this planet. Here is the example of self-control that all His followers and all men seeking spiritual perfection must strive to achieve.

POINTS TO REMEMBER

1. The test of Christ's disciple is a willingness to carry one's cross manfully and courageously. "If anyone wishes to come after me," says Jesus, "let him deny himself and take up his cross daily and follow me."

2. By His crucifixion Jesus transformed the cross from a symbol of shame to one of love.

3. Self-denial and sacrifice help to atone for sins and discipline the will to resist temptation.

4. The supreme objective in the spiritual life is the achievement of the highest holiness. This is attained "with the grace of God" chiefly through self-control.

5. Self-knowledge and self-reverence are most helpful in achieving self-control.

6. The more detached one is from sinful gratification, the more abundant is his spiritual life, freedom and joy.

7. Self-denial must be applied not only to the flesh but also to the intellect.

8. The holy season of Lent stresses the importance of self-denial and invites one to undergo voluntary mortifications.

9. Self-discipline requires one to subordinate his lower nature to the voice of conscience.

10. He who best knows how to endure will possess the greater peace.

11. Jesus offers us an example of perfect self-control.

II.

LOVING OUR NEIGHBOR

"Beloved, let us love one another, for love is from
God."—St. John

Linked to the first commandment, and indeed inseparable
from it, is the second: "Thou shalt love thy neighbor as thyself."
This is the basis of ethics and the most fundamental principle
and directive to guide us in our relations with our fellow men.
It sums up in a brief sentence all the directions spelled out in
detail in the seven last commandments of the decalogue.

Who is your neighbor? Those who live near you and others
with whom you associate? Yes, and every other human being as
well. Christ made it unmistakably clear that our love must embrace not only those near and dear to us but also the stranger,
the outcast, the leper and even our enemies. It must extend to
all who have been created in the image of God, regardless of
color, race, religion or nationality.

This was vividly brought out by our Lord when He answered
the question of the doctor of the Law: "Who is my neighbor?"
Jesus related the Parable of the Good Samaritan, in which a
Samaritan found a wounded Jew on the road leading from Jerusalem to Jericho. Moved with compassion, he bandaged the
wounds, brought the man to an inn, and paid for his lodging and
care. As there was marked enmity between Jews and Samaritans,
the parable makes it clear that one's neighbor is everyone in
need, Jew or non-Jew, friend or enemy.

Love Everyone?

Many people squirm and writhe in discomfort, if not in pain, at the thought that they are obliged to love everyone, no matter how unattractive, unpleasant or disagreeable he may be. They think this is going too far, that it is hopelessly idealistic and contrary to the grain of human nature. A student in one of my classes in ethics expressed this objection rather bluntly.

"Isn't it psychologically impossible," he asked, "to love people whom you positively dislike? There are some people who grate on your nerves, who irritate you, and in whose very presence you feel uncomfortable and on edge. How can you be expected to love them when you can scarcely refrain from hating them?"

The answer lies in securing a better understanding of the meaning of love. As mentioned in a previous chapter, love usually involves three elements: emotion, volition and action. Emotions are not always under the control of the will. Indeed we may not be able to generate the emotion of affection or fondness for every human being, and no one is held to the impossible.

Nevertheless we can love everyone in the sense that we sincerely wish him well: we desire all that is good for him, especially his true welfare and eternal salvation, and we stand ready to translate those wishes into action if the opportunity presents itself. By thus doing all that is in our power, we shall frequently find that, with God's grace, even an emotion of warmth, friendliness and affection creeps into our love for the person, though naturally it will not extend to his unlovely or bad traits or characteristics. This certainly has been the experience of many saints.

"My parish," John Wesley was wont to say, "is the world; my parishioners are all mankind." His words reflect the important truth that our concern, solicitude and love must not be limited to the members of our family or the circle of our friends and intimates but must extend to all men. We are the inhabitants not merely of a neighborhood, city, county, state and country

but of a planet, and our love must embrace every fellow traveler
on it. In this matter our political hindsight is beginning to catch
up with our spiritual insight.

Why Love
Our Neighbors?

Why should be love our neighbors? Because we are all the
children of God and are all therefore brothers and sisters. We
are all made in the image of God and we must see the lineaments of the divine countenance in every man and love him for
God's sake. It is this divine endowment which constitutes the
basis of the dignity of every person and makes him a being precious beyond all price. *It is the basis of the spiritual kinship of all
men, regardless of race or color.*

"God," declared Pope Pius XII, "did not create a human
family made up of segregated, dissociated and mutually inde-
pendent members."

Just as the moon derives its light from the sun, so man derives his right to respect and love from his kinship with God.
Our love for God must flow out to all creatures made in His
likeness: in loving them we are also loving Him. "God being
the principle of all good," points out St. Thomas Aquinas, "that
which a man loves in himself is the Divine Good communicated
to him, and he loves his neighbor by reason of fellowship in that
good." This is the line of reasoning which gives profound significance to the oft-quoted but insufficiently understood phrase,
the "Fatherhood of God and the Brotherhood of Man."

"Yes, God is our common Father and we are all brothers, and
we should love one another *as God loves us.* How simply and
beautifully the Beloved Disciple, St. John, privileged to rest his
head upon the bosom of Christ and hear the throbbing of the
divine heart, expresses this mighty truth: "Beloved," he says,
"let us love one another, for *love is from God.* And everyone
who loves is *born* of God. He who does not love does not know

God; for God is love . . . Beloved, if God has so loved us, we also ought to love one another."

Not content with the mere exposition of this mighty truth, the Beloved Disciple then proceeds to drive it home in a forceful manner, saying: "If anyone says, 'I love God' and hates his brother, he is a liar. For how can he who does not love his brother, whom he sees, love God, whom he does not see? And this commandment we have from him, that *he who loves God should love his brother also.*"

Living in abject poverty in the slums of Kobe, Toyohiko Kagawa was wont to pray: "O God! Make me a channel of Thy love." His life became the fulfillment of that prayer, as he shared his food, clothing and shelter with paupers and outcasts. Finding an abandoned baby on the verge of starvation, he took it to his room and nursed it back to life. We can see him holding the sleeping infant in his arms as he softly sings:

> My God is Love,
> My God is Love,
> Tender and deep.
> I feel His close sweet presence
> Looking down to see
> The beggar baby
> Lying in my arms asleep.

See God in Our Neighbor

By loving our neighbor for the sake of God, whose presence we see in him, we rise above considerations of mere kinship, patriotism, national solidarity or human fellowship to the higher view of our common divine adoption, heavenly heritage and eternal destiny. In this way we bring our brotherly love close to the love which God has for us, and achieve a kind of moral identity between Christ and our neighbor.

Whoever regards his fellow man in this light will see not so

much the individual's distinctive traits and peculiarities as the
image of God within him. Hence he will find it impossible to re-
strict his love to the members of his family, his friends, fellow
citizens or co-religionists, but must need extend it to all the
children of God.

This is vividly illustrated in the life of Father Damien. Learning of the sad plight of the lepers of Molokai, who were without
anyone to minister to their spiritual needs, he volunteered. The
faces of many of them were so badly disfigured with the disease
that they were indeed pitiful sights. But the young Belgian priest
had no eyes for those ulcerous sores: these lepers were his brothers and in each of them he saw the face of Christ and loved the
Christ within them.

With great tenderness and love he ministered to them, band-
aging their sores and whispering words of comfort and hope. He
cared for them as brothers until the dread disease caught up with
him twelve years later. Despite the inroads of the disease, he continued to minister for three more years when death called him
home. To these pitiable outcasts in the far Pacific, Joseph de
Veuster, known only as Father Damien—the saint whose name
he took at the time of his religious profession—had devoted his
entire priestly life and poured out his love upon them without
stint.

At an international missionary exhibit in Rome his deathbed
scene was reproduced with great realism. Grouped about him
were a number of lepers, their eyes moist with tears, their faces
aglow with love and gratitude for the man who had been all
things to them: spiritual shepherd, physician, nurse, carpenter
and comforter. He had brought something of God's boundless
love to them not so much by his words as by his deeds. The
scene has remained vividly in my mind over the years because
it was such an eloquent demonstration of the truth that when
one sees Christ in the faces of others, no matter how unattractive they may be, he loves them as he loves God—with his whole
heart, mind and soul.

The
Supreme Test

Such love does not shrink from paying the supreme sacrifice to aid one's neighbor in desperate need. This was demonstrated in a memorable and dramatic manner by the four heroic chaplains on the S.S. *Dorchester*, a 5,250 ton Army transport on February 3, 1943. The vessel carried a crew of 130 men of the Merchant Marine, a naval gun crew of 23, and 751 passengers, most of whom were army reinforcements for Greenland. Jeanne Dixon relates the stirring story in "Four Chaplains Join the Immortals" in the *Catholic Digest*. Here in condensed form are its highlights.

Among the passengers were four army chaplains, George L. Fox, a Methodist; Clark V. Poling of the Dutch Reformed Church; Alexander D. Goode, a rabbi; and John P. Washington, a Catholic priest. All were first lieutenants, brave and unselfish men and friends. As a soldier, Fox had won the *Croix de Guerre* in World War I. His little daughter in Chicopee, Massachusetts, had written him.

"Daddy, you'll be glad to know that I got good marks in all my studies."

"Yes, dear," he replied, "I'm not only glad, I'm proud of you. But I want you always to remember that kindness and charity and courtesy are much more important than marks."

Poling came from a long line of ministers; his brother is a Presbyterian and his father, Dr. Daniel A. Poling is the widely known and esteemed editor of the *Christian Herald*. Clark Poling was itching to share with the front-line soldiers the dangers and hardships of war. In his last letter to his wife he voiced the regret that he was being sent to a safe, lonely post instead of to the battlefront.

Goode had led his class and won letters in three sports at Eastern High in Washington, D.C. After he became a rabbi, he drove 45 miles daily to John Hopkins to earn a doctorate. This he did for three years; in the summertime he did social work.

He wanted to develop his many talents to the utmost so he could best serve his people.

Washington was the son of poor Irish immigrants and as a boy had a paper route in Newark, New Jersey. After ordination he served at St. Stephen's in Arlington, New Jersey, where he worked with youth, coaching the baseball and basketball teams. He won the hearts of young and old alike by his warm-hearted kindness. "Father John," an elderly parishioner recalled, "had a smile and a pat on the back for everyone. He brightened your whole day."

"Greater Love Than This . . ."

Of widely different backgrounds and faiths, the four were united in the common conviction that freedom of religious worship and of conscience is worth fighting for. They were ready to serve wherever they were sent.

At 3:55 in the morning of February 3, 1943, a German submarine released a torpedo that struck the *Dorchester* amidships. The abandon-ship order was given, and the vessel began to sink. Passengers rushed on deck, wild with terror. Afraid to remain, they were even more afraid to plunge into the bitterly cold sea. Men fought frantically for places in the few lifeboats and for the precious life jackets.

Hurrying on deck, John P. O'Brien, private first class, saw the four chaplains standing near the bridge. Fox and Goode were removing their own life preservers and giving them to two soldiers. The other two chaplains were taking life preservers from a rack and throwing them to men in the water. Just before jumping overboard, Sergeant Mike Bernstetter noticed one of the chaplains remove his own life belt and fasten it around the waist of a crying child.

On his way to the bridge to destroy the ship's confidential papers, Lieutenant William H. Arpaia saw the four chaplains seeking to calm the hysterical men around them. As he passed them, he heard the voice of Father Washington.

"Here, soldier," he was saying, "take my life preserver. I won't be needing it."

As the vessel sank, men struggling in the frigid sea saw an amazing sight: the four chaplains standing calmly on the bridge, their arms linked. A grateful government awarded each posthumously the Distinguished Service Cross. Better than any sermon ever preached, these four men dramatized on that cold February morning amid scenes of indescribable panic and terror the truth spoken by the gentle Christ: "Greater love than this no one has, that a man lay down his life for his friends."

Love
of Oneself

The practice of love would soon become imprudent or inoperative unless there is in this, as in all the moral virtues, a proper order. What then is the order in which our love is to be bestowed upon human beings? Love of one's own supernatural good, namely, the friendship of God and one's eternal salvation, comes first. Such love is not self-centered, nor opposed to humility, since it redounds to God's glory.

It is part of the divine plan that we should be sons of God, sharers in the divine nature, co-heirs with Christ and members of God's family on earth and in heaven. Such rational love of self is a presupposition of love for others, as evidenced in the words of Christ: "Thou shalt love thy neighbor as thyself." This means that we must first strive for God's grace and for the means necessary to attain our own eternal happiness.

No rational being can desire, or is ever asked to choose, his own permanent unhappiness. By virtue of his very nature man seeks his abiding happiness: this is one field in which the will is not free. Even when one appears to be deliberately choosing unhappiness by doing evil, he does so under the illusion that it will bring him happiness, at least temporarily. Herein lies the tragedy of all sin: the forfeiting of eternal happiness for a moment of present gratification.

> At the devil's booth are all things sold,
> Each ounce of dross costs its ounce of gold.
> For a cap and bells our lives we pay—
> Baubles we buy with a whole soul's tasking.

The craving for one's own happiness is so immediately apparent that the point need not be labored. It is sufficient to point out simply that love of neighbor never requires or permits an individual to sacrifice his own eternal happiness under the guise of helping his neighbor. This applies to our relations not only with our equals but also with our superiors. Here apply the memorable words of the Apostle Peter: "We must obey God rather than men."

"One of the principal causes of the enormous increase of alcoholics," reported an investigator, "is the growth of the custom of social drinking. Cocktails and other alcoholic beverages are now offered at so many social gatherings by overly hospitable hosts that it takes a person with a strong will to say 'No.' Under the mistaken impression that good fellowship requires one to take a drink whenever his host or companion hoists his glass, millions of well-meaning people have become alcoholics or near-alcoholics, and other millions are on their way. What people need to realize more clearly is that neighborliness, friendship and even warm regard for others impose no duty on one to drink to excess and thus undermine his own health and happiness."

How many violations of the moral law are traceable to a false sense of friendship and love. Many times their best expression would be a vigorous and resolute "No!" Everyone has an immortal soul to save and this requires that a decent regard for his own spiritual welfare is to take precedence over the imaginary or alleged claims of friendship and love. In short, one is never justified in committing a sin to please others.

Love for
One's Family

Second only to the duty of loving oneself in the sense of having a reasonable concern for one's welfare, temporal and eternal, is the duty of loving the members of one's own family. "Charity begins at home," is an old and true saying, but it should not end there. "But if anyone does not have a care of his own," says St. Paul, "and especially of his household, he has denied the faith and is worse than an unbeliever."

The home in which the members reinforce their love for one another with the love of God is like the house built not on shifting sands but upon solid bedrock. It will withstand the tumult of the storm and the fury of all the winds that blow. The home in which a deep and abiding love prevails is a home filled with peace and happiness.

Movies, television and trashy novels, featuring extramarital escapades and divorce, have done much in distorting the sacred character of conjugal love. Emphasizing the beauty and holiness of that love, the Apostle Paul says: "Husbands, love your wives, just as Christ also loved the Church . . . Even thus ought husbands also to love their wives as their own bodies. He who loves his own wife, loves himself. For no one ever hateth his own flesh; on the contrary he nourishes and cherishes it, as Christ also does the Church, because we are members of his body, made from his flesh and from his bones."

The love of husband and wife, elevated on their wedding day to a sacramental dignity, should deepen and grow with the passing years and spread its lovely aura throughout the home. One of the greatest menaces to that love is the angry word that cuts and burns. Spoken in a moment of irritation, it hurts and humiliates the person who is the closest and dearest of all to you and sears its ugly way into the memory. It acts as a termite that eats away the foundations and pulls the shining castle of love's dream into dust and ashes.

The
Second Vow

My first sick call was to a home on the verge of being destroyed by strife, kindled by angry bitter words. I was finally able to reconcile the couple and, to safeguard their marriage, had each kneel and repeat after me these words: "I solemnly promise on my word of honor that I shall never speak to my wife/husband an angry, bitter or spiteful word but shall discuss all differences in a kind and affectionate manner. So help me God!"

That is the simple promise with which I have had wedding couples supplement their conjugal vows for more than forty years. Never have I heard of one such marriage hitting the rocks or even being clouded by domestic strife. A mere resolution is not, of course, a panacea for unhappy couples. There is no magic elixir for any sickness of the heart. But this simple little vow is an effective technique of protecting the heart against its most common enemy: the angry bitter word that smarts and stings. If this enemy is excluded, kindness, sympathy, tenderness and love will flourish and they constitute a remedy more potent than any medicine doctors can devise. It is nature's remedy and God's as well.

Some years ago I told this story in some detail in an article called "The Second Vow in Marriage," in The Reader's Digest. Letters have come to me from grateful couples in many states, telling how much that simple little vow has done to preserve the happiness of their marriage and to keep their love in bloom. One bride, married now over twenty years, tells how it worked:

"Whenever one of us was about to blow his top, the other would say softly, 'Remember our second vow.' We'd clasp hands in silent prayer for a few moments and then quietly say whatever was in our minds. The irritation quickly passes under such treatment and we have been able to solve our problems without hurting one another or saying things we'd be sorry for later on. That bloom of love you spoke of on our wedding day is still there; it's made our home life beautiful and we'll hold fast to it to the end.

We wish others could share the secret—the precious secret—of our happiness: our love has never been sacrificed to the Moloch of the angry, spiteful word." Her letter is typical of hundreds.

Selfishness
—the Root

Since most people spend the greater part of their time at home, it is of the utmost importance to come to grips with the factors which mar the practice of love therein. I've been a marriage counselor to people of all faiths for many years and have listened to the stories of vexation and grief spelled out in endless detail by wrathful husbands and wives. There's no simple cure-all for their problems: each case has to be studied carefully to get to the underlying causes.

These are many, for people bring into marriage all the weakness, meanness and defects of their respective natures and dispositions. Love unfortunately doesn't eradicate them, though it may help to hold them in abeyance during courtship. But the more cases I'm called upon to treat, the more I'm convinced that selfishness, self-centeredness, egotism, call it what you will, is at the root of the trouble in most instances.

This, of course, is a violation of the law of love, which obliges us to love our neighbor as ourselves. "All things therefore whatsoever," says Jesus, "you would that men should do unto you, do you also to them: for this is the Law and the Prophets." If you wish to be loved, you must love others. It is of the very nature of love to give as well as to receive. The person always on the receiving end comes to believe that the world and all its inhabitants were created to minister to his comfort.

To help combat that self-centeredness it is of the utmost importance to try to understand the other person's position, to put yourself in his place and imagine how you would feel under the circumstances. To do this it is necessary to keep open the channels of communication, to listen as well as to speak, and indeed to encourage the other party to speak with complete candor. This can be done without shouting or screaming hysterically—which merely compounds the difficulty—and without stinging or sarcastic words.

Harsh Words
Are Termites

Few realize that harsh words are the termites that undermine the foundation of a happy home. Because words seem such little things, briefly spoken and so quickly gone, we must not minimize the destructive power which lies in their bitterness. They vie with atom bombs in their fury and destructiveness.

"I can readily forgive," a wife remarked to me, "the thoughtless actions of my husband, which have now and then embarrassed and mortified me, but I can never forget some of the bitter things he has said to humiliate and hurt me—not if I live to be a hundred. They rattlesnake through my mind at night when I lie awake and rankle anew. The memory of them still distills its poison."

Long ago the Latin poet Horace said, "A word once spoken can never be recalled." The subsequent ages have but confirmed his observation. A sword can be put back in its scabbard, but a word can never be caught and imprisoned behind the lips that uttered it.

When an angry word provokes a quarrel, each party has a position to defend. A "principle" is at stake, they assert, when in reality it is simply their vanity and pride. Reinforcements in the form of in-laws enter the picture: soon both sides are mobilized for all-out war. The peace that a simple, kindly word of apology could have quickly restored is now rendered exceedingly difficult.

The skeptic may ask: "Is not the vow against harsh words easily forgotten?" No, because, sadly enough, the occasions to remember it are too frequent. In disagreements, words of abuse and recrimination crowd the mouth like evil spirits clamoring to get out and do mischief. The problem generally occurs too often for the remedy to be forgotten.

The Mark
of an Adult

Anger begets stubbornness, and these two offer adamantine resistance to the voice of reason. An angry word provoked a quarrel between Donald and Edythe, married only seven months. When the dispute subsided, an atmosphere of sullen tension ensued. Both pouted in obdurate silence, each waiting for the other to make the first peace maneuver. This had gone on for three days when Edythe appealed to me over the phone to intervene.

"We're both miserable," she said, "and the situation is becoming increasingly ridiculous, if not tragic. Two people living together, eating together, and yet not speaking. Each is waiting for the other to speak first and each hesitates to do so, fearful that it will be considered a sign of weakness and an acknowledgment of having been in the wrong. Each is waiting for the other to break the ice. And as time goes on, it only freezes all the harder."

"I haven't come," I told them on arriving, "to decide who was in the right or wrong when this quarrel arose. But I have come to tell you that in perpetuating this state of silent tension you are *both* wrong, acting like two spoiled, pouting children—not like adults. If this conduct continues it will wreck your marriage.

"The mark of an adult of character and intelligence is the willingness to clear up a misunderstanding as quickly as possible—to say, 'I'm sorry. Please forgive me,' or 'Let's wash out the incident and forget about it.' Then heal it over with a kiss of understanding, sympathy, and love, and refrain henceforth from the angry word. If such bickerings, followed by sullen silences, are allowed to continue, they will destroy the happiness of the home and ultimately wreck the marriage."

Once again I had them kneel and solemnly promise to avoid
the angry word and seal their pledge with a kiss.

A Simple Rule

How many marriages go on the rocks through causes like this:
husband and wife still in love with each other but each waiting
for the other to make the first move toward reconciliation. The
most difficult words to pronounce in any tongue are: "I was at
fault . . . I'm sorry . . . Please forgive me."

Yet there are times when they must be pronounced if a marriage is to be salvaged. The person who first utters them proves
his superiority in character and in magnanimity and wins the
greater victory.

The technique of preventing such situations from arising is in
the observance of the simple rule: *Exclude the angry word.* For
it is chiefly through the ill-tempered word that strife enters the
home. When two individuals who should love each other more
than anyone else in the world begin to shout angry words at
each other, they are tarnishing the virginal beauty of their relationship, dispelling the illusions upon which love thrives, and
showing all too plainly that the idol has feet, if not a head, of
clay.

If not nipped in the bud, the tendency to quarrel is likely to
become chronic. If it persists, the young couple will succeed in
destroying the most beautiful and delicate flower in human life
—the sweet tender flower of conjugal love. Stark tragedy squats
brooding at the fireside. Soon the angry mills of the divorce
court will grind out one more home into dust and ashes and pile
the human debris mountain-high.

Tantrums
Accomplish Nothing

When people hear that the couples I marry remain together,
some retort that this claim is possible only because my faith for-

bids divorce. But the Church does not forbid separation; it is not
only divorce that I have to fight but also the breaking of part-
nership, estrangement, and the wrecking of the home through
prolonged separation.

There are also some who feel that an explosion of anger is a
relief to the feelings, a purge, good for body and soul. Such ad-
mirers of tantrums have misread both modern psychology and
medicine. The damage done by emotional hurricanes is not con-
fined to the object of wrath but extends to the wrathful as well.
In loss of adrenalin, in disruption of nervous force, in various
ways, mental and physical, frenzy can weaken us, body, mind,
and soul. Of course it is equally destructive to swallow grudges
and then nourish them quietly, but we can rid ourselves of re-
sentments without blowing up like a volcano.

People will receive virtually any suggestion if made in a
friendly manner, but they will bristle with porcupine fury and
resentment if it is shouted at them in an ill-tempered manner.
So instantly does the angry tone close the door of understanding
that the thought content never really crosses the threshold and
its worth is never weighed.

Home:
A House of God

I have stressed at some length the importance of the preserva-
tion of conjugal love on the part of both husband and wife
because their example has such a crucial influence upon the children. If they see each day the expression of the kindness, devotion, consideration and love of their parents, they will be
prompted to behave in the same manner toward one another
and toward their parents. The atmosphere of such a home will
be pervaded by the spirit of kindness and love.

In the dining room of such a home might well be framed the
words which St. Augustine had inscribed in his own: "Christ is
the head of this household. He is the witness of every deed, the

auditor of every spoken word." "A dining room table," observes Simeon Strunsky, "with children's eager, hungry faces around it, ceases to be a mere dining room table, and becomes an altar." Such a home will be a nursery of holiness, a school of virtue, a house of God and a gateway to heaven.

Parents are under a divine obligation to love their children and to rear them in the love and fear of God. Parents are a child's best teachers, and the lessons he learns at a mother's knee are the ones which he is most likely to carry to the journey's end. "Train up a child in the way he should go," says the Book of Proverbs, "and when he is old, he will not depart from it."

The only real cure for juvenile delinquency consists in proper parental care, direction and love. "A return to old-fashioned home and church life," says J. Edgar Hoover, "is essential if we are to provide an effective remedy for juvenile delinquency." "What is more noble," asks St. John Chrysostom, "than to form the minds of youth? He who fashions the morals of children performs a task in my judgment more sublime than that of any painter or sculptor." Parents sculpture the veined marble of flesh and blood into a living masterpiece which dwarfs into insignificance any inanimate statue.

Love
Your Enemies

Next to the members of one's home, a person's love should extend to his relatives, friends, associates, to the members of his community, state, nation and to all mankind. To His disciples Jesus said: "A new commandment I give you, that you love one another; that as I have loved you, you also love one another." This is the mark which is forever to distinguish His disciples, the unfailing credential by which they are to be recognized. So earnestly did the early Christians strive to fulfill this commandment that the Romans were wont to say, "See these Christians. How they love one another!"

Reflecting the supreme importance Christ attached to this commandment, St. Paul declares: "For the whole law is fulfilled in one word: Thou shalt love thy neighbor as thyself." Hence it is only when we strive with indomitable good will, day in and day out, to love one another that we are worthy of the name of Christians.

It is not too difficult to love those near and dear to us, those who are pleasant and agreeable to us and who love us. It is more difficult, however, to love those who are unattractive and disagreeable, who irritate, hate and hurt us. But even these we are called upon by Christ to love.

"You have heard," declared Jesus, "that it was said, 'An eye for an eye and a tooth for a tooth.' But I say to you not to resist the evildoer; on the contrary, if someone strikes thee on the right cheek, turn to him the other also; and if anyone would go to law with thee and take thy tunic, let him take thy cloak as well; and whoever forces thee to go for one mile, go with him two."

Does this sound like a strange and revolutionary doctrine? Yes, and it is. When it fell from the Savior's lips in the Sermon on the Mount it must have seemed incredibly odd to His hearers; even after the lapse of nineteen centuries it still seems strange. Yet there is no mistaking Christ's meaning, for He then proceeded to reiterate it with unequivocal clarity.

"You have heard," He continued, "that it was said, 'Thou shalt love thy neighbor, and shalt hate thy enemy.' But I say to you, love your enemies, do good to those who hate you, and pray for those who persecute and calumniate you, so that you may be children of your Father in heaven, who makes his sun to rise on the good and the evil, and sends rain on the just and the unjust. For if you love those who love you, what reward shall you have? Do not even the publicans do that? And if you salute your brethren only, what are you doing more than others? Do not even the Gentiles do that? You therefore are to be perfect, even as your heavenly Father is perfect."

This is not easy to do. It goes against the grain of our fallen human nature which clamors for vengeance and returns blow for blow and hate for hatred. But it is only in proportion as we go against the grain of the old Adam and rise above the instinctive urge for vengeance that we are worthy to be called followers of Christ. It is the unfailing mark of a true Christian.

We love a person by wishing him well, desiring his eternal salvation and by a willingness to help him achieve it. This is true and effective love; it is love not "in word or in tongue," as St. John says, "but in deed and in truth." How can anyone prove his love more effectively than by striving to help an individual achieve the greatest values in life and in eternity? By smothering our resentment, choking the instinctive clamor for vengeance, crowding back the hatred, and reaching out a hand to a brother in need, we demonstrate our love for him most authentically. Back of his scowling countenance we see the lineaments of the face of Christ and we seek to free the divine image within him from the fetters of hatred and sin. Surely that is love "in deed and in truth."

Lincoln's Example

Love is the best weapon with which to conquer one's enemies. Few, if any, of our statesmen perceived this truth so clearly as Lincoln. At a dinner in Washington he spoke kindly of some of the Confederates.

"I am surprised, Mr. President," remarked an elderly lady, "to hear you speak so kindly of our enemies. I should think you would seek to destroy them instead of trying to love them."

"But don't I destroy them as enemies," replied Lincoln, "when I make them our friends?"

Such a procedure is not only good Christianity but good statesmanship as well. How many millions of lives would have been spared if rulers had acted on such a principle and how much greater would be the ethical progress of mankind today.

Love Doesn't
Strike Back

One of the noblest Christian leaders of war-ridden Japan was Toyohiko Kagawa. An apostle of social justice, a champion of the rights of the poor and lowly, a pleader for peace amidst the raucous shouts of the Nipponese for war, Kagawa sought to put into daily practice the law of love.

He shared his little hut and his meager food with a homeless beggar. In that shack and in the jail cells into which he was repeatedly thrown for agitating for a living wage for workers, he wrote many of his inspiring books.

Knowing that Kagawa had a few coins in his pocket, a notorious bully accosted him.

"Give me your money," he threatened, "or I'll beat you up."

"No, I won't give it to you," he replied, "for you'll use it to get drunk."

Whereupon the bully rained blow after blow upon him, knocking out several of his front teeth and causing blood to stream from his lips. But Kagawa did not strike back. The law of love embraced even one's enemy and Kagawa did not hesitate to obey it—cost what it may. Love had clothed him with a coat of mail.

Terror-stricken at the sight of the man who made no attempt to defend himself, who did not hit back, the bully fled in dismay. There is something deep down in the heart of man that crumples at the sight of a person who innocent, defenseless and unafraid bears the buffetings and blows heaped upon him without striking back. Physical force falls on its knees in awe when confronted with the moral might of the naked human soul.

The power of an unselfish love has made Toyohiko Kagawa one of the most intrepid souls in Japan—a lion-hearted warrior battling for the rights of the toiling masses and the inarticulate poor, and using only the "feeble" weapons of kindness, sympathy and love.

Another remarkable example of love for one's enemy, reported by Arnold Lunn, was given by a priest during the Civil War in Spain. At Saragossa the communists were leading a group of priests and brothers to a place outside the city where they were to be shot.

Turning to his Red captor, an elderly priest said, "Will you please cut these ropes from my hands that I may bless you?"

"Yes," sneered the communist, "I'll cut them off you all right." Then he seized his sword and hacked off the priest's hands.

Raising those bleeding stumps aloft and tracing with them the Sign of the Cross, the priest said slowly, "God . . . God . . . forgive you, and bless you, and love you . . . as I do!"

Probably no more striking fulfillment of Christ's command to love your enemies and to pray for those who persecute you was given since Jesus, dying on the Cross, raised His eyes to heaven and prayed for His executioners, saying, "Father, forgive them for they know not what they do."

Love Washes Out Hatred

One afternoon a lady came into my office, looking discouraged and downcast. "I want," she said, "to live a Christian life and I've tried hard to do so. But I've failed miserably in this matter of loving my enemies. There's a woman who has spread lies about me and has repeatedly sought to injure my character. Hatred and bitterness well up in my mind whenever I think of her. I've tried to smother such feelings but I seem powerless to do so. What can I do?"

"Have you ever tried," I inquired, "to pray for her, earnestly, wholeheartedly and on your knees?"

"No. I thought that would be impossible."

"Try it," I suggested, "particularly whenever the thought of her comes to you. Recall how our Savior, dying on the Cross, not only forgave His enemies but also prayed for them. Follow His example. He will give you the grace and power to do so."

A few weeks later the woman returned. She was a different looking person. A new smile of confidence mantled a face that had been a picture of despondence.

"It was hard at first," she said, "but I stuck with it. To my amazement a feeling of peace and serenity gradually replaced the emotion of hatred. In praying sincerely that God would bless and help her in every way, my hatred has been replaced by love."

The amazing power of love to heal, to strengthen, to unify and integrate, and to uplift was recognized by William James. "Love your enemies," he said, "not simply those who happen not to be your friends, but your enemies, your positive and active enemies." This he prescribed not as an ethical precept but as a psychological principle and a guide to mental serenity, peace and happiness. It begets, he tells us, an emotion so unifying as to obliterate the differences between man and man, and thus strips enmity of the fangs which shoot their poison through the system.

More potent than all the medicine in the doctor's pills and bottles in washing away the green bile of envy, hatred, anger, fear and morbidity from the heart and soul of man is a generous dose of love which embraces even one's enemies. Such is the prescription, not of a moralist, but of a hard-headed psychologist who speaks not from theory but from scientifically verified facts.

Love for Underprivileged and Afflicted

We have developed at some length the duty of loving one's enemies because it is the acid test of Christ's discipleship and the sternest test of every religious person. Our love must go out likewise to the underprivileged, the handicapped and the afflicted. These frequently stand in the greatest need of our love and kindness.

Katherine Drexel of Philadelphia devoted her wealth, talents and tireless efforts to improve the lot of the underprivileged Indians and Negroes in our land. For 65 years she labored among them, bringing to them the tenderness and the love of Christ. Rose Hawthorne Lathrop, the daughter of the noted American novelist, Nathaniel Hawthorne, dedicated her life to care for the most pitiable class of all—the cancerous poor.

In thus serving them, both reached up gentle hands to take the glorious ideal of love of neighbor out of the blue of the skies and weave it into the warp and woof of their daily lives. In a world like ours such persons of undiscourageable good will and unfailing love are, in the words of George Eliot, like "a fine quotation from the Bible . . . in a paragraph of today's newspaper." Their lives show that love is the strongest force in the world.

The practice of love must not be a spasmodic, fitful affair but must be habitual; it must be woven into our character so that it becomes our second nature. It must enter into our spiritual bloodstream and permeate our whole being. Spiritual growth is essentially growth in love: without love all other growth is spurious, cancerous and destructive. We grow tall through stooping often to bring our love to the lowly, the needy, the underprivileged, the handicapped and the afflicted.

A Divine
Paradox

Through a divine paradox the person who loses his life for Christ's sake saves it; so too the person who pours out his love in sacrificial service to others finds that it comes back to him a hundredfold. In obeying the twofold commandment of love we are keeping all the commandments and thus are going *with*, not *against*, the grain of the moral universe. Love keeps a person from getting tangled in the flypaper of his own egotism; it is the best safeguard against excessive concern for health that leads to complexes of fear, anxiety and a fissured personality.

Dr. Karl Menninger, the famous psychiatrist, had given a lecture on mental health and was answering questions from the audience.

"What would you advise a person to do," asked a man, "if he felt that a nervous breakdown was coming on?"

Most people expected him to reply: "Consult a psychiatrist." To their astonishment, he said: "Lock up your house, go across the railway tracks, find someone in need and do something for him."

Yes, concern, solicitude and love for others, especially those in need or affliction, constitute the best brake against the downward slide into pathological preoccupation with oneself. It is to be noted that the safeguard which Dr. Menninger recommended was not an abstract theoretical love, but an intensely practical one that issued in concrete action for a needy person.

"The Greatest of These Is Charity"

In his inspired treatise on love, which he calls charity, in the thirteenth chapter of his first Letter to the Corinthians, the Apostle Paul trumpets with moving eloquence the supremacy of love among all the virtues. "If I have prophecy," he says, "and know all mysteries and all knowledge, and if I have all faith so as to remove mountains, yet do not have charity, I am nothing . . . Charity never fails, whereas prophecies will disappear, and tongues will cease, and knowledge will be destroyed."

Then the Apostle brings his presentation to the following glorious climax: "We see now through a mirror in an obscure manner, but then face to face. Now I know in part, but then I shall know even as I have been known. So there abide faith, hope and charity, these three; but the greatest of these is charity."

In short, love is the master key that fits the lock of every heart; it opens all doors on earth and in heaven. What the sun is to all vegetative life, love is to all human life: the source of its strength, vitality and happiness. What a world of meaning there is in the line with which Dante ends his great work, *The Divine Comedy:* "Love moves the sun in the heavens and all the stars."

Yes, love is the motivating force of the best and noblest deeds of all the human dwellers on this little planet speeding through immeasurable space to its rendezvous with destiny. It is the secret of happiness in this life and in eternity. The Beloved Apostle sums up the whole story in words so simple and so clear: "Beloved, let us love one another, for love is from God. And everyone who loves is born of God and knows God. He who does not love does not know God; for God is love." Between earth and heaven there is but one bridge and that bridge is love.

POINTS TO REMEMBER

1. The second great commandment of the Law is: "Thou shalt love thy neighbor as thyself."

2. By neighbor is meant not only those living near us but every human being and especially those in need.

3. We should love our neighbors because we are all the children of God and are all, therefore, brothers and sisters.

4. By loving our neighbor for the sake of God we bring our brotherly love close to the love which God Himself has for us, and thus achieve a kind of moral identity between Christ and our neighbor.

5. The order in which we should love is: God, ourselves, members of our family, relatives, friends, members of the community, state, nation and the world.

6. Selfishness and anger are root causes of domestic strife and should be avoided as a plague.

7. We can love our enemy by wishing him well, desiring his eternal salvation and by our willingness to help him achieve it.

8. Love washes out fear and contributes mightily to one's own peace of mind and happiness.

9. Solicitude and love for others, especially those in need or affliction, constitute the best brake against downward slide into unhealthy preoccupation with oneself.

10. Love is the master key that fits the lock of every human heart and opens all doors on earth and in heaven.

HOW YOU CAN CHANGE
THE WORLD

"Let your light shine before men."—*Jesus* (*Matthew 5:16*)

"It is better to light one candle than to curse the darkness."—*Chinese Proverb*

On a winter morning in 1933 a young Maryknoll priest, Father James Keller, stepped into the darkened Metropolitan Opera House to see its spacious and handsome interior. He waited in the rear while the manager, Earle Lewis, disappeared down the darkened aisle to turn on the lights. When he reached the stage, the manager lit a match to avoid stumbling over a piece of scenery.

Insignificant as was that tiny light, it was sufficient to penetrate the darkness. If that small flame were multiplied many times, the darkness would be banished. This is precisely what the manager then did. Crossing the stage, he turned on all the switches, flooding the spacious auditorium with brilliant light.

This was the incident which kindled the idea that led Father Keller to found the Christopher movement twelve years later in September 1945. Christopher means a Christ-bearer. The movement seeks to stir the sense of *personal responsibility in each individual and prompt him to do some specific job for the common good.* It endeavors to counteract the impression under which so many people labor today: there are so many powerful organizations in every field that *the individual* is powerless to accomplish anything significant.

Three Basic Truths

The movement focuses attention upon three basic truths.

1. *Every individual is a partaker in the divine.* God has instilled in each a small but precious bit of divine power.

2. *Every light counts.* The world will be changed for the better only in proportion as each person perceives his power to kindle at least one tiny flame and realizes too how much his pinpoint of light is needed.

3. *Each has a mission to fulfill.* This is the truth upon which Jesus laid such increasing emphasis: each individual is to serve as a channel of Christ's light and love to the world.

The movement draws much of its inspiration from the words addressed by Christ to all His followers: "You are the light of the world. A city set on a mountain cannot be hidden. Neither do men light a lamp and put it under the measure, but upon the lamp-stand, so as to give light to all in the house. Even so let your light shine before men in order that they may see your good works and give glory to your Father in heaven."

It is to be noted here that Christ stresses *works* and not mere *words.* While we tend to judge ourselves by our good intentions, others judge us by our deeds. They don't rate very high the noble plans that never get off the launching pad. They appreciate our high and holy principles only when we render them incarnate in good works.

Religion
in Action

In a small town in California a gasoline service station manager gave a part time job to a young Negro studying to be a teacher. He needed it to help support his wife and himself until he got his degree. But soon some customers began to complain: they wanted to buy gasoline only from white men. The manager was about to fire the boy when a woman customer learned of the situation.

"How many customers will you lose," she asked, "if you stand by this fellow?"

"About 18. Maybe 20."

"If I get you 20 new customers, will you keep him on?"

"You bet I will."

In a few days this aroused woman brought not only the required 20 new customers but five more for good measure. The woman was a Christopher and she was contributing her mite toward helping to change her tiny bit of the world into a better place to live. The incident is typical of what is taking place in thousands of communities because of the inspiration and practical suggestions provided by the Christopher movement.

It has no organization beyond its central headquarters at 16 East 48th Street, New York 17, N.Y. It has no chapters, no meetings, no memberships, no dues and no fund-raising drives. Yet it stimulates millions of people in all walks of life to take a personal initiative in support of worthy causes through the following means: 1) Monthly *Christopher Notes* which are sent free to 1,250,000 persons; 2) 14 Christopher paperback books which are in circulation here and overseas; 3) 106 daily newspapers carrying a syndicated Christopher column; 4) 306 television stations which present a half-hour Christopher program once a week. 5) 811 radio stations broadcasting a fifteen-minute weekly program, and 6) 1725 radio stations broadcasting a one-minute Christopher thought each day.

In a small town in Idaho a Christopher housewife and mother of four children was appalled at the small number of people who turned out to vote. She decided to do something to stimulate more voters to use their precious privilege. She enlisted a small group of helpers, which encountered the usual apathy and difficulties. But they worked on, year after year, and finally got the desired results.

"Four years ago," she related, "only 200 people turned out to vote. At the election two years later we got out 400. We kept hammering away and at the last election we got out the record-breaking total of 1000!"

Two
Important Truths

In the Italian elections of 1948 the communist party was so well organized, formidable and active that it appeared almost certain to win the majority of offices. Philip Cancellieri, a barber in Southampton, Long Island, decided to write to his relatives in St. Catherine, Sicily, describing his happy life here. Next he wrote to his wife's relatives. Then he got his son, a doctor, and his daughter, a dietician, to write. He appealed to newspaper editors and even to President Truman to help enlist the nation.

The steady trickle of letters gradually swelled into a mighty torrent. Millions of letters from people of Italian descent in the U.S.A. streamed into the homes of relatives in the old country encouraging them to vote against communist tyranny. They resulted in a democratic victory which heartened all Europe.

One man helped to start that flood because he lifted himself out of his own narrow, selfish cubicle into the larger world with all its tremendous and breathtaking potentialities. It was an affirmation of two important truths: 1) *The individual does count.* 2) *The greatest achievements begin with the thought and action of a single person.*

How apt are the words of Shakespeare:

> How far that little candle throws his beams!
> So shines a good deed in a naughty world.

Constructive Action
Needed

Discouraging mere criticism and condemnation as wasteful and ineffective, Christophers stress the positive approach: prompt, vigorous and constructive action. They have been profoundly influenced by the words of the great Apostle to the Gentiles: *"Be not overcome by evil but overcome evil by good."* This important truth shines forth in the motto of the whole movement: "It is better to light one candle than to curse the darkness." Millions are ready to find fault, but few are willing to take constructive action to correct the evil.

"The champions of a Christian order of society," observes Dr. J. Messner, "are at a disadvantage because they do not offer *concrete positive pictures* of what they aim at. They remain too much on the defensive, in a negative attitude, condemning the state of things as well as revolutionary movements for changing it."

Good ideas bear no fruit until they are translated into action. Too many people let their good intentions die stillborn because they lack the initiative to make them realities through determined and resolute action. Stressing the need for action instead of mere talk, President Abraham Lincoln wrote to Major General David Hunter on December 31, 1861: "He who does *something* at the head of one regiment will eclipse him who does *nothing* at the head of a hundred."

Do noble deeds, not dream them all day long,
And so make life, death and the hereafter one grand sweet song.

A pan of dough remains just that until a cake of yeast is added; the latter penetrates it and raises every tiny bit of its mass. With the grace of God you can be a particle of divine yeast, penetrating the mass of society in your neighborhood and leavening every member. This is what Jesus means when He says, "Let your light shine before men that they may see your good works and give glory to your Father in heaven."

Your light and your good works are distinctive of you and different from all others. Each one is endowed with a personality so unique as to have no double either in the long past history of the race or in the future, no matter how far it may stretch. Just as there are no two leaves, no two blades of grass identically alike, so neither are there any two personalities exactly the same. In consequence there is a contribution to society which only you can make.

"No matter who you are," says Father Keller, "or what you are, or where you may be, you can do something to change the world for the better. You, as an individual, are important. You count!" The truth of these words is illustrated in the following dramatic incident.

What Can I Do?

When Madame Oksana Kasenkina jumped from the third floor of the Russian consulate in New York on August 12, 1948, the crash of her body on the pavement, like the shots fired at Concord, was heard around the world. Back of that spectacular leap for freedom is the story of Louise McKeon, a young housewife of Ridgefield, Connecticut, who started the fateful chain of events. A friend of Father Keller, she had become convinced that ordinary people by selfless acts can bring about extraordinary changes in the world.

"But what can I do?" Louise had asked Father Keller only months before. "A busy housewife, buried in Connecticut, can't change the world." In "Whose Business Was It?" in The Reader's Digest, Fulton Oursler describes the chain reaction which she triggered. Here, in condensed form, are its highlights.

"I don't care if you are buried in Alaska," replied the Maryknoll priest. "Drop that feeling of personal futility and just try something sometime. When you do, you won't be alone. The good Lord will be right there helping you."

On Sunday, August 8, 1948, Louise, her husband Dan and their six children had just returned from Mass and were seated around the breakfast table at their farm home. The Sunday newspapers carried the story of the sensational kidnaping of Madame Kasenkina by Soviet agents. They were intent upon sending back to Russia, perhaps for liquidation, this woman who wanted to become an American citizen.

That news story was being read that same Sunday by millions of other Americans, but it didn't occur to any of them to do something about it. Louise realized that for her the "sometime" spoken of by Father Keller had arrived.

"Why don't we do something about it?" she asked.

"But," replied Dan, "what can you or I possibly do in a case like this? Only the State Department can deal with Soviet Russia."

"Just the same, I am going to do *something!*" Louise blazed.

Looking up from his paper, Dan saw a glow of dedication on his wife's face, a flame of fierce determination in her eyes.

"All right, darling, I'm with you," he said. "Your brother Pete is coming up from New York today. He's a lawyer, and we'll talk to him."

Whose Business Is It?

Peter W. Hoguet had just recently passed the state bar examinations. He too was indignant over the action of the Russians, but he didn't see that there was anything he could do.

"But no American could kidnap another American and get away with it, could he?" argued Louise. "Are Russians allowed to break our laws?"

"Sis," he explained, "this isn't our business."

"Well, if it's not our business," retorted Louise, "whose business it it?"

Those words struck home. They continued to echo in Peter's mind as he rode back to Manhattan Monday evening. Peter enlisted the co-operation of Christopher Emmet of Common Cause, Inc., and the two of them applied to Justice Samuel Dickstein of the New York Supreme Court for a writ of *habeas corpus.* Older than Magna Carta, this principle asserts the right of any citizen, convinced that another is illegally detained, to bring that person into a court where the facts can be ascertained.

So well reasoned were Peter's arguments that he secured the precious writ, commanding Jacob M. Lomakin, Soviet Consul General, to be in Manhattan Supreme Court at Foley Square at

ten o'clock the following morning and to have with him "the
body of Oksana Stepanovna Kasenkina by you detained and imprisoned, as it is said."

Peter served the writ on the elusive Lomakin. Not knowing
that the Soviet ship on which Madame Kasenkina was to be
shanghaied was to sail at midnight of this same Thursday, the
court granted a delay. Imprisoned in her room, Madame heard
over the radio the exciting news of the efforts being made to
rescue her. The fate of a solitary stranger evidently meant something in America.

She saw the crowds swarming around the consulate. Two
floors below she spied a telephone line strung across the court.
It was now or never. Aiming her body at that wire, she jumped.
Though it nearly severed her hand, the wire broke her fall and
saved her life. The news of her spectacular leap for freedom
spread like lightning around the world, and brought inspiration
and hope to oppressed people everywhere.

The incident provides a striking and dramatic demonstration
of the truth of Louise McKeon's belief that *every individual can
help to change the world if he will be but put his spiritual ideals
into action.* By weaving the shining ideals and principles of
religious faith into the fabric of society, the humblest individual
can accomplish something worth while. Indeed he may even
set in action a chain of events that will affect the lives of uncounted millions.

Hidden Potentialities
in Every Soul

Christ emphasized the importance of the individual and the
dignity and worth of his soul in the memorable words: "What
does it profit a man if he gain the whole world, but suffer the
loss of his own soul? Or what will a man give in exchange for
his soul?" Place on one side of the scales a single soul and on the
other side put all the gold, silver, diamonds, pearls and riches of

of the world. That one soul will outweigh in value all the wealth of the universe.

This truth will help each individual to realize that he is a being of supreme worth and that he counts where it is most important, namely, in the eyes of God. Hence he must never feel helpless or impotent when he looks at society with its numerous organizations, corporations, trusts, cartels and institutions. All these have been created by society to minister to the individual, just as the state itself has been established to serve him and promote his welfare.

In the soul of the humblest individual there are potentialities that have scarcely been scratched. This was demonstrated in 1914 when Sir Ernest Shackleton placed a "want ad" in a London newspaper, advertising an expedition he was about to lead into the Antarctic. The ad read:

> Men wanted for hazardous journey—small wages, bitter cold, long months of complete darkness, constant danger, safe return doubtful. Honor and recognition in case of success.

Though the ad would seem so forbidding as to deter almost everyone, more than 5,000 men applied! Of these, 28 were chosen, and they learned that the ad was not exaggerating when it represented the journey as "hazardous." Their ship, the "Endurance," was crushed by tons of ice, forcing the crew to spend 21 months on drifting ice floes, with three small boats providing the only hope of a return to civilization.

Despite piercing bitter cold, howling gales and blizzards, shortage of provisions and terrifying experiences in the vast Antarctic wastes, all 28 survived. They reached home safe and sound, two years after they had started their perilous adventure. Coming from prosaic walks of life, these brave men probably had but the vaguest idea of the extraordinary power hidden within them. Only a great and daring challenge could bring it out.

Besides the 5000 men who applied for the jobs, there were doubtless hundreds of thousands of other readers who felt at least momentarily the ad's challenge. It made many of them yearn for the opportunity to prove their mettle and make a worthwhile contribution to life, even at the cost of hardship and suffering. In the depths of every human soul God has put a bit of potential greatness. Without any formidable challenge, however, it lies dormant and the individual never achieves the greatness and the heroism of which he is capable.

This is the tragedy of many lives. It can be avoided by espousing great and difficult causes, fighting against overwhelming odds for victory. Even if they lose the battle, they achieve greatness.

It is not in the power of mortals to command success, but they can fight with such courage, gallantry and daring as to deserve it. That is what counts with God, who is able to transmute defeat into victory. "He who loses his life," says Jesus, "for my sake and for the gospel's sake will save it." It is not the victory, but the cause for which one battles that merits the reward.

What One Woman Accomplished

Here is the story of a housewife, the mother of two children, who battled for one of the noblest causes: the right of the unorganized poor for a decent living wage. She believes that spiritual and religious ideals should not be kept in moth balls but should be put to work to leaven society and to promote social justice. Her achievement shows what one woman can do. In "The Lady and the Gangsters" in *The Reader's Digest*, Lester Velie tells the inspiring story. Here are its highlights in condensed form.

Min Lurye Matheson is a regional manager of the International Ladies' Garment Workers Union (ILGWU) in Wilkes-Barre, Pennsylvania. The wives and daughters of idle miners were paid as little as $16 weekly for sewing work. Min espoused their cause. She would secure decent wages by unionizing them. This pitted her against the terror and power of the big underworld of racketeers and gangsters.

Her brother Will had given up his $150-a-week job as presser to join up as an $80-a-week union organizer. His first assignment was to captain a picket line blockading a shop protected by a partner of Albert Anastasia of Murder, Inc. The next day he was jammed into a telephone booth by two gangsters who stabbed him to death.

"Tell your boss," the girl pickets were told, "to lay off our union. Or she'll get what her brother got."

"To live by permission of goons," replied Min over the radio, "is worse than death. Hoodlums, I don't scare easily."

At the risk of her life, Min stayed on the job and signed up all but a few of the 150 garment factories in her area, including all the once "protected" shops. The $16-a-week victims of sweatshops are now averaging $65 for a 35-hour week in an industry that has become so stabilized it is the economic backbone of many Pennsylvania communities.

Here was a battle in which the hazards were as great as those which faced the members of Shackleton's expedition in the Antarctic. In grateful recognition of Min's pluck and valor Wilkes-Barre sent her to Washington to speak for the city before a Senate committee probing distress areas. Because one woman believed strongly enough in overcoming evil by good, a new way of life has opened up for thousands of people in that area.

What One Man Can Do

This is an era of multi-megaton atomic weapons and multi-billion-dollar military budgets administered by a Pentagon of incredible size. As a consequence many people have the depressing conviction that there is nothing the ordinary citizen can do to change the course of events. He feels dwarfed and helpless in the presence of the vast complex organizations which characterize our era.

It is fortunate that there are some exceptions: individuals who still believe they can change the world and help shape history, at least within their own domain. One such individual is Mr. W. O. Biernacki-Poray, a Polish-born architect, of Montclair, New Jersey. He endeavored to translate into the realities of the twentieth century the age-old command of Christ: "Let the little children come unto me, and do not hinder them, for of such is the kingdom of God." In February 1958, his three-year-old daughter Christina was stricken with a mysterious virus infection.

"The vigil of that agonizing night," he said, "brought to a focus the real need for a practical way to help the sick children of countries which, like my native Poland, have grossly inadequate medical facilities. Within three days Christina was on her way to recovery. But meanwhile I had formulated the idea of building in Poland a medical center for children."

Poland lost six million people during World War II and another eleven million through post-war boundary reshuffling. Her economy is badly crippled and her medical facilities are pitifully inadequate. With this picture in his mind Mr. Biernacki-Poray went to Washington to "sell" his proposal to government officials. He encountered the customary obstacles and even resistance from officials already burdened with many pressing problems.

But this architect was not easily discouraged. He kept calling at office after office until he had secured pledges of co-operation from the State Department, the Polish government, CARE, Senators Humphrey and Javits, Representative Zablocki, and John Richardson, Jr., who had previously done a superb job in getting medical supplies for Poland. Struggling through a maze of difficulties, he kept pushing his project until on June 17, 1960, the Mutual Securities Appropriations Bill was amended to permit the expenditure of $3,500,000 for the American Research Hospital for Children.

Designed by Mr. Biernacki-Poray and his staff, all donating their services, the 400-bed structure incorporates the latest features for medical facilities. It is being erected on a high plateau overlooking the city of Krakow, whose university is the oldest medical center in Europe.

Scheduled for completion in 1964, the hospital will have a stimulating effect on standards of medical practice throughout the Middle and East European countries. Scarcely less important, *it will stand as an affirmation to people everywhere that individual initiative and dedication can still accomplish wonders,* despite the baffling complexities of the era in which we live. On its cornerstone might well be inscribed: "What One Man Can Do."

A Pioneer
in Many Fields

Whenever an individual struggles with courage, determination and persistence to weave the ethical ideals of Christ into the fabric of society instead of allowing them to remain as mere abstractions, he never fails to change his community for the better. Whether he knows it or not, he is a Christopher, bearing something of the light and love of Christ into the hearts and minds of people, and enabling them to share in the more abundant life Jesus came on earth to bring. This is vividly illustrated in the life of Jane Addams. The inspiring story is brilliantly told by Karl Detzer in "What We Owe to Jane Addams of Hull House" in *The Reader's Digest.* Here in condensed form are its highlights.

Born of well-to-do parents in 1860, Jane got her first glimpse of a slum area when, as a child of seven, she was riding in the family carriage through the mean back streets of Freeport, Illinois.

"When I'm grown up," she said, "I'm going to have a big house, but I don't want it to be near other pretty houses. I'm going to live right next door to poor folks, and invite them in." Little did she then realize how literally her prophecy was to be fulfilled.

From infancy Jane suffered from a slight curvature of the spine that twisted her head to one side. Before it was corrected by surgery, it gave to the young girl a strange pigeon-toed gait. This may have helped to deepen her sympathy for the poor, the underprivileged and the afflicted, which was to characterize her whole subsequent career.

On a trip through Europe Jane was more impressed by the misery and poverty in which so many people lived than by its famous museums and historic relics. She spent some time at Toynbee Hall in London, the world's first social settlement. Deeply stirred by what she saw, Jane returned to Chicago to set up a similar establishment.

Walking through the slum section of Chicago's west side, she spied the "big house" of her childhood dreams. A once-stately mansion erected in 1856 by a man named Hull, it was surrounded by dirty, overcrowded shacks. Newly arrived Italian, Polish, Greek, German and Lithuanian immigrants swarmed in the ramshackle area. Few homes had running water, the streets were deep with mud, the garbage was rarely collected, and a horrible stench pervaded the area.

Jane Addams Finds Her Clients

Here Jane settled, and here she found her clients and her life work. Because of dirt, ignorance and malnutrition babies were dying by the hundreds. Tuberculosis was rampant, milk was tainted, sanitation was only a word in the dictionary. Jane brought the babies into her home for baths and then went out to the tenements to fix decent places for them to sleep.

Within a year 20 volunteers joined her. Working 12-hour days at Hull House, she still found time to tell her story wherever she could find an audience. After one of her talks a wealthy property owner approached her.

"Miss Addams," he asked, "is there anything I might do to help?"

"Yes," she replied, looking him straight in the eye. "You own several filthy firetraps, occupied by prostitutes. Tear down the shacks and turn the lots into playgrounds."

Stung to the quick, the man stormed out of the hall. But her words haunted him. A few weeks later he gave her the lots. On May 1, 1892, Jane Addams opened the first free public playground in Chicago.

Next Jane turned her attention to the shocking conditions in factories where women and children were working—children for four cents an hour. Her demand for factory safety laws and prohibition of child labor provoked a storm of protests from employers, slum parents and venal politicians. A prominent factory owner called on her.

"If you'll stop this agitation," he said, "I'll give you $50,000 for the support of your Hull House work."

"Not for $50,000,000," replied Jane, "will I call off this campaign. Child labor must stop. Laws must be enacted to protect the lives of women workers in these horrible sweatshops. There can be no compromise on either of these two demands."

A Warrior
for Peace

Through her efforts the first factory safety laws in Illinois were enacted, and the start was made on the abolition of child labor throughout the country. She had a profound concern for children, and was instrumental in the establishment of a juvenile court—the first of its kind in the world.

Miss Addams was particularly proud of her appointment as

garbage collector, for it enabled her to eliminate some of the chief sources of disease. From six o'clock in the morning, Jane followed the collectors on their smelly rounds, and gradually got the nine garbage wagons in the ward increased to 17. Soon the whole sprawling metropolis was cleanliness-conscious, and gave itself its first thorough housecleaning.

An unflinching opponent of war as an instrument for settling disputes, Miss Addams voiced her sentiments at every opportunity. This brought down upon her severe criticism from "patriotic societies" and in one of its conventions the American Legion booed her name. But scholars and statesmen of vision throughout the world knew that she was right, and the Nobel Peace Prize for 1931 was conferred jointly upon her and Dr. Nicholas Murray Butler, president of Columbia University.

I heard her address the students and faculty at the University of Illinois on the subject of peace in the early thirties. Speaking simply and clearly, without notes, she held the vast audience enraptured. "War settles nothing," she said, "and after all the destruction and bloodshed are over, reason must resume its task of solving the controversy according to the principles of right and justice."

After two world wars most of humanity has finally learned the lesson she strove so valiantly a generation ago to teach. Tardily and gropingly the United Nations Organization is seeking to weave her principles into the practice of all civilized people.

Jane Addams was a pioneer in racial integration. She appointed a Negro as the first doctor at Hull House. Thither she brought Negroes both as guests and residents, placing them at her dinner table. Confronted with such an unusual spectacle some visitors left in anger. But Jane did not back down. She lived to see most of the forlorn causes for which she battled so valiantly win out.

Sanitary codes, day nurseries, public playgrounds became universal; her cherished child-labor laws were enacted in most states, and safeguards established for both men and women in industry. Slum clearance has become an established policy in all large cities, and woman suffrage, for which she pioneered, has become a reality not only in the U.S.A. but also in many other lands.

A True Christopher

Visitors from all parts of the world came to see her; legislators, scholars, social workers, statesmen and presidents sought her counsel. Woodrow Wilson said he was "strengthened" by her aid, and Theodore Roosevelt named her "America's most useful citizen." When Jane Addams died on May 21, 1935, the whole world paid her honor. Thousands knelt in the streets and wept as they bade farewell to the frail kindly little woman who had taken them all to her heart.

Can anyone look at her life and fail to see the secret of its greatness? If there is one lesson more than any other which her life teaches, it is this: *Greatness lies not in paying lip-service to the noble ethical, spiritual and religious ideals taught by Jesus, but in putting them into practice in daily life.*

Often Jane Addams must have reflected upon the words of Christ: "Amen, I say to you, as long as you did it for one of these, the least of my brethren, you did it for me . . . Whoever wishes to become great among you shall be your servant." No greater tribute can be paid to Jane Addams—or to any man or woman—than to say: "She was a Christopher, and carried the light and life and love of Christ to the people of her day. She helped to make the world a better place in which to live."

POINTS TO REMEMBER

1. God has instilled in each person a small but precious bit of divine power.

2. The world will be changed for the better only in proportion as each person does his part to kindle at least one tiny flame.

3. Every individual must serve as a channel of Christ's light and love to the world.

4. The greatest achievements begin with the thought and action of a single person.

5. It is better to light one candle than to curse the darkness.

6. In spite of the complexity of modern life individual initiative and dedication can still accomplish wonders.

7. Every person who bears something of the light and love of Christ to others is a Christopher.

8. Greatness consists in putting spiritual ideals into daily practice.

13.

HOW TO ACHIEVE
SPIRITUAL SERENITY

"Why are you fearful, O you of little faith?"—*Jesus*
(*Matthew 8:26*)

"Peace I leave with you, my peace I give to you;
not as the world gives do I give to you."—*Jesus*
(*John 14:27*)

In the last fifty years two world wars, two depressions and
a half dozen recessions have shaken our world to its very foundations and banished the complacency, confidence and easy-
going self-assurance which had so long characterized our nation.
These memories of suffering and disaster still haunt us and, with
the threat of a thermonuclear war hanging like the sword of
Damocles over our worried heads, we can find no relief. We are
tense, nervous, jittery, scared stiff at the thought of multimega-
ton bombs blasting our cities, reducing civilization to shambles
and converting our planet into a vast cemetery.

These tensions are rendered more acute by the far-reaching
changes which, like tornadoes, have swept across our land, up-
rooting people and hurling them like specks of dust into new
industries and communities in which they are strangers to one
another. Here they live like dwellers in a tower of Babel, friendless and forlorn. Gone are the social sanctions of the old neighborhood where they lived among friends and relatives. *Rootlessness* and *loneliness* are the two outstanding characteristics of
man today.

"We moved to Chicago from a little town in Texas," said a

young wife, "when Jim's company transferred him to the home office. Back home we knew everyone. Among the millions of people here we feel friendless and alone. We don't know a soul in our apartment building, and no one even bids us the time of day. It's like living in a foreign land, and it's getting on our nerves."

Is it any wonder then that people are jittery, that fear stalks our streets and anxiety throbs in the hearts of millions, making their waking hours a fever and filling their intermittent sleep with nightmares? Has religion any message for this "shook-up" generation? What can it do to bring peace of mind and serenity to people sick with fear and anxiety?

Religion has a message of the utmost consequence. It penetrates to the very heart of the matter. It comes to grips with the human soul wherein all hope of tranquility lies. It supplies us with the profound truths by which we can conquer our fears and acquire that spiritual serenity without which life is little more than a series of plagues and a tortured nightmare. What depth is to the ocean, roots to the tree, peace to the home and rest to the body, serenity is to the mind. It is a great spiritual resource which cushions the jars and jolts of life and makes smooth our voyage.

Millions seek tranquility through the increasing use of alcohol, barbiturates, Miltowns and other so-called tranquilizers. These at best, however, yield but temporary relief and after their effect wears off, the individual is confronted with the same chronic tensions and fears, often in more acute form. Others haunt the offices of doctors, psychiatrists and psychoanalysts; they may gain some temporary relief from their obsessive anxieties but seldom a permanent cure if the malady is deep-rooted and the patients are in the second half of their lives. We shall cite the testimony of psychotherapists themselves on this point.

"I haunted the offices of psychiatrists seeking peace of mind," related a middle-aged businessman, "but I didn't find it till I consulted my pastor."

"What did he tell you?" I asked.

" 'Stop playing around with other women. Be true to your marriage vows.' I followed his prescription, and it has worked like magic."

Since peace of mind and spiritual serenity have their roots in the spiritual realm, it follows that the remedies for disorders in this domain must be basically spiritual. This does not minimize or disparage in the slightest the immense and invaluable service which psychiatrists render to patients afflicted with various mental ills. It simply recognizes the large number of cases wherein the loss of peace of mind and serenity is traceable basically to spiritual maladies and where in consequence the remedies must be essentially spiritual in character.

Contentment stems not from external things: drugs, potions, riches, fame or high position. It is found *within* or not at all. It is rooted in the heart at peace with God and man. Well does Shakespeare portray Henry VI as saying:

> My crown is in my heart, not on my head;
> Not decked with diamonds and Indian stones,
> Nor to be seen: my crown is call'd content;
> A crown it is that seldom kings enjoy.

Faith in God

The first great truth which religion offers for our peace of mind and serenity is: *Have a profound and unshakeable faith in God*, the Ruler of the universe and the Creator of mankind. He is the infinite and omnipotent Being who has fashioned billions of planets, stars and galaxies and sent them coursing in their appointed orbits through the immeasurable universe. In the last analysis we all rest in the palm of His mighty hand. No external force can really hurt us. The human soul is indestructible and immortal: it will survive in all its power, beauty and goodness even though the heavens fall and the body returns to the dust from which it came.

. . . And behind the dim unknown,
Standeth God within the shadow, keeping watch above His own.

How vividly and dramatically Jesus drove this basic truth
home to His disciples! One day He was riding with them in
a boat on the Sea of Galilee when suddenly a storm arose. The
winds whipped the sea into a fury: tumultuous waves threatened
at any moment to capsize the boat. The Savior was resting,
asleep, in the rear of the vessel. Unable any longer to restrain
their fear, the disciples awakened Jesus.

"Lord, save us!" they pleaded. "We are perishing!"

"Why are you fearful," asked Jesus, "O you of *little* faith?"

Then He extended His hands over the sea and rebuked the
winds.

"Peace," He said, "be still!"

Immediately there came a great calm.

"What manner of man is this," exclaimed the disciples, "that
even the winds and the sea obey Him?"

The Power
of Faith

What a lesson for all of us! Jesus teaches us that if we but
believe and *trust* in Him, nothing can hurt us. Here is revealed
the amazing power of faith: it can move mountains. "All things
whatsoever you shall ask in prayer," says Jesus, "*believing*, you
shall receive . . . If thou canst believe, all things are possible
to him that *believeth* . . . Amen, amen I say to you, he that
believeth in me, the works that I do, he also shall do; and greater
than these shall he do."

Faith in God bestows serenity upon a person even in the
midst of tribulation and suffering. Robert Louis Stevenson was
plagued with a multitude of afflictions: sciatica, hemorrhage
and ophthalmia which threatened him with permanent loss of
vision. At times, cramps in both arms prevented him from
writing.

"I suppose," remarked his wife cynically, "you will say as usual that things have fallen out for the best, if only we look at them in the right way."

"Why now," he replied, smiling, "it's odd you should say that, for that's exactly what I have been thinking. What I needed was a rest, and this has forced me into it."

When the cramp left his right arm, he took up his pen and wrote articles so full of courage and valor that something of their gallantry rubs off on the minds of all his readers even to this day.

It was Job's invincible trust in God that enabled him not only to bear without complaint the series of afflictions which fell like rain upon him but also to bid defiance even to death itself. "Though he slay me," he cries, "yet will I trust in him." What nobler profession of indomitable faith can be found in all the pages of Holy Writ?

Faith in God implies belief in His Providential love and care of His creatures. As a father provides for the support and welfare of the members of his family, so Almighty God provides for the needs of His children. "All events that take place in this world," points out St. Thomas Aquinas, "even those apparently fortuitous or casual, are comprehended in the order of divine Providence."

His infinite power is able to transmute apparent defeat into glorious victory. By His Resurrection Jesus transformed the cross from a symbol of shame and defeat into an emblem of honor and triumph. This too He can do with any apparent tragedy that befalls His children.

"Bob was getting impossible to live with," the wife of a sales manager related, "when he was averaging $2,000 a month. He was arbitrary, inconsiderate and despotic at home, and domineering at the office. When the depression came and the sales dropped to near the vanishing point, he changed his tune. Before he had had no time for God or religion. Now he gets down on his knees and really prays. He's a different man. His old kindness has returned and he realizes there are things infinitely more important than money. That depression for Bob and our family was a blessing in disguise."

> God moves in a mysterious way
> His wonders to perform;
> He plants His footsteps in the sea
> And rides upon the storm.

God Dwells
Within Us

Walking through Athens, the Apostle Paul saw an altar bearing the inscription, "To the Unknown God." It afforded him an excellent opportunity to tell the Athenians about the true God. To a crowd in the Areopagus the Apostle said: "What therefore you worship in ignorance, that I proclaim to you. God, who made the world and all that is in it, since He is Lord of heaven and earth . . . it is He who gives to all men life and breath and all things."

Then he astonished them by telling them that God is not distant from them. "In him," said St. Paul, "we live and move and have our being." Thus God dwells in the very heart of those who love and serve Him. He is their strength in time of weakness, their aid in time of danger and affliction.

This is the note he sounds again in his letter to the Philippians: "The Lord is near. Have no anxiety, but in every prayer and supplication with thanksgiving let your petitions be made known to God. And may the peace of God which surpasses all understanding guard your hearts and your minds in Christ Jesus." Then a few verses later he utters the great truth: "I can do all things in Him who strengthens me." Here is the mighty truth of God's unfailing Providence, which is sufficient to banish fear from the heart of every sincere Christian.

What gives these words of St. Paul special significance is the fact that he wrote them from his gloomy prison cell in Rome. Instead of being downcast and depressed in his dark Mamertine dungeon, he sings a song of joy, exulting over "the peace that surpasses all understanding," with which God had filled his soul. Instead of feeling weak and helpless, he is conscious of his ability to do all things through the power of God *dwelling within him.*

"I Have Kept the Faith"

The great Apostle not only preached a joyous confidence in God but also practiced it in season and out of season. He suffered shipwreck, scourgings, stonings, beatings, imprisonment and martyrdom, but none of these impaired in the slightest his robust faith and stout-hearted trust in his Lord and Redeemer. On the contrary, they seem to have increased both. As his end drew near, the crescendo of his exultant confidence in God echoed in the last words written in his prison cell.

"I am already being poured out in sacrifice," he writes, "and the time of my deliverance is at hand. I have fought the good fight, I have finished the course, *I have kept the faith.*" He turns now with exuberant and boundless confidence to the divine Redeemer whose name he has carried afar unto the Gentiles. "For the rest," he continues, "there is laid up for me a crown of justice, which the Lord, the just judge, will give to me in that day . . . The Lord will deliver me from every work of evil, and will preserve me for his heavenly kingdom; to whom be the glory forever and ever. Amen."

This is the invincible faith and the unconquerable trust in God and in His Providence that will stand like a mighty Rock of Gibraltar, against which the tempests and tumults of earthly vicissitudes will beat in vain. More potent than all the medicines in the pharmacopoeia of all the druggists and all the therapeutic techniques of all the psychiatrists in banishing obsessive fear and brooding anxiety are simple faith and trust in God.

"I'm Ruined"

A man in his late fifties called at my office one rainy autumn day. There was a dazed look in his eyes, and his hands were trembling. He was so jittery and upset that he could scarcely talk.

"I'm ruined," he burst out, "after a lifetime of work. I invested virtually all my savings in some mining stock that I was assured was the very best buy on the market. It was expected to double in value in the next five years. Now I learn that the ore is of such poor quality that it is not worth the cost of mining. It means that $50,000 has gone down the drain.

"I'm too old to start over again. The bottom has dropped out, and I've been going around in circles. I haven't the courage to break the news to my wife. It will crush her."

He paused. His voice broke and tears filled his eyes. He was the picture of gloom and despair.

"Let us see," I said, "what's left. You have a good job. You own your home. Your three children are married and on their own. You have your health and your good name. You've made a mistake in judging the earning power of that stock. But it was an honest mistake, such as thousands of others have made. You've committed no crime.

"Your wife loves you and she will stick with you. Confide in her and see what retrenchments are in order. You won't starve. Time, patience and persevering work will put you back on your feet again."

"What About Your Faith in God?"

"But the problem," I continued, "is deeper than mere economics. It's basically a spiritual one. What about your faith in God? As long as you have God with you, in your heart and mind, standing by you and willing to help you if you but turn to Him, what have you really to fear? Rekindle your faith and trust in

Him. He will wash away your anxiety and give you the courage to start again. Remember the words of St. Paul: "I can do all things in him who strengthens me!"

His clouded face began to clear and a glimmer of hope shone in his eyes.

"I'm afraid," he said, "that you've put your finger on the real trouble. God has receded into the background in my life. I've put my trust in the almighty dollar, and I see where *that* has got me. I'll try to put God back in first place and build my life and hope around Him. Then I won't ever again think that my sole hope of security and happiness lies in my bank account."

"Yes," I said, "you can learn a much needed lesson from this and emerge a wiser and a better man. Spend at least fifteen minutes daily in prayer. After your evening meal you and your wife can read slowly a chapter or two of the New Testament and let its great truths sink deep into your minds. These spiritual exercises will enable you to achieve a closer union with God, in whom you can place your hope and trust. With God in the center of your life, you have nothing to fear."

I gave him a framed copy of the little verse which St. Theresa had written on a card which she used as a bookmark. I've quoted it in a previous chapter, but it's worth repeating here.

> Let naught disturb thee,
>   Naught fright thee ever.
> All things are passing,
>   God changeth never.
> Patience e'er conquers.
>   With God for thy own
> Thou nothing dost lack,
>   He sufficeth alone.

"Where Your Treasure Is, There Your Heart . . ."

Some five months later my friend stepped into the office for a visit. He was a different looking man. Gone were the gloom and despair. His eyes were beaming; there was a smile of confidence on his face. He was the picture of cheerfulness, peace of mind and serenity.

"It was tough going for the first few weeks," he said. "But gradually peace of mind came back. We've resumed our practice of attending Sunday services, and we get more out of the service because we come in a spirit of humility, seeking God's guidance and blessing. We've kept up that practice of prayer and Bible reading and it has changed our whole outlook on life.

"The pay-off came one evening," he continued, "when we reached the twelfth chapter of St. Luke's Gospel, where Christ relates the parable of the rich man. He pulled down his barns and built larger ones in which he stored all his grain and possessions. 'Soul,' he said, 'thou hast many good things laid up for many years; take thy ease, eat, drink and be merry.'

"But God said to him, 'Thou fool, this night do they demand thy soul of thee; and the things thou hast provided, whose will they be?' 'So,' says Jesus, 'is he who lays up treasure for himself, and is not rich as regards God.' That parable hit me right between the eyes."

"It's an important lesson for us all," I remarked. "Twelve verses later the Savior enunciates the principle which should guide us all in these matters. 'Make for yourselves,' He says, 'purses that do not grow old, a treasure unfailing in heaven, where neither thief draws near nor moth destroys. For where your treasure is, there your heart also will be.'"

Psychologists and Psychiatrists Testify

The Scripture testimony concerning the power of deep religious faith to wash out every vestige of fear and worry is reinforced by the testimony of noted psychologists and psychiatrists. William James said: "The sovereign cure for worry is religious faith. . . . It gives a new zest for life . . . more life, a larger, richer, more satisfying life."

Why does religious faith bring one such repose and peace of mind? James answers: "The turbulent billows of the fretful surface leave the deep parts of the ocean undisturbed; and to him who has a hold on vaster and more permanent realities, the hourly vicissitudes of his personal destiny seem relatively insignificant things. The really religious person is accordingly *unshakeable and full of equanimity*, and calmly ready for any duty that the day may bring forth."

One of the towering figures in modern psychiatry is Dr. Carl Jung of Zurich University, Switzerland. In his great work, *Modern Man in Search of a Soul*, he points out that the basic and ultimate solution of virtually every psychiatric trouble is found in a deep religious faith and outlook.

"During the past thirty years," he says, "people from all the civilized countries of the earth have consulted me. I have treated many hundreds of patients. Among all my patients in the second half of life—that is to say, over 35—*there has not been one whose problem in the last resort was not that of finding a religious outlook on life*. It is safe to say that every one of them fell ill because he had lost that which the living religions of every age have given to their followers, and *none of them has been really healed who did not regain his religious outlook*."

Another distinguished psychiatrist, Dr. A. A. Brill of Columbia University, confirms the conclusion reached by Jung. "Anyone," he says, "who is truly religious does not develop a neurosis." Stressing the same important truth, Dr. Alexis Cassel says: "Those who keep the peace of their inner self in the midst of tumult are immune from nervous and organic diseases." Religious faith enables one to create for himself an oasis of peace and repose amidst the hustle and bustle of modern life. It sharpens one's consciousness of the presence of God in our hearts. Since He is infinitely powerful, no harm can possibly come to one in whose heart He dwells.

We Are
Not Alone

It was the keen consciousness of this truth which exercised such a powerful influence in the life of Dr. Joseph R. Sizoo, for many years the president of New Brunswick Theological Seminary in New Jersey. For several years Dr. Sizoo was co-chairman with Rabbi Maurice Eisendrath and myself of the commission on interreligious activities of the National Conference of Christians and Jews, whose purpose is to eradicate religious prejudice and bigotry.

"Years ago," Dr. Sizoo relates, "in a day of uncertainty and disillusionment, when my whole life seemed to be overwhelmed by forces beyond my control, one morning quite casually I opened my New Testament and my eye fell upon this sentence, *'He that sent me is with me—the Father hath not left me alone.'* My life has never been the same since that hour. . . . Many have come to me for counseling during these years, and I have always sent them away with this sustaining sentence. I have walked with it and I have found in it my peace and strength."

In 1934 Admiral Charles Byrd spent five months alone in a hut buried beneath the icecap of Ross Barrier deep in the Antarctic. With blizzards raging around him, and the cold plunging to 82 degrees below zero, Byrd was engulfed in unending night. Fumes of carbon dioxide from his stove were slowly poisoning him. It would take several months for any aid to reach his lonely outpost.

In this crisis Byrd's deep religious faith came to his rescue. It brought him the comforting assurance that he was not alone, that God with all His infinite power was with him. To that God he turned in humble prayer and he received the calmness, courage and fortitude to work his way out of his desperate situation. Speaking of his religious faith, Byrd said, *"I know it pulled me through."*

Persons who go through life without any vital religious faith have no spiritual resources to fall back upon when stark tragedy strikes. They feel like rats caught in the trap of a universe void of purpose, meaning or significance. Only God and His Providential care and love for His children give meaning to human existence. To the believer there is no such thing as irredeemable failure, for with God's aid defeat can be transformed into victory and failure into a stepping stone for greater achievement.

Inner Secret
of Serenity

What a world of meaning there is in the words uttered by St. Paul after the Resurrection: "This corruptible body must put on incorruption and this mortal body must put on immortality. But when this mortal body puts on immortality, then shall come to pass the word that is written, 'Death is swallowed up in victory! O grave where is thy victory? O death where is thy sting?' " Hence the Christian goes through life with the inspiring and cheerful confidence that enables him to say: "If my bark sinks 'tis to another shore."

"Certainly there is a way of life," says Dr. Harry Emerson Fosdick, "known to those in whom religion has become a vital reality, which can in many cases forestall the need of psychiatry. One factor in that way of life is an *inner secret of serenity*. Multitudes today have no place inside themselves where, in a noisy and turbulent world, they can calm down and be quiet." Such a sanctuary is provided by religion. There the individual communes with God and emerges refreshed and comforted with the knowledge that he can do all things when strengthened by divine power.

In ever increasing numbers psychiatrists are recognizing the power of religion to establish peace of mind and spiritual serenity. Thus Dr. J. A. Hadfield, one of England's foremost psychiatrists, says: "Speaking as a student of psychotherapy who, as such, has no concern with theology, I am convinced that the Christian religion is a most valuable and potent influence for producing that harmony and peace of mind and that confidence of soul needed to bring health and power to most nervous patients."

The spiritual serenity of which we speak is not a form of ivory tower escapism from the hectic hurly-burly of an active and busy life. Neither is it a sort of anaesthesia in which one remains insensitive to the pressing social, economic and political problems of the day. On the contrary, it requires the conscientious fulfillment of all one's duties in the practical concerns of daily life. Indeed poise and serenity afford a basis for purposeful activity, a solidity within one to lean his lever on.

"Do Not
Be Afraid"

It is not the feverishly excited but the calm poised individual who can think most clearly, see the farthest and bring the best judgment to the solution of urgent social and economic problems. "No reconstructed society," observes Joshua Loth Liebman, "can be built on unreconstructed individuals. Personal unbalance never leads to social stability. And peace of mind is the indispensable prerequisite of individual and social balance."

At the heart of religious faith is the belief in God's Providential care and love of His children. No earthly father can discern the needs of his children so clearly or minister to them so effectively as our heavenly Father. This is the mighty truth which Jesus repeatedly emphasizes. "Are not five sparrows sold for two farthings?", He asks. "And yet not one of them is forgotten before God. Yes, the very hairs of your head are all numbered. Therefore do not be afraid, you are of more value than many sparrows."

These words must have been in the mind of Telemachus on that memorable day in 404 when, holding aloft a crucifix, he rushed into the arena of the Roman Colosseum. Silence and astonishment fell upon the thousands of spectators as they saw this frail figure approach the two gladiators who were about to fight for their lives.

"Stop this barbarous slaughter!" cried Telemachus. "Stop in the name of Jesus Christ!"

"Who is that?" asked the Emperor Honorius.

"It's the monk, Telemachus," replied a soldier.

Angry at the thought of being deprived of their bloody sport, the crowd jeered and booed.

"Kill him! Kill him!" they shouted.

Whereupon one of the gladiators hacked off his head. The fighting went on. But the emperor was haunted by the memory of the brave monk who serenely entered the area to give his life to end the slaughter. Two months later he terminated the cruel sport.

The consciousness of God's fatherly solicitude and love for us is the best antidote for obsessing fear and worry. Since God is all-powerful, it follows that his solicitude is efficacious, if we but co-operate with His grace. Only we can stand in the way of our happiness; only we can hurt ourselves. God's hand is stretched out to us in all times of danger and temptation; we have only to clasp that divine hand to be delivered from evil.

This is a favorite theme of our Lord's and He comes back to it again. "Which of you," He asks, "by being anxious about it can add to his stature a single cubit? Therefore if you are not able to do even a very little thing, why are you anxious concerning the rest? See how the lilies grow; they toil not, nor spin, yet I say to you that not even Solomon in all his glory was arrayed as one of these. But if God so clothes the grass which today is alive in the field and tomorrow is thrown into the oven, how much more you, O you of little faith!"

Here Jesus ends with the same word of gentle rebuke that He addressed to the disciples when they were fearful that He would allow their vessel to sink. In both instances their anxiety stemmed from a lack of faith in God's Providential care of His children. Jesus seeks to teach them the importance of having a proper sense of values, of putting first things first.

Seek First
the Kingdom of God

"And as for you," Christ continues, "Do not seek what you shall eat, or what you shall drink . . . your Father knows that you need these things. But seek the kingdom of God, and all these things shall be given you besides." How much anxiety and worry are traceable to a grossly disproportionate emphasis upon superfluous material things to the neglect of spiritual values—the things really worth while?

Families with good homes, abundant food and clothing, and two cars in the garage continue to stew and fret, exhausting their energies in the continued pursuit of the almighty dollar. They must not only "keep up with the Joneses": they must surpass them. It is in the pursuit of these unprofitable and unworthy goals that millions wear themselves to exhaustion and end up nervous wrecks. Peace of mind, like Maeterlinck's bluebird of happiness, was at their very door. But they failed to find it.

It is the failure to lift our eyes from the things of earth to those of heaven that is the fertile cause of much of our panic and fears. Frederick H. Ecker, the former president of Metropolitan Life Insurance Company, relates that when the Metropolitan Tower was nearing completion in 1909, he and the architect made a personal inspection above the 50th floor, where the elevators ended. They had to climb by ladders outside the building to the top of the tower some 55 stories above the street.

"The architect," he recalls, "warned me not to look down, but instinctively I did, and my knees began to tremble. Then I began looking up, as the architect had advised, and found that my fear vanished. Ever since, I've remembered that in any worrisome situation it pays to look up, not down. Looking up—and adding a smile if possible—relieves the tension and banishes the fear."

A Good Conscience
Brings Serenity

To achieve tranquillity of soul one must not only have a religious faith but also practice it. He must not only say, "O God! I believe in Thee," but he must also keep His commandments. It is in the *fulfillment* of the law that one best proves his faith and secures the testimony of a good conscience. Herein is found the secret of that inner serenity, for which men search in vain among exterior things. Surveying man's desperate and frantic search for peace of mind, Empedocles the Greek philosopher says: "We would have inward peace but will not look within. . . ."

Only in the joy of a good conscience can that inward peace be found. Even in the midst of adversity a good conscience buoys up the heart with joy, while in the midst of external rejoicing an evil conscience scourges one with remorse and fear. The wicked are strangers to true joy because their conscience robs them of interior peace. Even the applause of multitudes can't bring them real joy because it reaches only their ears and not their hearts.

"Great tranquility of heart hath he," says Thomas à Kempis, "who careth neither for praise nor blame. Easily will he be content and at peace whose conscience is undefiled. Thou art not more holy for being praised, nor the worse for being blamed. What thou art, that thou art; nor canst thou be said to be greater than God seeth thee to be. If thou attend diligently to what thou art interiorly, thou wilt not regard what men say of thee. . . . Have a good conscience and thou shalt always have joy."

Coming back from Europe recently on the *Queen Elizabeth*, we ran into some stormy weather. Despite the high waves, however, the great vessel moved steadily and smoothly along with no disruption of the activities of the passengers. I could not help but contrast its even steady balance with the pitch and roll of the vessels on which I had crossed forty years ago.

"How," I asked one of the ship's officers, "are you able to maintain such balance and smoothness despite the heavy seas?"

"We have a spinning gyroscope," he replied, "which enables the vessel to resist the roll of the seas and serves as a stabilizer. It's a great invention and eliminates much of the discomfort and seasickness which passengers formerly suffered."

Conscience: The Gyroscope of the Soul

A good conscience is the gyroscope of the soul, the *inner stabilizer of our serenity*, enabling us to pass through the storms and tempests of adversity, calm and undisturbed. It provides us with shockproof passage over the rocks and boulders with which life's highway is strewn. Religious faith is the magnetic needle which points the pathway to our destination, but it needs the inner stabilizer of a good conscience to enable us to reach that haven with our serenity intact.

The secret of St. Paul's marvelous inner tranquillity amidst all his trials and difficulties was the good conscience which brought to him the assurance of God's abiding presence and unfailing help. This was evidenced when he was on trial before Felix, the Roman governor. He frankly acknowledged that he was a servant of the God of the Christians, spreading His faith and looking forward to the Resurrection. In all these activities he said that he strove "always to have a clear conscience before God and before men."

A good conscience gives a person strength to face any ordeal with cheerful courage. This is shown by Christian martyrs who in every age welcomed the opportunity to give their lives rather than deny their God. During the persecution under the Emperor Antoninus in the second century, the Christian widow Felicitas and her sons were brought before Publius, the prefect of Rome.

"Take pity, Felicitas, on your children," he said. "They are in the bloom of youth, and may aspire to the greatest honors."

"Your pity," replied the mother, "is really impiety. The compassion to which you exhort me would make me the most cruel of mothers."

Turning toward her sons, she said:

"My sons, look up to heaven, where Jesus Christ with His saints expects you. Be faithful in His love, and fight courageously for Him."

With smiling faces, the mother and her sons, singing hymns of praise to God, walked to their martyrdom. Nothing can terrify or daunt a person with a good conscience. God clothes him with His power and might and safeguards him from all harm.

A good conscience is a soft pillow upon which one can sleep amidst the roar of thunder and the crash of lightning. It clothes each day with the joy of Christmas and robs even death of its sting. Shakespeare declared that a still and quiet conscience brings "a peace above all earthly dignities." An approving conscience enables one to rejoice in the midst of adversity.

A guilty conscience is the worst prison into which one can be thrown; in it he gets a taste of hell, and from it there can be no escape. "Every guilty person," said Seneca, "is his own hangman." Ransack the universe and you will find neither serenity nor happiness unless you bring them with you in the form of a good conscience. George Crabbe epitomizes many volumes on the role of conscience in the memorable lines:

Oh! Conscience! Conscience! man's most faithful friend,
Him canst thou comfort, ease, relieve, defend;
But if he will thy friendly checks forego,
Thou art, oh! woe for me, his deadliest foe!

Love
of Neighbor

Another factor in the achievement of spiritual serenity is *love of neighbor*. The person who cherishes grudges can secure the counsel of psychiatrists and use all their therapeutic techniques, but he will find no tranquillity as long as hatred and revenge flame within him. Hatred sets up a tension and a restless feverish brooding, which bar the door to tranquillity and peace of mind. Only love can relax the tension, quiet the anxiety, extinguish the vengeful flame and bring peace to the troubled soul.

This is shown in the experience of a regiment of Scottish Highlanders, captured by the Japanese at the fall of Singapore. In the article, "It Happened on the River Kwai," in *The Reader's Digest*, Ernest Groton tells the story to Clarence W. Hall. Here in condensed form are its highlights. The prisoners were set to work in the jungle of Thailand to build the infamous "Railway of Death," the 250-mile railroad which the Japanese thought would facilitate their push into Burma and India. The prisoners were forced to toil from dawn to dusk, barefooted and bareheaded in temperatures as high as 120 degrees in the sun. Fed starvation rations, they were soon reduced to living skeletons.

Hatred and revenge burned within them. Desperate and starving, they stole one another's food and clothes; some curried the favor of the guards by telling on others. Morale was at its lowest. Then something happened. Two corporals, Miller a Protestant, and Moore a Catholic, introduced a new spirit. They gave portions of their own meager rations to the more needy; they went into the hospitals and ministered to the sick and dying.

Finding Captain Ernest Groton, ridden with malaria, amoebic dysentery, beriberi and scabies, paralyzed from the waist down, they carried him to a little bamboo shack which they had made in the woods. They shared their food with him and took turns in nursing him.

"In two and a half months," said Groton, "they had given me back my life. But more important, they gave me another life. Under their care I became aware that these lads had something that the rest of us had missed, something beyond the reach of the evil about them, something that could not be beaten out of them, or starved, or kicked to death.

"That something was the greatest force on earth—*love*. Love that quite literally 'casts out fear.' Love that loses life in order to gain it. And suddenly I knew that I, and all others in Chungkai, must have that kind of love, must be its bearers, or *we would all perish*."

That spirit of mutual love and solicitude effected a moral revolution among the prisoners. Instead of stealing their comrades' food, they were sharing their own with the sick, giving the other fellows "all the breaks." Moore and Miller organized prayer meetings. At one of these, a young private was leading the Lord's Prayer. When he came to "Forgive us . . . as we forgive those who trespass against us," he found himself saying it alone.

He paused a moment and then repeated the line. This time a hundred voices spoke it with him, firmly, resolutely, some with a sob. In the fellowship of suffering these prisoners made an amazing discovery: hatred is poisonous and self-defeating, mutual love is healing and self-liberating, and forgiveness of enemies brings a quiet peace and an inner serenity.

They learned too that "God is love, and he who abides in love abides in God and God in him." Yes, love is the best antidote for the poisonous fears spawned by hatred. The forgiveness of our enemies brings us the peace of mind and spiritual serenity which forever elude the vengeful spirit.

Espouse
a Noble Cause

Unselfish devotion to noble causes is another method of achieving spiritual serenity. The more we forget ourselves and think of others, the better off we are. The more closely we attach ourselves to the promotion of worthy causes, the greater becomes our peace of mind. The individual who is forever concentrating on his health, concerned with every petty ache and possible symptom of disease is headed straight for the miserable ranks of the hypochondriacs. Fearful and suspicious of every imaginable ailment, he works himself into a chronic sickness, compounded of his own motley brood of anxieties.

The remedy is decentralization—the submergence of the ego to higher values. Put some worthy cause before you, attach yourself to it unselfishly and through a divine paradox you grow in richness and beauty of personality and find yourself. "He who loses his life for my sake," says Jesus, "will find it."

What a world of truth, both spiritual and psychological, is contained in that brief sentence! There are not a few scholars who consider it one of the most arresting and revealing in all the Bible. The truth it expresses has been verified whenever it has been put into practice. Dr. Gordon Allport, professor of psychology at Harvard, expresses the same truth when he says: "Paradoxically, 'self-expression' requires the capacity to lose oneself in the pursuit of objectives not primarily referred to the self."

Individuals who try to escape from their emotional prisons by giving free rein to their lusts find they have engaged not in self-expression but in self-explosion, to the detriment of both their character and personality. Visit a sanitarium for alcoholics and you will see the tragic price paid by those who sought to escape from their troubles only to find they have multiplied them a hundredfold. They have jumped from the frying pan into the fire.

One night Frederick Ozanam, a lonely and reflective student at the Sorbonne, walked through a slum section of Paris. He was deeply stirred by the abject poverty and misery of the people. He wanted to do something to help them. He had lodgings with Ampère, who was to become an illustrious physicist. Frederick confided his ambition to Ampère who said: "I should possess everything in the world to make me happy did I possess *nothing at all but the happiness of others.*" Ozanam made that the guiding principle of his life.

He organized a group of laymen who devoted themselves to the poor and needy. Its members visited them in their homes, brought them food and clothing and, when their homes were unheated, brought them fuel. The ideal animating them was that expressed by Christ: "As long as you did it for one of these, the least of my brethren, you did it for me."

In the fulfillment of that ideal they found that inner serenity which is the source of our deepest happiness. Today the Society of St. Vincent de Paul, with its thousands of members carrying on its works of mercy and charity in more than a score of countries, is the lengthened shadow of its founder, Frederick Ozanam.

Defenders
of the Oppressed

At the wicket gate that leads to the kingdom of the tranquil and serene are barred all those in whom hatred, revenge, jealousy, greed, envy, anger or lust has gained dominion. But all who bear a card stamped Defenders of the Oppressed find ready admittance. There is a special type of nobility attached to those who devote themselves to the oppressed, the persecuted and the downtrodden. Victims of *oppression and discrimination* are rarely able to defend themselves. They are scarcely ever even given a hearing. They desperately need defenders, spokesmen and advocates.

In 1610 when Peter Claver, a young Jesuit missionary from Spain, landed at Cartagena, a seaport in Colombia and the center of the slave trade in the New World, he witnessed an appalling sight. Negro slaves were being unloaded from a nearby vessel. Covered with sores, vermin and filth, they were pathetic sights. For weeks they had been packed in bundles of six, with chains around their ankles, wedged in the hold where sunshine never entered. So great was the stench that no white officer ever descended into it.

When Peter saw these miserable victims of human brutality and oppression, he knew that he had found his clients and his life work. For 44 years he was their tireless servant, their fearless defender and their unfailing friend. Meeting every boat, Peter would bathe the slaves, dress their sores, clothe them and speak words of comfort to them. In each fear-crazed countenance, he saw the lineaments of the face of Christ and loved them as Christ did.

With stouthearted courage he struggled to end the traffic in "black cattle" and fought for their rights as human beings. In his long ministry among them, he is reputed to have baptized more than 300,000 slaves. Peter also ministered to the lepers at St. Lazarus. Thither he brought lint, bandages, ointments and material for mosquito nets. He dressed their sores, and was continually giving the mantle of his cassock as a robe for the leprous, a veil for lupus-gnawed faces and a pillow for the dying.

Toward the end of his life, Peter was so worn out by his labors that he had to be strapped to his horse to make his rounds of the slave cabins, the harbor, prison and leper house.

Finding
a More Abundant Life

"These are my children," he said to those who tried to dissuade him, "and no father can be happy if he doesn't see his children. When I come, their faces light up with new hope and courage. They look for me, and I can't disappoint them."

When he died on September 8, 1654, throngs of Negroes rushed to his home. They broke through the guard at the door to gaze for the last time upon the face of their servant, defender and friend, dearer to them than all the world. Stooping, they kissed the floor of the room that held his body, so sure were they that he was a man filled full of God, and was now His saint.

Unable to believe that he was gone from them, children in the streets started calling, "Father Peter! Father Peter!" This was the cry that had brought an answer to their every need.

No king expiring upon the silken cushions of his regal bed ever left such emptiness in the hearts of his subjects as did Peter Claver in the hearts of the slaves, prisoners and lepers of Cartagena. He had declared himself "the slave of the Negroes forever," and they made him their uncrowned king. Today more than a hundred churches are named in honor of the Apostle to · the Negroes—St. Peter Claver.

In his 44 years of tireless ministry for the most pitiful victims of man's cruelty, oppression and discrimination, Peter never lost that *inner serenity* through which shone the radiance of God within him. In losing his life for the least of his brethren, he found a larger, more abundant and glorious one.

To sum up: Spiritual serenity, the source of our inner peace and happiness, is achieved through a deep and unshakeable faith and trust in God, in the realization that He loves us and dwells within us, that He is ready to answer our every cry for help. It is achieved through a good conscience, love of neighbor, the espousal of noble causes, especially those in behalf of the oppressed and persecuted, and the victims of man's brutality and discrimination. Whatsoever we do for others, especially for the least of the brethren, comes back to us a hundredfold. In seeking first the kingdom of God, His justice, and the welfare of our neighbor we find peace of mind and spiritual serenity—the source of our deepest happiness here and the blessed harbinger of our abiding happiness hereafter.

POINTS TO REMEMBER

1. The two outstanding characteristics of man today are rootlessness and loneliness.

2. The first great truth which religion offers for peace of mind and serenity is: Have a profound and unshake-

able faith in God, the Ruler of the universe and the Creator of mankind.

3. Since God dwells within us, we should have no anxiety but should place all our confidence and trust in Him.

4. Spiritual exercises enable you to achieve a closer union with God. Make Him the center of your life, and you have nothing to fear.

5. Memorize the quotation on St. Theresa's bookmark and recite it daily.

6. Psychiatrists testify to the power of a deep religious faith to wash out every vestige of fear and worry. Dr. Jung states that none of his patients over 35 years of age achieved inner serenity without a religious outlook on life.

7. Spiritual serenity is not a form of ivory tower escapism; it requires the conscientious fulfillment of all one's duties in daily life.

8. At the heart of religious faith is the belief in God's Providential care and love of His children. This is the best antidote for fear and worry.

9. The failure to lift our eyes from the things of earth to those of heaven is the fertile cause of much of our panic and fears.

10. To achieve tranquillity one must not only have a religious faith but also practice it. This brings one the joy of a good conscience, in which all peace of mind must be anchored.

11. A good conscience is the gyroscope of the soul, the inner stabilizer of our serenity, enabling us to pass calm and undisturbed through the storms and tempests of adversity.

12. Love of neighbor is also a powerful factor in the achievement of spiritual serenity. The individual who cherishes grudges will find no tranquillity even though he secures the services of many psychiatrists.

13. Unselfish devotion to noble causes is an effective method of achieving inner serenity. The more we forget ourselves and think of others, the better off we are.

14. Hatred, revenge, jealousy, anger and lust rob the individual of inner peace and make him restless and ill at ease.

15. In seeking the kingdom of God and the welfare of our neighbor we find peace of mind and inner serenity—the source of our deepest happiness here and of abiding happiness hereafter.